T0255620

Lecture Notes in Computer Science 10688

Commenced Publication in 1973
Founding and Former Series Editors:
Gerhard Goos, Juris Hartmanis, and Jan van Leeuwen

Editorial Board

David Hutchison
    Lancaster University, Lancaster, UK
Takeo Kanade
    Carnegie Mellon University, Pittsburgh, PA, USA
Josef Kittler
    University of Surrey, Guildford, UK
Jon M. Kleinberg
    Cornell University, Ithaca, NY, USA
Friedemann Mattern
    ETH Zurich, Zurich, Switzerland
John C. Mitchell
    Stanford University, Stanford, CA, USA
Moni Naor
    Weizmann Institute of Science, Rehovot, Israel
C. Pandu Rangan
    Indian Institute of Technology, Madras, India
Bernhard Steffen
    TU Dortmund University, Dortmund, Germany
Demetri Terzopoulos
    University of California, Los Angeles, CA, USA
Doug Tygar
    University of California, Berkeley, CA, USA
Gerhard Weikum
    Max Planck Institute for Informatics, Saarbrücken, Germany

More information about this series at http://www.springer.com/series/7409

Patrick Horain · Catherine Achard
Malik Mallem (Eds.)

Intelligent Human Computer Interaction

9th International Conference, IHCI 2017
Evry, France, December 11–13, 2017
Proceedings

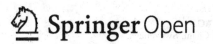

Editors
Patrick Horain
Telecom SudParis
Evry
France

Malik Mallem
Univ. Evry, Paris Saclay University
Evry
France

Catherine Achard
Pierre and Marie Curie University
Paris
France

![CC BY]

ISSN 0302-9743   ISSN 1611-3349 (electronic)
Lecture Notes in Computer Science
ISBN 978-3-319-72037-1   ISBN 978-3-319-72038-8   (eBook)
https://doi.org/10.1007/978-3-319-72038-8

Library of Congress Control Number: 2017960864

LNCS Sublibrary: SL3 – Information Systems and Applications, incl. Internet/Web, and HCI

© The Editor(s) (if applicable) and The Author(s) 2017. This book is an open access publication.

Open Access This book is licensed under the terms of the Creative Commons Attribution 4.0 International License (http://creativecommons.org/licenses/by/4.0/), which permits use, sharing, adaptation, distribution and reproduction in any medium or format, as long as you give appropriate credit to the original author(s) and the source, provide a link to the Creative Commons license and indicate if changes were made.

The images or other third party material in this book are included in the book's Creative Commons license, unless indicated otherwise in a credit line to the material. If material is not included in the book's Creative Commons license and your intended use is not permitted by statutory regulation or exceeds the permitted use, you will need to obtain permission directly from the copyright holder.

The use of general descriptive names, registered names, trademarks, service marks, etc. in this publication does not imply, even in the absence of a specific statement, that such names are exempt from the relevant protective laws and regulations and therefore free for general use.

The publisher, the authors and the editors are safe to assume that the advice and information in this book are believed to be true and accurate at the date of publication. Neither the publisher nor the authors or the editors give a warranty, express or implied, with respect to the material contained herein or for any errors or omissions that may have been made. The publisher remains neutral with regard to jurisdictional claims in published maps and institutional affiliations.

Printed on acid-free paper

This Springer imprint is published by Springer Nature
The registered company is Springer International Publishing AG
The registered company address is: Gewerbestrasse 11, 6330 Cham, Switzerland

Preface

The international conference on Intelligent Human Computer Interaction (IHCI) is a forum for the presentation of research results and technological advances at the crossroads of human-computer interaction, artificial intelligence, signal processing, and computer vision. It brings together engineers and scientists from around the world focussing on theoretical, practical, and applicational aspects of the field.

The 9th event, IHCI 2017, took place during December 11th–13th, 2017 in Evry, France. The present proceedings consist of papers presented at the conference.

The call for papers attracted 25 submissions from around the world, which have been reviewed by at least two and up to four members of the International Program Committee. Fifteen oral communications have been selected, the authors of which come from ten countries and four continents. The summary of one of the invited talks is also included. We thank all the invited speakers, authors, and members of the Program Committee for their contribution in making IHCI 2017 a stimulating and productive conference.

Finally, we gratefully acknowledge Telecom SudParis, Pierre and Marie Curie University, and Evry Val d'Essonne University for jointly sponsoring the conference. Special thanks go to the Telecom SudParis staff for their assistance and hard work in organizing the conference on campus and providing the logistics.

October 2017

Patrick Horain
Catherine Achard
Malik Mallem

Organization

Program Committee

Catherine Achard	Pierre and Marie Curie University, France (Chair)
Patrick Horain	Telecom SudParis, France (Co-chair)
Malik Mallem	Univ. Evry, Paris Saclay University, France (Co-chair)
Ajith Abraham	Machine Intelligence Research Labs, USA
Rahul Banerjee	BITS Pilani, India
Amrita Basu	JU India, India
Samit Bhattacharya	IITG - CSE, India
Plaban Kumar Bhowmick	Indian Institute of Technology Kharagpur, India
Jérôme Boudy	Telecom SudParis, France
Thierry Chaminade	Institut de Neurosciences de la Timone, France
Richard Chebeir	Université de Pau et des Pays de l'Adour, France
Amine Chellali	Univ. Evry, Paris Saclay University, France
Mohamed Chetouani	Pierre and Marie Curie University, France
Keith Cheverst	Lancaster University, UK
Gérard Chollet	CNRS, France
Partha P. Das	IIT KGP, India
Alok Kanti Deb	IIT Delhi, India
Laurence Devillers	LIMSI, Univ. ParisSud, Paris Saclay University, France
Gaël Harry Dias	CNRS & University of Caen Basse-Normandie, France
Bernadette Dorizzi	Telecom SudParis, France
Shen Fang	Pierre and Marie Curie University, France
Tom D. Gedeon	Australian National University, Australia
Alexander Gelbukh	Mexican Academy of Science, Mexico
Martin A. Giese	CIN/HIH University Clinic Tuebingen, Germany
David Antonio Gomez Jauregui	ESTIA, France
Michele Gouiffes	LIMSI, Univ. ParisSud, Paris Saclay University, France
David Griol Barres	Carlos III University of Madrid, Spain
Nesma Houmani	Telecom SudParis, France
Ekram Khan	AMU, India
Geehyuk Lee	KAIST, South Korea
Atanendu Sekhar Mandal	CERRI, Pilani, India
José Marques Soares	Universidade Federal do Ceará, Brazil
Marion Morel	Pierre and Marie Curie University, France
Galina Pasko	Uformia, Norway
Dijana Petrovska	Telecom SudParis, France

Jan Platoš	VŠB-TU Ostrava, Czech Republic
Jaroslav Pokorný	Charles University, Prague, Czech Republic
A. G. Ramakrishnan	Indian Institute of Science, India
Geoffrey Vaquette	Commissariat à l'énergie atomique et aux énergies alternatives, France
Alexandre Vervisch-Picois	Telecom SudParis, France
Daniel Wesierski	Gdansk University of Technology, Poland

Additional Reviewers

Lopamudra Choudhury	Jadavpur University, Kolkata, India
Maria Stylianou Korsnes	University of Oslo, Norway
Kavita Vemury	IIIT Hyderabad, India

Sponsors

Telecom SudParis

Telecom SudParis is a leading public graduate school of engineering in Information and Communication Technologies (ICT). It is part of the Institut Mines Télécom, France's leading group of engineering schools, supervised by the Ministry of Industry. It is part of the Université Paris-Saclay, the first French research cluster in sciences and technologies of information. The 105 full-time professors of Telecom SudParis contribute to the education of 1,000 students including 700 engineers and Master students and more than 150 doctoral students.

Univ. Evry, Paris Saclay University

The University of Evry-Val d'Essonne was created in 1991 as part of the development of higher education in the Ile-de-France region. It is multidisciplinary and there are more than 160 curricula, over half of which are professionally-oriented. The University offers courses and research in Science, Technology, Law, Economics, Management, and the Social Sciences. It is part of the Université Paris-Saclay, the first French research cluster in sciences and technologies of information. The 500 full-time professors of the university contribute to the education of more than 10,000 students including 3,000 Master students and more than 300 doctoral students.

Pierre and Marie Curie University

UPMC represents French excellence in science and medicine. A direct descendant of the historic Sorbonne, UPMC is the top French university by the Shanghai world rankings, 7th in Europe, and 36th in the world. UPMC encompasses all major sciences, such as mathematics (5th in the world); chemistry; physics; electronics; computer science; mechanics; Earth, marine, and environmental sciences; life sciences; and medicine.

Invited Papers

Optimizing User Interfaces for Human Performance

Antti Oulasvirta

School of Electrical Engineering, Aalto University, Espoo, Finland

Abstract. This paper summarizes an invited talk given at the 9th International Conference on Intelligent Human Computer Interaction (December 2017, Paris). Algorithms have revolutionized almost every field of manufacturing and engineering. Is the design of user interfaces the next? This talk will give an overview of what future holds for algorithmic methods in this space. I introduce the idea of using predictive models and simulations of end-user behavior in combinatorial optimization of user interfaces, as well as the contributions that inverse modeling and interactive design tools make. Several research results are presented from gesture design to keyboards and web pages. Going beyond combinatorial optimization, I discuss self-optimizing or "autonomous" UI design agents.

Simplexity and Vicariance:
On Human Cognition Principles
for Man-Machine Interaction

Alain Berthoz

Collège de France
French Academy of Science and Academy of Technology

Abstract. The study of living bodies reveals that in order to solve complex problems in an efficient, fast and elegant way, evolution has developed processes that are based on principles that are neither trivial nor simple. I called them "simplexes". They concern for example detours, modularity, anticipation, redundancy, inhibition, reduction of dimensionality etc. They often use detours that seem to add an apparent complexity but which in reality simplifies problem solving, decision and action. Among these general principles, "vicariance" is fundamental. It is the ability to solve some problem by different processes according to the capacity of each one, the context, etc. It is also the ability to replace a process by another in the case of deficits. It is also the possibility to create new solutions. Indeed, it is the basis of creative flexibility.

I will give examples borrowed from perception, motor action, memory, spatial navigation, decision-making, relationship with others and virtual worlds. I will show its importance for the compensation of neurological deficits and the design of humanoid robots for example. Finally, I will mention their importance in the fields of learning and education.

Interpersonal Human-Human and Human-Robot Interactions

Mohamed Chetouani

Pierre and Marie Curie University, Paris, France

Abstract. Synchrony, engagement and learning are key processes of interpersonal interaction. In this talk, we will introduce interpersonal human-human and human-machine interactions schemes and models with a focus on definitions, sensing and evaluations at both behavioral and physiological levels. We will show how these models are currently applied to detect engagement in multi-party human-robot interactions, detect human's personality traits and task learning.

Contents

Applications

Machine Perception of Humans

Smart Interfaces

Optimizing User Interfaces for Human Performance

Antti Oulasvirta[✉]

School of Electrical Engineering, Aalto University, Espoo, Finland
antti.oulasvirta@aalto.fi

Abstract. This paper summarizes an invited talk given at the 9th International Conference on Intelligent Human Computer Interaction (December 2017, Paris). Algorithms have revolutionized almost every field of manufacturing and engineering. Is the design of user interfaces the next? This talk will give an overview of what future holds for algorithmic methods in this space. I introduce the idea of using predictive models and simulations of end-user behavior in combinatorial optimization of user interfaces, as well as the contributions that inverse modeling and interactive design tools make. Several research results are presented from gesture design to keyboards and web pages. Going beyond combinatorial optimization, I discuss self-optimizing or "autonomous" UI design agents.

Talk Summary

The possibility of mathematical or algorithmic design of artefacts for human use has been a topic of interest for at least a century. Present-day user-centered design is largely driven by human creativity, sensemaking, empathy, and creation of meaning. The goal of computational methods is to produce a full user interface (e.g., keyboard, menu, web page, gestural input method etc.) that is good or even "best" for human use with some justifiable criteria. Design goals can include increases in speed, accuracy, or reduction in errors or ergonomics issues. Computational methods could speed up the design cycle and improve quality. Unlike any other design method, some computational methods offer a greater-than-zero chance of finding an optimal design. Computational design offers not only better designs, but a new, rigorous understanding of interface design. Algorithms have revolutionized almost every field of manufacturing and engineering. But why has user interface design remained isolated?

The objective of this talk is to outline core technical problems and solution principles in computational UI design, with a particular focus on artefacts designed for human performance. I first outline main approaches to algorithmic user interface (UI) generation. Some main approaches include: (1) use of psychological knowledge to derive or optimize designs [1–3], (2) breakdown of complex design problems to constituent decisions [4], (3) formulation of design problems as optimization problems [5], (4) use of design heuristics in objective functions [6], (5) use of psychological models in objective functions [7,8], (6) data-driven

© The Author(s) 2017
P. Horain et al. (Eds.): IHCI 2017, LNCS 10688, pp. 3–7, 2017.
https://doi.org/10.1007/978-3-319-72038-8_1

methods to generate designs probabilistically, (7) formulation of logical models of devices and tasks to drive the transfer and refinement of designs [9], and (8) learning of user preferences via interactive black-box machine learning methods [10]. I ask: Why is there no universal approach yet, given the tremendous success of algorithmic methods across engineering sciences, and what would a universal approach entail? I argue that successful approaches require solving several hard, interlinked problems in optimization, machine learning, cognitive and behavioral sciences, and design research.

I start with an observation of a shared principle across the seemingly different approaches: The shared algorithmic basis is *search*: "To optimize" is the act and process of obtaining the best solution under given circumstances. Design is about the identification of optimal conditions for human abilities. To design an interactive system by optimization, a number of decisions is made such that they constitute as good whole as possible. What differentiates these approaches is what the design task is, how it is obtained, and how it is solved. Four hard problems open up.

The first problem is the definition of design problems: algorithmic representation of the atomic decisions that constitute the design problem. This requires not only abstraction and mathematical decomposition, but understanding of the designer's subjective and practical problem. I show several definitions for common problems in UI design and discuss their complexity classes. It turns out that many problems in UI design are exceedingly large, too large for trial-and-error approaches. To design an interactive layout (e.g., menu), one must fix the types, colors, sizes, and positions of elements, as well as higher-level properties, such as which functionality to include. The number of combinations of such choices easily gets very large. Consider the problem of choosing functionality for a design: If for n functions there are $2^n - 1$ candidate designs, we already have 1,125,899,906,842,623 candidates with only 50 functions, and this is not even a large application.

The second problem is the definition of meaningful objective functions. The objective function is a function that assigns an *objective score* to a design candidate. It formalizes what is assumed to be 'good' or 'desirable' – or, inversely, undesirable when the task is to minimize. In applications in UI design, a key challenge is to formulate objective functions that encapsulate goodness in both designer's and end-users' terms. In essence, defining the objective function "equips" the search algorithm with design knowledge that tells what the designer wants and predicts how users interact and experience. This can be surface features of the interface (e.g., visual balance) or expected performance of users (e.g., 'task A should be completed as quickly as possible'), users' subjective preferences, and so on. However, it is tempting but naive to construct objective function based on heuristics. Those might be easy to express and compute, but they might have little value in producing good designs. It must be kept in mind that the quality of a interface is determined not by the designer, nor some quality of the interface, but by end-users, in their performance and experiences. I argue that an objective function should be essentially viewed as a predictor:

a predictor of quality for end users. It must capture some essential tendencies in the biological, psychological, behavioral, and social aspects of human conduct. This fact drives a departure from traditional application areas of operations research and optimization, where objective functions have been based on natural sciences and economics. I discuss the construction of objective function based on theories and models from cognitive sciences, motor control, and biomechanics.

A key issue we face in defining objective functions for interface design is the emergent nature of interaction: the way the properties of the design and the user affect outcomes in interaction unfolds dynamically over a period of time in the actions and reactions of the user. A key issue is people's ability to adapt and strategically change. The way they deploy their capacities in interaction complicates algorithmic design, because every design candidate generated by an optimizer must be evaluated against how users may adapt to it. I discuss approaches from bounded agents and computational rationality toward this end. Computational rationality (CR) [11] assumes an ideal agent performing under the constraints posed by the environment. This assumption yields good estimates in performance-oriented activities, but complicates computation remarkably.

The third problem is posed by algorithmic methods. I discuss trade-offs among modern method, which can be divided into two main classes: (i) heuristics such as genetic algorithms and (ii) exact methods such as integer programming. Exact methods offer mathematical guarantees for solutions. However, they insist on rigorous mathematical analysis and simplification of the objective function, which has been successful in only few instances in HCI this far. Black-box methods, in contrast, can attack any design problem but typically demand empirical tuning of the parameters and offer only approximate optimality. Here the design of the objective function and design task come to fore. The choice of modeling formalism is central, as it determines how design knowledge is encoded and executed, and how interaction is represented.

Fourth is the definition of task instances. In optimization parlance, task instance is the task- and designer-specific parametrization of the design task: "What constitutes a good design in this particular case?" There are two main sources of information when determining a task instance. To capture a *designer's* intention, interactive optimization can be used. Characteristic of interaction design is that the objectives can be under-determined and choices subjective and tacit [12]. The known approaches in design tools can be divided according to four dimensions: (1) interaction techniques and data-driven approaches for specification of a design task for an optimizer, (2) control techniques offered for steering the search process, (3) techniques for selection, exploration and refinement of outputs (designs), (4) level of proactivity taken by the tool, for example in guiding the designer toward good designs (as determined by an objective function). Principled approaches like robust optimization or Bayesian analysis can be used. I discuss lessons learned in this area.

However, the designer may not always be able to report all design-relevant objectives. For a full specification of a design task, one may need to algorithmically elicit what *users* "want" or "can" from digitally monitorable traces.

This is known as the inverse modeling problem [13]. I discuss probabilistic methods for cognitive models. These may disentangle among beliefs, needs, capabilities, and cognitive states of users as causes of their observations. Alternatively, black box models can be used. The benefit of white-box models, however, is that they allow the algorithm in some cases to predict the consequences (costs, benefits) of changing a design on user.

To conclude, perhaps the most daring proposition made here is that essential aspects of design, which has been considered a nuanced, tacit, and dynamic activity, can be abstracted, decomposed, and algorithmically solved, moreover in a way that is acceptable to designers. I review empirical evidence comparing computationally to manually designed UIs. However, much work remains to be done to identify scalable and transferable solution principles.

Even more critical is the discussion of what "design" is. Interaction design is characterized as "the process that is arranged within existing resource constraints to create, shape, and decide all use-oriented qualities (structural, functional, ethical, and aesthetic) of a digital artefact for one or many clients" [14]. Some scholars go as far as claiming that interaction design is through-and-through subjective and experiential [15]. It is about conceptualizing product ideas and designing their behavior from a user's perspective. In this regard, computational methods still cover a limited aspect of design. Transcending beyond optimization, I end with a discussion of what *artificially intelligent UI design* might mean. I claim that "AI for Design" must meet at least five defining characteristics of design thinking: (1) agency, (2) problem-solving, (3) sense-making, (4) speculation, and (5) reflection. So far, no approach exists that – in a unified fashion and with good results – achieves this.

Acknowledgements. The work of AO has received funding from the European Research Council (ERC) under the European Union's Horizon 2020 research and innovation programme (grant agreement No. 637991).

References

1. Dvorak, A., Merrick, N.L., Dealey, W.L., Ford, G.C.: Typewriting Behavior. American Book Company, New York (1936)
2. Fisher, D.L.: Optimal performance engineering: good, better, best. Hum. Factors J. Hum. Factors Ergon. Soc. **35**(1), 115–139 (1993)
3. Wickens, C.D., Kramer, A.: Engineering psychology. Ann. Rev. Psychol. **36**(1), 307–348 (1985)
4. Card, S.K., Mackinlay, J.D., Robertson, G.G.: A morphological analysis of the design space of input devices. ACM Trans. Inf. Syst. (TOIS) **9**(2), 99–122 (1991)
5. Burkard, R.E., Offermann, D.M.J.: Entwurf von schreibmaschinentastaturen mittels quadratischer zuordnungsprobleme. Z. für Oper. Res. **21**(4), B121–B132 (1977)
6. O'Donovan, P., Agarwala, A., Hertzmann, A.: Learning layouts for single-pagegraphic designs. IEEE Trans. Vis. Comput. Graph. **20**(8), 1200–1213 (2014)
7. Gajos, K., Weld, D.S.: Supple: automatically generating user interfaces. In: Proceedings of the 9th International Conference on Intelligent User Interfaces, pp. 93–100. ACM (2004)

8. Oulasvirta, A.: User interface design with combinatorial optimization. IEEE Comput. **50**, 40–47 (2017)
9. Eisenstein, J., Vanderdonckt, J., Puerta, A.: Applying model-based techniques to the development of UIS for mobile computers. In: Proceedings of the 6th International Conference on Intelligent User Interfaces, pp. 69–76. ACM (2001)
10. Shahriari, B., Swersky, K., Wang, Z., Adams, R.P., de Freitas, N.: Taking the human out of the loop: a review of Bayesian optimization. Proc. IEEE **104**(1), 148–175 (2016)
11. Gershman, S.J., Horvitz, E.J., Tenenbaum, J.B.: Computational rationality: a converging paradigm for intelligence in brains, minds, and machines. Science **349**(6245), 273–278 (2015)
12. Cross, N.: Designerly Ways of Knowing. Springer, Heidelberg (2006)
13. Kangasrääsiö, A., Athukorala, K., Howes, A., Corander, J., Kaski, S., Oulasvirta, A.: Inferring cognitive models from data using approximate Bayesian computation. In: Proceedings of the 2017 CHI Conference on Human Factors in Computing Systems, pp. 1295–1306. ACM (2017)
14. Löwgren, J., Stolterman, E.: Thoughtful Interaction Design: A Design Perspective on Information Technology. The MIT press, Cambridge (2004)
15. Goodman, E., Stolterman, E., Wakkary, R.: Understanding interaction design practices. In: Proceedings of the SIGCHI Conference on Human Factors in Computing Systems, pp. 1061–1070. ACM (2011)

Open Access This chapter is licensed under the terms of the Creative Commons Attribution 4.0 International License (http://creativecommons.org/licenses/by/4.0/), which permits use, sharing, adaptation, distribution and reproduction in any medium or format, as long as you give appropriate credit to the original author(s) and the source, provide a link to the Creative Commons license and indicate if changes were made.

The images or other third party material in this chapter are included in the chapter's Creative Commons license, unless indicated otherwise in a credit line to the material. If material is not included in the chapter's Creative Commons license and your intended use is not permitted by statutory regulation or exceeds the permitted use, you will need to obtain permission directly from the copyright holder.

Geometrical Shapes Rendering on a Dot-Matrix Display

Yacine Bellik[(✉)] and Celine Clavel

LIMSI, CNRS, Univ. Paris-Sud, Université Paris-Saclay, Rue John von Neumann,
Campus Universitaire d'Orsay, 91405 Orsay cedex, France
{Yacine.Bellik,Celine.Clavel}@limsi.fr

Abstract. Using a dot-matrix display, it is possible to present geometrical shapes with different rendering methods: solid shapes, empty shapes, vibrating shapes, etc. An open question is then: *which rendering method allows the fastest and most reliable recognition performances using touch?* This paper presents results of a user study that we have conducted to address this question. Using a 60 * 60 dot-matrix display, we asked 40 participants to recognize 6 different geometrical shapes (square, circle, simple triangle, right triangle, diamond and cross) within the shortest possible time. Six different methods to render the shapes were tested depending on the rendering of shape's outline and inside: static outline combined with static or vibrant or empty inside, and vibrating outline combined with static or vibrant or empty inside. The results show that squares, right triangles, and crosses are more quickly recognized than circles, diamonds, and simple triangles. Furthermore, the best rendering method is the one that combines static outline with empty inside.

Keywords: Touch · Dot-matrix display · Graphics · Geometry

1 Introduction

Blind people can have access to digital documents using specific software called "screen readers". Screen readers can present in a linear way, either through speech synthesis or braille, the content of a document or elements of a graphical interface. However, access to graphics and other two-dimensional information is still severely limited for the blind. It is not easy for them to explore 2D structures such as mathematical formulas, maps, electronic circuit diagrams...) using a screen reader. The user is then faced with many problems such as disorientation and difficulty to memorize and to build a correct mental model.

The work presented in this paper is a first step of a larger project that aims at defining new ways for the blind to have access to electronic documents while preserving spatial layout of the document. The main idea of the project is to use a dot-matrix display to present the general spatial layout of the document. Each element of the document structure (title, paragraph, image, etc.) will be represented by a geometrical form that will reflect the size and the position of the element in the document. When the user explores this spatial layout, he/she will be able to access to the detailed content of the element

© The Author(s) 2017
P. Horain et al. (Eds.): IHCI 2017, LNCS 10688, pp. 8–18, 2017.
https://doi.org/10.1007/978-3-319-72038-8_2

that is currently under his/her fingers, through another modality such as speech synthesis or braille.

As a preliminary step, two questions should be addressed. First, which geometrical form should be used? Obviously, using rectangles is the first idea that comes in mind but is it possible to use other forms depending for instance on the information type? Second, which rendering method allows the best and faster recognition process?

2   Related Work

Different methods exist to translate graphical information into a tactile form to make it accessible to a blind person [2, 3]. 3D printing, collage, thermoforming and embossed paper [8] are great for educational purposes but they all have the same drawback: they produce static documents which prevents useful interactive operations such as zooming and scrolling. This leads to a drastic reduction of information density due to the limited resolution of the skin. Furthermore, their quality decreases with use and they require huge space to be stored.

Other devices that allow refreshable tactile display, exist. They can be classified into two main categories. The first category concerns the devices that allow a tactile exploration of a virtual large surface using a small tactile device. A typical example of such devices is the VTPlayer mouse [9, 10] that can be used as a classical mouse to explore a virtual surface while receiving tactile stimuli through the index finger thanks to its 4 * 4 Braille dots. The main advantage of this device is its low cost and portability. However, exploration is generally done using only one finger which leads to important time exploration before achieving recognition even of very simple shapes.

Another similar device is the Tactograph [11, 12]. The Tactograph includes a STReSS^2 tactile display (see Fig. 1) [5] which allows the production of a variety of tactile stimuli providing richer rendering of textures using thin strips for stretching the skin of the finger. However, it still allows only a single finger exploration.

(a)   (b)   (c)

Fig. 1.   (a) Active area of the STReSS^2 tactile display, (b) STReSS^2 mounted on a planar carrier, and (c) usage of the device. Extracted from Levesque's website (http://vlevesque.com/papers/Levesque-HAPTICS08/)

The second category concerns the devices that allow the tactile exploration of a large physical surface using several fingers of both hands [6, 7]. The surface is generally composed by a matrix of a high number of Braille dots which play the same role as pixels in screens. An example of such device is the dot-matrix display designed by Shimada et al. [4] which offers 32 × 48 Braille dots. The main drawback of this kind of devices is their cost.

In this paper, we present a study conducted using a device of this second category to identify the rendering features that allow the fastest and most reliable recognition of geometrical shapes. The protocol of this study was inspired by a study conducted by Levesque and Hayward [1] on a device of the first category (the STReSS^2 device).

3   User Study

For this study, we have used a 3600-dot-matrix display (60 × 60 dots) from metec AG. The display surface is 15 × 15 cm^2. The dots can be only in 2 states: up or down. The device is presented in Fig. 2. It has also a set of buttons (some of them can be used as a braille keyboard) and a scrollbar.

Fig. 2. The dot-matrix display used in the study

3.1   Experimental Conditions

Shapes. Six different shapes were used in the experiment. We choose the same shapes as the ones used in [1]. As shown in Fig. 3 these shapes are: square, circle, simple triangle, right triangle, diamond and cross.

Fig. 3. The six shapes used in the study

Size of shapes. In [1] the shapes were selected to fill a 2 or 3 cm square, leading to two different sizes: *small* and *large*. In our experiment, we used three different sizes: *small*, *medium,* and *large*. Our small and medium sizes correspond respectively to small and large sizes of Levesque's study (2 and 3 cm). Our large size corresponds to a 4-cm bounding square. We added this larger size because the dot-matrix display has less resolution than the STReSS^2 tactile display [5]. In the STReSS^2 device, the center-to-center distance between adjacent actuators is 1.2×1.4 mm and the actuators can deflect toward the left or right by 0.1 mm. In our dot-matrix display, the horizontal and vertical distances between the dots centers are the same and are equal to ~2.5 mm. The diameter of each dot is ~1 mm. So, we kept the same sizes as in [1] but added a supplementary (larger) one in case recognition performances would be affected by poorer resolution of the dot-matrix display.

Rendering of shapes. Six different rendering methods were used during the experiment depending on the way the outline[1] and the inside of the shapes are displayed. Each of these two elements can be rendered in 3 different ways: static, vibrating, empty. The vibration effect is obtained by putting the dots up and down alternatively with a 10 Hz frequency to not damage the device. Theoretically this should lead to 9 different Rendering Methods (RM) as shown in Table 1.

Table 1. Features of different renderings of shape.

Outline / Inside	Static	Vibrating	Empty
Static	RM1	RM4	RM7
Vibrating	RM2	RM5	RM8
Empty	RM3	RM6	RM9

However, if we look deeper at these 9 rendering methods, we can see that 3 of them (RM7, RM8, RM9) are not pertinent. RM9 displays nothing since both the outline and the inside of the shape are empty. RM7 represents the same rendering method as RM1 because only the size of the shape is a little smaller if we remove the outline. Similarly, RM8 and RM5 represent the same rendering method for the same reason. Since the size factor is evaluated separately, we have decided to not consider RM7 and RM8. Figure 4 illustrates examples of the 6 RMs that were kept. Note that in [1], only RM1, RM3 and RM6 were used.

RM1   RM2   RM3   RM4   RM5   RM6

Fig. 4. The six rendering methods used in the study.

---

[1] The width of the outline is composed by the width of one dot, so ~1 mm.

3.2 Participants

Data were collected from 40 sighted subjects (31 men and 9 women), aged from 18 to 40 (M age = 23.7; SD age = 5.2). Many participants were people with a computer science background. All participants filled out a background questionnaire, which was used to gather information on personal statistics such as age and education level. Our sample was composed by 34 right-handers and 6 left-handers. All participants were naive with respect to the experimental setup and purpose of the experiment.

3.3 Protocol

First, each participant is invited to sign an informed consent and then an overview of the experiment is provided. The experiment was conducted in two main phases:

1. A training phase (~5 min) allowing each participant to become familiar with the geometrical shapes and the rendering methods used during the experiment. The six geometrical shapes are presented to the subject (who cannot see them thanks to a raised cover that hides the dot-matrix display) and then we ask him/her to name them. This step is complete when the subject is able to recognize the six shapes.
2. A phase of test where subjects were asked to recognize and to name shapes as fast as possible. This phase was decomposed in three continuous sessions (with a short break between them). The duration of the whole process (3 sessions) was under 1 h of time.

During the test, shapes varied according to the geometrical form, the size, and the rendering method. The order of the forms, sizes and rendering methods was randomly generated across participants. In all, each participant had to recognize 324 shapes (6 forms × 3 sizes × 6 rendering methods × 3 sessions).

3.4 Measures

For each shape, we recorded time to recognize it (in milliseconds) and participant's answer. The participants used a button to display/hide the figure (which starts/stops the chronometer). The answers were given verbally. We developed a program to extract dependent variables from the log files that were generated during the test.

4 Results

The results presented in this section are considered statistically significant when $p < 0.05$. Results are explicitly referred as a "trend" if p is between 0.05 and 0.1. We applied the Shapiro-Wilk test to verify that the variables succeed to satisfy normality assumptions. This is only verified for the recognition time variable. Recognition time was analyzed by means of ANOVAs[2] with shape, shape size, and combination of rendering methods of shape's outline and shape's inside. ANOVAs were calculated

---

[2] Regarding each factor, a one-way ANOVA was conducted for the recognition time.

using Statistica 9. Post hoc comparisons used the Student's t-test. A Chi 2 test was performed for the recognition rate.

4.1 Recognition Rate

We first analyzed the results by considering all answers given by the subjects and we conducted an analysis of Chi 2. Results show that recognition rate do not vary according to the geometrical form, the size, and the rendering method. The global mean of the recognition rate is 95%. Table 2 provides the detailed percentages of recognition in each category. Chi 2 analysis reveals that shapes are well recognized whatever the geometrical form, the size, and the rendering.

Table 2. Recognition rate according the shape, the size, and the rendering.

		Circle	Diamond	Cross	Square	Simple Triangle	Right Triangle	Total
Small	RM1	85%	91%	98%	98%	93%	96%	94%
	RM2	93%	92%	99%	96%	96%	89%	94%
	RM3	100%	88%	100%	96%	91%	95%	95%
	RM4	88%	83%	96%	95%	92%	97%	92%
	RM5	75%	82%	89%	89%	93%	90%	86%
	RM6	97%	75%	91%	90%	84%	93%	88%
	All	90%	85%	95%	94%	92%	93%	92%
Medium	RM1	91%	98%	100%	98%	98%	98%	97%
	RM2	98%	95%	98%	99%	97%	99%	98%
	RM3	100%	93%	100%	98%	94%	95%	97%
	RM4	94%	97%	100%	99%	95%	97%	97%
	RM5	83%	88%	97%	98%	96%	93%	92%
	RM6	99%	87%	93%	96%	94%	95%	94%
	All	94%	93%	98%	98%	96%	96%	96%
Large	RM1	96%	95%	100%	99%	96%	97%	97%
	RM2	98%	98%	100%	99%	98%	96%	98%
	RM3	100%	94%	99%	98%	97%	96%	97%
	RM4	94%	97%	100%	99%	94%	96%	97%
	RM5	92%	91%	98%	98%	97%	96%	95%
	RM6	98%	91%	95%	99%	93%	98%	96%
	All	96%	94%	99%	99%	96%	96%	97%
All	RM1	91%	95%	99%	98%	96%	97%	96%
	RM2	96%	95%	99%	98%	97%	95%	97%
	RM3	100%	92%	100%	97%	94%	95%	96%
	RM4	92%	92%	99%	98%	94%	96%	95%
	RM5	83%	87%	95%	95%	95%	93%	91%
	RM6	98%	84%	93%	95%	90%	96%	93%
	All	93%	91%	97%	97%	94%	95%	95%

4.2 Recognition Time

Shape effect. We observed a main effect of the geometrical shape on the recognition time ($F(5, 195) = 39,295$, $p < 0,001$ see Fig. 5). Post hoc comparisons suggested that participants tended to recognize more quickly crosses, squares, and right triangles than circles, diamonds, and simple triangles. There was no significant difference between crosses, squares, and right triangles. In addition, there was no significant difference between circles, diamonds, and simple triangles.

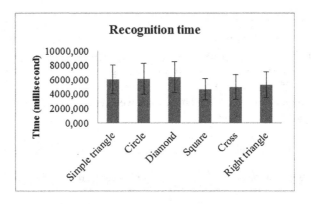

Fig. 5. Recognition time according the geometrical shapes.

Size effect. We observed a main effect of the size on the recognition time ($F(2, 78) = 86,157; p < 0,001$). Post hoc comparisons suggested that participants recognized more slowly small shapes (*Mean* = 6219,87; *SD* = 1996,642) than medium (*Mean* = 5300,23; *SD* = 63838,58) or large shapes (*Mean* = 5242,80; *SD* = 1674,63). There was no significant difference between the medium and large shapes.

Rendering method effect. We observed a main effect of the rendering method on the recognition time ($F(5, 195) = 73,237, p < 0,001$ see Fig. 6). Post hoc comparisons suggested that the best configuration is when the rendering method combines static

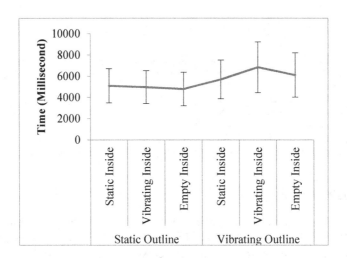

Fig. 6. Recognition time according the combination of inside and outline rendering.

outline with empty inside. Participants recognize faster the shapes with this configuration compared to other configurations. In addition, post hoc comparisons suggested that the worst configuration is when the rendering method combines vibrating outline with vibrating inside. Participants recognize more slowly the shapes with this configuration compared to other configurations. Finally post comparisons suggested that the recognition time varies according to the combination of rendering methods.

5   Discussion

The previous section revealed three important results.

- First, the forms are well recognized regardless of the geometrical shape, the size, or the rendering method.
- Second the recognition times appears to be significantly better with crosses, squares, and right triangles than with circles, diamonds, and simple triangles. This result provides an interesting cue about the exploration strategy that participants followed. Some of them said that they start by looking for right angles in the shape which help them to rapidly identify the form (only 1 right angle for right triangles, 4 for squares and a lot (12) for crosses).
- Third, the rendering methods that include vibrations seem to disrupt the participants even if there is no impact on the recognition rate. Participants spend more time to recognize the shapes rendered with vibrations than those rendered with static outline and empty or static insides. This result differs from Levesque and Hayward study [1] which obtained better identification for the shapes rendered with vibrations or dots than the ones rendered with grating. We think that this is due to the better resolution of the STReSS^2 which allows a less "aggressive" perception of the vibrations.

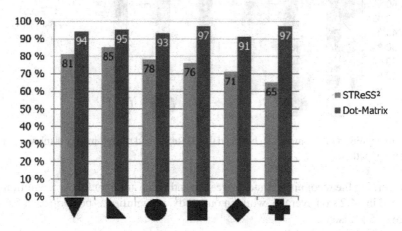

Fig. 7. Recognition rate comparison between the STReSS^2 and the dot-matrix display according to shapes.

However, and even though the following results should be taken with care due to different experimental conditions, a comparison with Levesque and Hayward results shows that recognition of geometrical shapes is better with a dot-matrix display than with a STReSS^2 device in all cases. Figures 7, 8 and 9 show the comparison between our average recognition rates (Dot-Matrix) and theirs (STReSS^2) depending respectively, on shapes, sizes, and rendering methods.

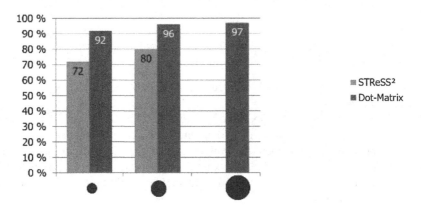

Fig. 8. Recognition rate comparison between the STReSS^2 and the dot-matrix display according to size.

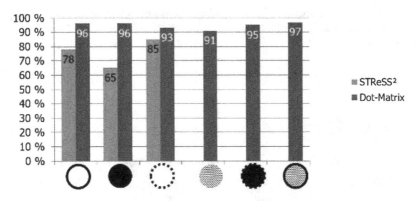

Fig. 9. Recognition rate comparison between the STReSS^2 and the dot-matrix display according to rendering method.

Concerning the recognition time, Levesque and Hayward found that recognition was performed in 14,2 s on average, while in our study, recognition is performed in 5,6 s on average (2,5 × faster).

6   Conclusion

This article explored several haptic rendering methods to present geometrical shapes through the touch using several fingers on a large physical surface: the dot-matrix display. The presented study allowed us to collect 12960 recognition times and 12960 recognition scores (324 shapes × 40 participants). Results show that the best rendering method is the one that combines static outline with empty inside and that squares, right triangles, and crosses are more quickly recognized than circles, diamonds, and simple triangles. These results are interesting for our project concerning spatial access to documents by the blind.

The protocol of the presented study was inspired by a similar study conducted by Levesque and Hayward on a smaller device that allows exploring a virtual surface using only one finger: the STReSS^2 device. The comparison of results shows that the recognition rates and times on a dot-matrix display are better in all cases. However, further investigations are needed to determine if this is due to mono-finger vs multi-finger exploration or for other reasons.

Next step of this work will be to reproduce the same experiment with visually impaired people. It would be also interesting to study the effects of different vibration frequencies and different outline widths as well to compare the performances of the dot-matrix display with those of a vibrotactile device such as in [13].

References

1. Levesque, V., Hayward, V.: Tactile graphics rendering using three laterotactile drawing primitives. In: Proceedings of the 16th Symposium on Haptic Interfaces for Virtual Environment and Teleoperator Systems, Reno, NV, USA (2008)
2. Vidal-Verdu, F., Hafez, M.: Graphical tactile displays for visually-impaired people. IEEE Trans. Neural Syst. Rehabil. Eng. **15**(1), 119–130 (2007)
3. Edman, P.K.: Tactile Graphics. American Foundation for the Blind Press, New York (1992)
4. Shimada, S., Shinohara, M., Shimizu, Y., Shimojo, M.: An approach for direct manipulation by tactile modality for blind computer users: development of the second trial production. In: Miesenberger, K., Klaus, J., Zagler, W.L., Karshmer, A.I. (eds.) ICCHP 2006. LNCS, vol. 4061, pp. 1039–1046. Springer, Heidelberg (2006). https://doi.org/10.1007/11788713_152
5. Wang, Q., Hayward, V.: Compact, portable, modular, high-performance, distributed tactile transducer device based on lateral skin deformation. In: Proceedings of HAPTICS 2006, pp. 67–72 (2006)
6. Zeng, L., Weber, G.: Exploration of location-aware you-are-here maps on a pin-matrix display. IEEE Trans. Hum. Mach. Syst. **46**(1), 88–100 (2015)
7. Prescher, D., Weber, G., Spindler, M.: A tactile windowing system for blind users. In: Proceedings of the 12th International ACM SIGACCESS Conference on Computers and Accessibility, ASSETS 2010, pp. 91–98 (2010)
8. McCallum, D., Ungar, S.: An introduction to the use of inkjet for tactile diagram production. Br. J. Vis. Impairment **21**(2), 73–77 (2003)
9. Jansson, G., Juhasz, I., Cammilton, A.: Reading virtual maps with a haptic mouse: effects of some modifications of the tactile and audiotactile information. Br. J. Vis. Impairment **24**(2), 60–66 (2006)

10. Pietrzak, T., Pecci, I., Martin, B.: Static and dynamic tactile directional cues experiments with VTPlayer mouse. Proc. Eurohaptics **2006**, 63–68 (2006)
11. Petit, G., Dufresne, A., Levesque, V., Hayward, V., Trudeau, N.: Refreshable tactile graphics applied to schoolbook illustrations for students with visual impairment. In: Proceedings of the 10th International ACM SIGACCESS Conference on Computers and Accessibility, ASSETS 2008, pp. 89–96 (2008)
12. Petit, G.: Conception, prototypage et évaluation d'un système pour l'exploration audio-tactile et spatiale de pages web par des utilisateurs non-voyants. Ph.D. thesis, Université de Montréal (2013)
13. Safi, W., Maurel, F., Routoure, J.-M., Beut, P., Dias, G.: An empirical study for examining the performance of visually impaired people in recognizing shapes through a vibro-tactile feedback. In: 17th International ACM SIGACCESS Conference on Computers & Accessibility (ASSETS 2015), Lisbon, Portugal, 26–28 October 2015

Open Access This chapter is licensed under the terms of the Creative Commons Attribution 4.0 International License (http://creativecommons.org/licenses/by/4.0/), which permits use, sharing, adaptation, distribution and reproduction in any medium or format, as long as you give appropriate credit to the original author(s) and the source, provide a link to the Creative Commons license and indicate if changes were made.

The images or other third party material in this chapter are included in the chapter's Creative Commons license, unless indicated otherwise in a credit line to the material. If material is not included in the chapter's Creative Commons license and your intended use is not permitted by statutory regulation or exceeds the permitted use, you will need to obtain permission directly from the copyright holder.

Dynamic Hand Gesture Recognition for Mobile Systems Using Deep LSTM

Ayanava Sarkar[1], Alexander Gepperth[2(✉)], Uwe Handmann[3], and Thomas Kopinski[4]

[1] Computer Science Department, Birla Institute of Technology and Science, Pilani, Dubai Campus, Dubai, UAE
[2] Computer Science Department, University of Applied Sciences Fulda, Fulda, Germany
`alexander.gepperth@cs.hs-fulda.de`
[3] Computer Science Department, University of Applied Sciences Ruhr West, Mülheim, Germany
[4] Computer Science Department, University of Applied Sciences South Westphalia, Iserlohn, Germany

Abstract. We present a pipeline for recognizing dynamic freehand gestures on mobile devices based on extracting depth information coming from a single Time-of-Flight sensor. Hand gestures are recorded with a mobile 3D sensor, transformed frame by frame into an appropriate 3D descriptor and fed into a deep LSTM network for recognition purposes. LSTM being a recurrent neural model, it is uniquely suited for classifying explicitly time-dependent data such as hand gestures. For training and testing purposes, we create a small database of four hand gesture classes, each comprising 40×150 3D frames. We conduct experiments concerning execution speed on a mobile device, generalization capability as a function of network topology, and classification ability 'ahead of time', i.e., when the gesture is not yet completed. Recognition rates are high (>95%) and maintainable in real-time as a single classification step requires less than 1 ms computation time, introducing freehand gestures for mobile systems.

Keywords: Mobile computing · Gestural interaction · Deep learning

1 Introduction

Gestures are a well-known means of interaction on mobile devices such as smart phones or tablets up to the point that their usability is so well-integrated into the interface between man and machine that their absence would be unthinkable. However, this can only be stated for touch gestures as three-dimensional or freehand gestures have to yet find their way as a means of interaction into our everyday lives. While freehand gestures are steadily being included as an additional means of control in different various fields (entertainment industry,

© The Author(s) 2017
P. Horain et al. (Eds.): IHCI 2017, LNCS 10688, pp. 19–31, 2017.
https://doi.org/10.1007/978-3-319-72038-8_3

infotainment systems in cars), within the domain of mobile devices a number of limitations present obstacles to be overcome in order to make this an unequivocally seamless interaction technique.

First and foremost, data has to be collected be in an unobtrusive manner, hence no sensors attached to the user's body can be utilized. As mobile devices have to remain operable independent of the user's location the number of employable technologies is drastically reduced. Eligible sensor technology is mainly limited to Time-of-Flight (TOF) technology as it is not only capable to provide surrounding information independent of the background illumination but moreover can do so at high frame rates. This is the presupposition to realize an interface incorporating freehand gesture control as it allows for the system's reaction times to remain at a minimum. TOF technology has to yet be established as a standard component in mobile devices (as e.g. in the Lenovo PHAB2 Pro) and it moreover suffers from a comparatively small resolution, potentially high noise and heat development. Despite these drawbacks it is a viable choice since the benefits outweigh the disadvantages as will be presented in this contribution. Realizing freehand gestures as an additional means of control not only overcomes problems such as usage of gloves or the occlusion of the screen interface during touch gesture interaction. It moreover also allows for increased expressiveness (with additional degrees of freedom) which in turns allows for a completely new domain of novel applications to be developed (especially in the mobile domain). This can be corroborated by the fact that car manufacturers, which have always been boosting innovations by integrating new technologies into the vehicle, have recently begun incorporating freehand gestures into the vehicle interior (e.g. BMW, VW etc.). The automotive environment faces the same problems such as stark illumination variances, but on the other hand can compensate difficulties such as high power consumption.

In this contribution we present a light-weight approach to demonstrate how dynamical hand gesture recognition can be achieved on mobile devices. We collect data from a small TOF sensor attached to a tablet. Machine Learning models are created by training from a dynamic hand gesture data base. These models are in turn used to realize a dynamic hand gesture recognition interface capable of detecting gestures in real-time.

The approach presented in this contribution can be set apart from other work in the field of Human Activity Recognition (HAR) by the following aspects: We utilize a single TOF camera in order to retrieve raw depth information from the surrounding environment. This allows for high frame rate recordings of nearby interaction while simultaneously making the retrieved data more robust vs. nearby illumination changes. Moreover, our approach is viable using only this single sensor, in contrast to other methodology where data coming from various kinds of sources is fused. Furthermore, data acquired in a non-intrusive manner allows for full expressiveness in contrast to data coming from sensors attached to the user's body. The process as a whole is feasible and realizable in real-time insofar as that once the model is generated after training, it can be simply transferred onto a mobile device and utilized with no negative impact on the device's performance. The remaining sections are organized as follows: Work presented in this contribution is contrasted to state of the art methodology within the domain of dynamic freehand gesture recognition (Sect. 1.1). The Machine Learning models are trained on a database described in Sect. 2.1. Data sample/s are transformed and presented to the LSTM models in the manner outlined in Sect. 2.2. The LSTM models along with the relevant parameters are subsequently explained in Sect. 2.3. The experiments implemented in this contribution are laid out in Sect. 3 along with the description of the parameter search (Sect. 3.1) and model accuracy (Sect. 3.3). The resulting hand gesture demonstrator is explained in Sect. 5 along with an explanation of its applicability. Section 6 sums up this contribution as a whole and provides a critical reflection on open questions along with an outlook on upcoming future work.

1.1 Dynamic Hand Gesture Detection - An Overview

Recurrent Neural Networks (RNNs) are employed for gesture detection by fusing inputs coming from raw depth data, skeleton information and audio information [4]. Recall (0.87) and Precision rates (0.89) peak, as expected, when information is fused from all three channels. The authors of [5] present DeepConvLSTM, a deep architecture fusing convolutional layers and recurrent layers from an LSTM for Human Activity Recognition (HAR). Data is provided by attaching several sensors to the human body and therewith extracting accelerometric, gyroscopic and magnetic information. Again, recognition accuracy improves strongly as more data is fused. Their approach demonstrates how HAR can be improved with the utilization of LSTM as CNNs seem not to be able to model temporal information on their own. The authors of [6] utilize BLSTM-RNNs to recognize dynamic hand gestures and compare this approach to standard techniques. However, again body-attached sensors are employed to extract movement information and results are comparatively low regarding the fact that little noise is present during information extraction. No information is given with regard to execution time raising the question of real-time applicability.

2 Methods

2.1 The Hand Gesture Database

Data is collected from a TOF sensor at a resolution of 320×160 pixels. Depth thresholding removes most of the irrelevant background information, leaving only hand and arm voxels. Principal-Component Analysis (PCA) is utilized to crop most of the negligible arm parts. The remaining part of the point cloud carries the relevant information, i.e., the shape of the hand. Figure 1 shows the color-coded snapshot of a hand posture.

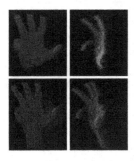 

Fig. 1. Data and data generation. Left: Sample snapshot of a resulting point cloud after cropping from the front (left) and side view (right) during a grabbing motion. The lower snapshot describes the hand's movement for each viewpoint (left and right respectively). Right: The Setup - tablet with a picoflexx (indicated with yellow circle). (Color figure online)

We recorded four different hand gestures from a single person at one location for our database: close hand, open hand, pinch-in and pinch-out. The latter gestures are performed by closing/opening two fingers. For a single dynamic gesture recording, 40 consecutive snapshots (no segmentation or sub-sampling) are taken from the sensor and cropped by the aforementioned procedure. In this manner, 150 gesture samples at 40 frames per gesture are present per class in the database, summing up to a total of 24.000 data samples.

2.2   From Point Clouds to Network Input

Description of a point cloud usually is implemented by so-called descriptors which, in our case, need to describe the phenomenology of hand, palm and fingers in a precise manner at a certain point in time. The possibilities of describing point cloud data are confined to either utilizing some form of convexity measure or calculating the normals for all points in a cloud. Either way, it has to remain computationally feasible in order to maintain real-time capability. In this contribution, the latter methodology is implemented: for a single point cloud, the normals for all points are calculated. Then, for two randomly selected points in a cloud, the PFH metric is calculated [7,8]. This procedure is repeated for up to 5000 randomly selected point pairs extracted from the cloud. Each computation results in a descriptive value which in turn is binned into a 625-dimensional histogram. Therefore, one such histogram provides a description of a single point cloud snapshot at a single point in time. These histograms form the input for training and testing the LSTM models.

2.3   LSTM Model for Gesture Recognition

In our model for dealing with the video frames sequentially, we use a deep RNN with LSTM model neurons, where the LSTM term for neurons is "memory cell" and the term for hidden layer is "memory cell". At the core of each memory cell is a linear unit supported by a single self-recurrent connection whose weight is initialized to 1.0. Thus, in the absence of any other input, this self-connection serves to preserve the cell's current state from one moment to the next. In addition to the self-recurrent connection, cells also receive input from input units and other cell and gates. The key component of a LSTM cell inside the memory block is its cell state, referred to as C_t or the cell state at time step t. This cell state remains unique for a cell and any change to the cell state is done with the help of gates - input gate, output gate and the forget gate. The output of the gates is a value between 0 and 1, with 0 signifying not "let anything through the gate" and 1 signifying "let everything through the gate". The input gate determines how much of the input to be forwarded to the cell, then the forget gate calculates how much of the cell's previous state to keep depending on how much to let the input affect the cell state, thus, the extent to which a value remains in the cell state and finally, the output gate computes the output activation, thereby, determining how much of the activation of the cell to be output.

At a time step t, the input to the network is x_t and h_{t-1}, where the former is the input and the latter is the output at time step $t-1$. For the first time step, the h_{t-1} is taken to be 1.0. In the hidden layers or the memory blocks, the output of one memory block forms the input to the next block. The following are the equations revolving around the inner complexities of an LSTM model, where W refers to the weights, b refers to the biases and the σ refers to the sigmoidal function, outputting a value between 0 and 1:

$$i_t = \sigma(W_{ix}x_t + W_{ih}h_{t-1} + b_i) \tag{1}$$

Equation 1 refers to the calculation of the input gate. Final output of the input gate is a value between 0 and 1.

$$f_t = \sigma(W_{fx}x_t + W_{fh}h_{t-1} + b_f) \tag{2}$$

Equation 2 refers to the calculation of the forget gate. Final output of the forget gate is a value between 0 and 1.

$$o_t = \sigma(W_{ox}x_t + W_{oh}h_{t-1} + b_o) \tag{3}$$

Equation 3 refers to the calculation of the output gate. Final output of the output gate is a value between 0 and 1.

$$g_t = \tanh(W_{gx}x_t + W_{gh}h_{t-1} + b_g) \tag{4}$$

Equation 4 refers to the calculation of g_t that gives a value between -1 and 1, specifying the amount of importance of the input that is relevant to the cell state, where the tanh function outputs a value between -1 and 1. Here, g_t refers to the new candidate values that must be added to the existing or the previous cell state.

$$c_t = f_t c_{t-1} + i_t g_t \tag{5}$$

Equation 5 refers to the calculation of the new cell state, replacing the old one.

$$h_t = \tanh(c_t) o_t \tag{6}$$

Equation 6 refers to the calculation of the hidden state or the output of that particular memory block, which then serves as the input to the next memory block. The tanh function allows it to output a value between -1 and 1. Further information about these equations can be found in [1].

The final output of the LSTM network is produced by applying a linear regression readout layer that transforms the states C_t of the last hidden layer into class membership estimates, using the standard softmax non-linearity leading to positive, normalized class membership estimates.

3   Experiments and Observations

The implementation has been done in TensorFlow using Python. There is a total 150 video files for each of the 4 classes of hand gestures. The model is trained on $N_{tr} = 480$ total samples, with 120 samples belonging to each of the 4 classes of hand gestures. The model is then evaluated using a total of $N_{te} = 120$ samples, with 30 samples belonging to each of the 4 classifying classes. The three parts of the experiment adhere to this partitioning of the data. In our implementation, each gesture is represented by a tensor of 40×625 numbers, while the input of the deep LSTM network corresponds to the dimension of a single frame, that is 625 numbers.

3.1   Model Parameters

Network training was conducted using the standard tools provided by the TensorFlow package, namely the Adam optimization algorithm [2,3]. Since the performance of our deep LSTM network depends strongly on network topology and the precise manner of conducting the training, we performed a search procedure by varying the principal parameters involved here. These are given in Table 1, as well as the range in which they were varied.

Table 1. Principal parameter for network topology and training. The last column indicated the range of values that were exhaustively tested for these parameters.

Symbol	Meaning	Variability
B	Batch size	2, 5, 10
M	# of Memory Blocks (MB)	1–4
C	# of LSTM Cells per MB	128, 256, 512
I	SGD training iterations	A = 100, B = 500, C = 1000
η	Learning rate	0.1, 0.001, 0.0001, 0.00001

3.2 Deep LSTM Parameter Search

Initially with $B = 2, 5, 10$, M is varied from 1 to 4 for each value of B, C is varied with 128, 256 and 512 for each value of B and M, and I has been varied between 100, 500 and 1000 for each value of the other three parameters. The learning rate is kept constant at 0.0001. Thus, for all combinations of the B, M, C and I, a total of 108 experiments has been carried out.

Now let the predictions for each sample data entered into the model be denoted by $\boldsymbol{P}_i$, where i refers to the index of the sample data in the test data. $\boldsymbol{P}_i$ is calculated for all frames of a test sample i, where the prediction obtained at the last frame defines $\boldsymbol{P}_i$. It is also possible to consider $\boldsymbol{P}_i$ for frames <40, achieving ahead-of-time guesses at the price of potentially reduced accuracy. $\boldsymbol{P}_i$ is a vector of length 4, since there are 4 classes for classification in the experiment. We take the argmax of these 4 elements to indicate the predicted class as shown in Eq. 7. Now to test if the prediction is correct or not it is compared with the label of the data sample, l_i.

$$\tilde{p}_i = \text{argmax}(\boldsymbol{P}_i) \tag{7}$$

$$\xi = 100\frac{\#(\tilde{p}_i = l_i)}{N_{te}} \tag{8}$$

Equation 8 refers to the simple formula used for calculating the accuracy.

3.3 Measuring Accuracy as a Function of Observation Time

In the second part of our experimentation, we train the model similar to Sect. 3.2, however in the testing phase, we calculate the predictions at different in-gesture time steps (frames) t. Let $\boldsymbol{P}_{i,t}$ denote the prediction for sample i at $t < 40$. In order to obtain an understanding of how the prediction varies more frames are processed, we calculate the predictions $\boldsymbol{P}_{i,t}$ at time steps $t = \{10, 20, 25, 30, 39, 40\}$. Here, we perform class-wise analysis to determine which classes lend themselves best to ahead-of-time "guessing" which can be very important in practice.

3.4   Speedup and Optimization of the Model

The implementation shown so far is focused on accuracy alone. Since mobile devices in particular lack faster and more capable processing units, the aim of this part of the article is to speed-up gesture recognition as much as possible by simplifying the LSTM model, if possible without compromising its accuracy. To this end, B has been kept constant at 2, while M is taken to be 1 in all the experiments. The number of memory cells in the single memory block is taken as either 8 or 10. Now, with such a small network, we are able to greatly speed up the system as well as minimize the computation complexities involved regarding the entire model.

4   Experimental Results

4.1   Deep LSTM Parameter Search

With the 108 experiments conducted by varying B, M, C and I, 20 accuracies have been reported in Table 2, with the idea of covering the diversity of the experimental setup of 108 experiments.

From the observations, it can be concluded that for a given M, C and I, the accuracy improves with the increase in the value of B. Thus, $B = 10$ will have a greater accuracy on the test data as compared to $B = 2$ or $B = 5$. This can be explained by the fact that for a given I, the model undergoes a total of (I X B) times of training in this experimental setup. Thus, as the number of B increases, so does the value (I X B) and consequently the accuracy of prediction. Now, for a given B, C and I, if M is varied between 1 to 4, it has been observed that with the increase in the number of hidden layers or M, the accuracy of prediction improves significantly. This is because, as the number of layers increases, the network becomes more complex with the ability to take into account more complex features from the data and hence, account for more accurate predictions. Similarly, when keeping B, M and I constant and varying C between 128, 256 and 512, we observe that accuracy increases with the increase in the number of memory cells in each memory block, thereby bearing a directly proportional relationship. Similar results were observed when I is varied, keeping

Table 2. Results for exhaustive parameter search in topology space. In total, we conducted 108 experiments by varying the network topology and training parameters. The best 18 results are shown here. The column headings correspond to the symbols defined in Table 1.

B	2	5	10	10	5	2	10	5	5	10	10	5	2	5	2	5	5	2
M	1	1	4	3	2	1	3	2	4	1	2	1	4	4	2	4	2	1
C	512	256	128	512	128	256	256	512	128	128	128	512	128	512	512	256	128	128
I	C	C	B	B	B	C	B	C	C	B	C	C	C	B	C	C	C	C
ξ	100	96.7	100	98.3	100	95	96.7	96.7	100	97.5	99.2	100	100	99.2	100	100	95.8	96.7

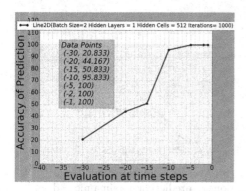 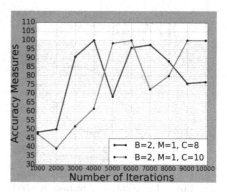

Fig. 2. Left: accuracy of prediction of a single test data sample, with B = 2, M = 1, C = 512 and I = 1000, at different in-gesture time steps t. Right: accuracy of prediction (taken at the end of a gesture) depending on training iterations for a small LSTM network size.

B, M and C as constant parameters, which can be explained by the fact that the model has more time or iterations to adjust its weight in order to bring about the correct prediction. Further, Table 2 shows the accuracies for the different combinations of the network parameters.

4.2 Measuring Accuracy as a Function of Observation Time

In this part we calculate different quality measures as a function of the frame t they are obtained. The graph in Fig. 2 shows that as the number of time steps increases, the accuracy increases until the maximum accuracy is reached in the last 5 time steps. Furthermore, we can also evaluate the confidence of each classification: as classification of test sample i is performed by taking the argmax of the network output P_i, the confidence of this classification is related to max P_i. We might expect that the confidence of classification increases with $t < 40$ as well as more frames have been processed for higher t. Now, Fig. 3a and b depicts the average maxima plus standard deviations (measured on test data) as a function of their class. We observe that, in total coherence to the increase in accuracy over in-gesture time t, the certainty of predictions increases as well, although we observe that this is strongly depending on the individual classes, reflecting that some classes are less ambiguous than others.

4.3 Speedup and Optimization of the Model

We observe that as the size of the network is greatly reduced comprising a single memory block and the number of memory cells being either 8 or 10, the accuracy is not as great as observed in Sect. 4.1. Hence, in order to accomplish the same level of accuracy as obtained in Sect. 4.1, the number of iterations for the training process was increased. The performances can be referred to in Fig. 2, showing

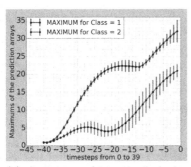 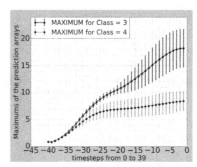

(a) Average and standard deviations of prediction maxima plotted against in-gesture time for classes 1 and 2

(b) Average and standard deviations of prediction maxima plotted against in-gesture time for classes 3 and 4

Fig. 3. "Ahead of time" classification accuracy for classes 1 and 2 (left) as well as 3 and 4 (right).

that 100% accuracy can be achieved even with small networks, although training time (and thus the risk of overfitting) increases strongly.

5   System Demonstrator

5.1   Hardware

The system setup consists of a Galaxy Notepro 12.2 Tablet running Android 5.02. A picoflexx TOF sensor from PMD technologies is attached to the tablet via USB. It has an IRS1145C Infineon 3D Image Sensor IC chip based on pmd intelligence which is capable of capturing depth images with up to 45 fps. VCSEL illumination at 850 nm allows for depth measurements to be realized within a range of up to 4 m, however the measurement errors increase with the distance of the objects to the camera therefore it is best suited for near-range interaction applications of up to 1 m. The lateral resolution of the camera is 224×171 resulting in 38304 voxels per recorded point cloud. The depth resolution of the picoflexx depends on the distance and with reference to the manufacturer's specifications is listed as 1% of the distance within a range of 0.5–4 m at 5 fps and 2% of the distance within a range of 0.1–1 m at 45 fps. Depth measurements utilizing ToF technology require several sampling steps to be taken in order to reduce noise and increase precision. As the camera allows several pre-set modes with a different number of sampling steps we opt for 8 sampling steps taken per frame as this resulted in the best performance of the camera with the lowest signal-to-noise ratio. This was determined empirically in line with the positioning of the device. Several possible angles and locations for positioning the camera are thinkable due to its small dimensions of 68 mm $\times$ 17 mm $\times$ 7.25 mm. As we want to setup a demonstrator to validate our concept the exact position of the camera

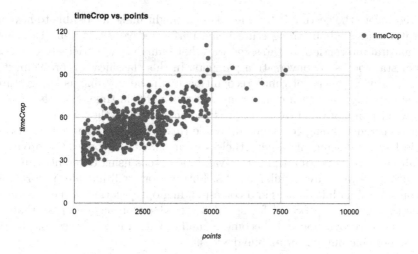

Fig. 4. Graph plotting the time required to crop the hand and reduce the number of relevant voxels with respect to the number of total points in the cloud.

is not the most important factor however should reflect a realistic setup. In our situation we opted for placing it at the top right corner when the tablet is placed in a horizontal position on the table. However, it should be stated here that any other positioning of the camera would work just as well for the demonstration presented in this contribution.

5.2 System Performance

One classification step of our model takes about [1.6e−05, 3.8e−05] of compu-tation time (in s). As Fig. 4 indicates, the time required to crop the cloud to its relevant parts is linearly dependent on the number of points within the cloud.

This is the main bottleneck of our approach as all other steps within the pipeline are either constant factors or negligible w.r.t. computation time required. During real-time tests our systems achieved frame rates of up to 40 fps.

6 Conclusion

We presented a system for real-time hand gesture recognition capable of run-ning in real time on a mobile device, using a 3D sensor optimized for mobile use. Based on a small database recorded using this setup, we prove that high speed and an excellent generalization capacity are achieved by our combined pre-processing+deep RNN-LSTM approach. As LSTM is a recurrent neural network model, it can be trained on gesture data in a straightforward fashion, requiring no segmentation of the gesture, just the assumption of a maximal duration cor-responding to 40 frames. The preprocessed signals are fed into the network frame by frame, which has the additional advantage that correct classification is often achieved before the gesture is completed. This might make it possible to have an "educated guess" about the gesture being performed very early on, leading to more natural interaction, in the same way that humans can anticipate the reactions or statements of conversation partners. In this classification problem, it is easy to see why "ahead of time" recognition might be possible as the gestures differ sufficiently from each other from a certain point in time onwards.

A weak point of our investigation is the small size of the gesture database which is currently being constructed. While this makes the achieved accuracies a little less convincing, it is nevertheless clear that the proposed approach is basically feasible, since multiple cross-validation steps using different train/test subdivisions always gave similar results. Future work will include performance tests on several mobile devices and corresponding optimization of the used algorithms (i.e., tune deep LSTM for speed rather than for accuracy), so that 3D hand gesture recognition will become a mode of interaction accessible to the greatest possible number of mobile devices.

References

1. Hochreiter, S., Schmidhuber, J.: Long short-term memory. Neural Comput. **9**(8), 1735–1780 (1997)
2. Kingma, D., Ba, J.: Adam: a method for stochastic optimization. arXiv preprint arXiv:1412.6980 (2014)
3. Bengio, Y.: Practical recommendations for gradient-based training of deep architectures. In: Montavon, G., Orr, G.B., Müller, K.-R. (eds.) Neural Networks: Tricks of the Trade. LNCS, vol. 7700, pp. 437–478. Springer, Heidelberg (2012). https://doi.org/10.1007/978-3-642-35289-8_26
4. Neverova, N., et al.: A multi-scale approach to gesture detection and recognition. In: Proceedings of the IEEE International Conference on Computer Vision Workshops (2013)
5. Ordóñez, F.J., Roggen, D.: Deep convolutional and LSTM recurrent neural networks for multimodal wearable activity recognition. Sensors **16**(1), 115 (2016)
6. Lefebvre, G., Berlemont, S., Mamalet, F., Garcia, C.: BLSTM-RNN based 3D gesture classification. In: Mladenov, V., Koprinkova-Hristova, P., Palm, G., Villa, A.E.P., Appollini, B., Kasabov, N. (eds.) ICANN 2013. LNCS, vol. 8131, pp. 381–388. Springer, Heidelberg (2013). https://doi.org/10.1007/978-3-642-40728-4_48
7. Rusu, R.B., et al.: Aligning point cloud views using persistent feature histograms. In: IEEE/RSJ International Conference on Intelligent Robots and Systems, IROS 2008. IEEE (2008)
8. Caron, L.-C., Filliat, D., Gepperth, A.: Neural network fusion of color, depth and location for object instance recognition on a mobile robot. In: Agapito, L., Bronstein, M.M., Rother, C. (eds.) ECCV 2014. LNCS, vol. 8927, pp. 791–805. Springer, Cham (2015). https://doi.org/10.1007/978-3-319-16199-0_55

Open Access This chapter is licensed under the terms of the Creative Commons Attribution 4.0 International License (http://creativecommons.org/licenses/by/4.0/), which permits use, sharing, adaptation, distribution and reproduction in any medium or format, as long as you give appropriate credit to the original author(s) and the source, provide a link to the Creative Commons license and indicate if changes were made.

The images or other third party material in this chapter are included in the chapter's Creative Commons license, unless indicated otherwise in a credit line to the material. If material is not included in the chapter's Creative Commons license and your intended use is not permitted by statutory regulation or exceeds the permitted use, you will need to obtain permission directly from the copyright holder.

Adjustable Autonomy for UAV Supervision Applications Through Mental Workload Assessment Techniques

Federica Bazzano[1(✉)], Angelo Grimaldi[1], Fabrizio Lamberti[1],
Gianluca Paravati[1], and Marco Gaspardone[2]

[1] Dip. di Automatica e Informatica, Politecnico di Torino,
Corso Duca degli Abruzzi, 24, 10129 Turin, Italy
{federica.bazzano,angelo.grimaldi,fabrizio.lamberti,
gianluca.paravati}@polito.it
[2] TIM JOL Connected Robotics Applications LaB,
Corso Montevecchio 71, 10129 Turin, Italy
marco.gaspardone@telecomitalia.it

Abstract. In recent years, unmanned aerial vehicles have received a significant attention in the research community, due to their adaptability in different applications, such as surveillance, disaster response, traffic monitoring, transportation of goods, first aid, etc. Nowadays, even though UAVs can be equipped with some autonomous capabilities, they often operate in high uncertainty environments in which supervisory systems including human in the control loop are still required. Systems envisaging decision-making capabilities and equipped with flexible levels of autonomy are needed to support UAVs controllers in monitoring operations. The aim of this paper is to build an adjustable autonomy system able to assist UAVs controllers by predicting mental workload changes when the number of UAVs to be monitored highly increases. The proposed system adjusts its level of autonomy by discriminating situations in which operators' abilities are sufficient to perform UAV supervision tasks from situations in which system suggestions or interventions may be required. Then, a user study was performed to create a mental-workload prediction model based on operators' cognitive demand in drone monitoring operations. The model is exploited to train the system developed to infer the appropriate level of autonomy accordingly. The study provided precious indications to be possibly exploited for guiding next developments of the adjustable autonomy system proposed.

Keywords: Adjustable autonomy · Mental workload
Supervisory control · Decision-making system

Work reported has been partially funded by TIM JOL Connected Robotics Applications LaB (CRAB).

© The Author(s) 2017
P. Horain et al. (Eds.): IHCI 2017, LNCS 10688, pp. 32–44, 2017.
https://doi.org/10.1007/978-3-319-72038-8_4

1   Introduction

In recent years, the field of aerial service robotics applications has seen a rapidly growing interest in the development of Unmanned Aerial Vehicles (UAVs) equipped with some autonomous capabilities. However, since UAVs often operate in high uncertainty and dynamic scenarios characterized by unpredictable failures and parameter disturbances, no totally-autonomous control system has emerged yet [1]. Supervisory systems including human in the control loop are required to both monitor UAV operations and assist UAV controllers when critical situations occur [2,3].

Systems equipped with flexible levels of autonomy (LOAs) and decision-making capabilities in uncertain environments may be exploited to dynamically allocate human-machine functions by discriminating situations where operators' skills are sufficient to perform a given task from situations where system suggestions or interventions may be required [4–6]. The assessment of operator multi-tasking performance as well as the level of his/her mental effort for monitoring UAVs, generally termed as *"cognitive or mental workload"* [7], may be used to determine which LOA is needed for the system.

By leveraging the above considerations, this paper reports on the activities that have been carried out at Politecnico di Torino and at TIM JOL Connected Robotics Applications LaB (CRAB) to develop, through an assessment of humans' mental workload, an adjustable autonomy system equipped with some decision-making capabilities in UAV-traffic monitoring scenarios. The system, later referred to as *"control tower"*, was devised to autonomously infer the appropriate level of autonomy by exploiting a mental workload prediction model built on operators' cognitive demand in monitoring a growing number of UAVs with an increasing level of risk.

A simulation framework was developed to reproduce both swarm of autonomous drones flying in a 3D virtual urban environment and critical conditions they could be involved into. Afterwards, a user interface showing the 2D map of the city was developed to both display drones' positions and drones' flight information and allow human operators to monitor and intervene when critical conditions occur. A Bayesian Network (BN) classifier was exploited in this work to build the mental workload prediction model described above. This classifier was also leveraged as learning probabilistic model due to its capability to solve decision problems under uncertainty [8].

A user study was carried out with several volunteers, who were asked to perform some supervision and monitoring tasks of a variable number of drones with a growing level of risk. During each experiment, participants were asked to evaluate their perceived mental workload in order to train the system developed inferring the appropriate level of autonomy accordingly.

The rest of the paper is organized as follows. In Sect. 2, relevant literature in the area of adaptive autonomy systems is reviewed. In Sect. 3, the architecture of the system proposed in this study is described. Section 4 provides an overview of the user interface exploited in this study. Section 5 introduces the methodology that has been adopted to perform the experimental tests and discusses results obtained. Lastly, Sect. 6 concludes the paper by providing possible directions for future research activities in this field.

2   Related Work

Many studies in aerial robot applications domain have investigated the evaluation and classification of cockpit operator's workload.

A number of studies have revealed the advantages in exploiting dynamic function allocations for managing operator workload and maintaining him or her focused in control loops [9,10]. In literature, several criteria have been investigated to evaluate human's cognitive load. The main measurement techniques have been historically classified into three categories: physiological, subjective, and performance-based [11]. Different techniques for mental workload assessment and classification have been proposed in this field.

Many research studies have focused on physiological measurements for assessing operator cognitive load in real time. For instance, Scerbo et al. [12] proposed the EEG power band ratios as example of workload measurement in adaptive automation. Wilson et al. [13] exploited EEG channels, electrocardiographic (ECG), electrooculographic (EOG), and respiration inputs as cognitive workload evaluation and an Artificial Neural Network (ANN) as classification methodology. Magnusson [14] examined the pilots' Heart Rate (HR), Heart Rate Variability (HRV), and eye movements in simulator and real flight.

Despite these studies have provided evidences in merging more than one physiological measurements to improve the accuracy of workload classification [13,15], such approaches have proved to be very infeasible from a measurement perspective, affected by the emotional state of the operator and impractical in aircraft cockpits application due to the need of wearing different devices at the same time [16].

In parallel to these studies, other approaches were investigated involving physiological measures in combination with other classes of workload assessment techniques. As a matter of examples, in [8] the authors performed operator's workload evaluation in piloting a flying aircraft by using EEG signal with NASA-TLX questionnaire as subjective measure and a Bayesian Network as classification method. Di Nocera et al. in [17] have investigate operator's workload evaluation engaged in simulated flight employing the eye fixations measure and NASA-TLX questionnaire as assessment methodology and Nearest Neighbor algorithm (NN) as classification method. In [16], the authors investigated different classes of cognitive workload measures by merging cardiovascular activity and secondary task performance (a performance-based technique), as inputs to an Artificial Neural Network (ANN) for operator cognitive state classification during a simulated air traffic control task.

Based on the short but representative review above, it can be observed that the panorama of mental workload assessment and classification techniques in aerial robotics applications is quite heterogeneous. By taking into account advantages and drawbacks of the above solutions, the system proposed in this paper combines subjective workload assessment techniques with a probabilistic Bayesian Network classifier to support UAV controllers in monitoring operations by autonomously inferring the appropriate LOA for the specific situation.

3 Proposed System

In the following, the adjustable autonomy system will be introduced, by providing also some implementation details.

3.1 Architecture Overview

The Adjustable Autonomy System Architecture (AASA) implementing the basic idea inspiring the present paper is illustrated in Fig. 1. It consists of three main components: *UAVs Simulator* (left), *Bandwidth Simulator* (right) and *Adjustable Autonomy Control Tower* (down). More specifically, the *UAVs Simulator* is the block devoted to load the 3D urban environment and execute the 3D drones flight simulation in it. A 3D physics engine was also exploited to test different flying scenarios in conditions as similar as possible to a realistic environment. The *Bandwidth Simulator* block was used to reproduce the network transmission rate of the simulated city. Since drones communicate or send information through the network, a low bandwidth connection could lead to critical conditions for UAV controllers. The *Adjustable Autonomy Control Tower* hosts *Alert* and *Decision* modules. The former determines the state for each drone by mapping the set of information collected by *UAVs* and *Bandwidth Simulators*, i.e., drones' battery level, their distance from obstacles, with different levels of risk, later referred to as *"Alert"*. Three different levels are used to discriminate the drone's level of risk, namely: *"Safe"*, *"Warning"* and *"Danger"*. The latter is responsible for establishing the appropriate level of autonomy by elaborating both the operator's mental workload and his performances via the *"Alert"* level of each drone.

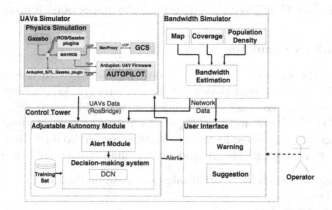

Fig. 1. Adjustable autonomy system architecture.

3.2 UAVs Simulator

The *UAVs Simulator* is the module responsible for performing the 3D drones'
simulation in an urban environment. It consists of three different modules namely
Autopilot, *Physics Simulation* and *Ground Control Station (GCS)*.

The *Autopilot* module contains the flight software allowing drones to fly sta-
ble during the flight. More specifically, the Software-In-The-Loop (SITL)[1] simulator was exploited to run the UAV flight code without any specific hardware.
Within this simulation tool, the un-compiled autopilot code, which normally
runs on the drone's onboard computer, is compiled, simulated and run by the
SITL simulation software itself. In the specific case, the SITL software was used
to run the PX4 Autopilot Flightcode[2], an open source UAV firmware of a wide
range of vehicle types.

The *Physics Simulation* module is responsible for replicating the real world
physics of drones' flight. In this work, Gazebo[3] was exploited as a real-time
physics engine in order to emulate the 3D models of UAVs, their physic properties
and constraints and their sensors (e.g. laser, camera) in a 3D urban environment.
Gazebo runs on Robot Operating System (ROS)[4], which is a software framework
developed for performing robotics tasks.

The *Ground Control Station (GCS)* module contains the software needed
to setup drones' starting GPS locations, get real-time flight information, plan
and execute drones' missions. The communication between the PX4 Autopilot
Flightcode and the GCS module is provided by the Micro Air Vehicle ROS
(MAVROS) node with the MAVLink communication protocol. As illustrated in
Fig. 1, MAVProxy node acts as an intermediary between the GCS and UAVs
supporting MAVLink protocol.

Lastly, as illustrated in Fig. 1, this module provides UAVs information data
to the Adjustable Autonomy Module by means of the RosBridge Protocol[5]. More
specifically, these information regarding drones' battery level, later abbreviated
b and their distance from obstacles (e.g. buildings), later abbreviated o, are
gathered from the Alert Module to determine the status of each drone.

3.3 Bandwidth Simulator

In this work, the network transmission rate was assumed to depend on two
different variables: population density of the city sites (parks, stadiums, schools,
etc.) and the network coverage. Three different values, in the range [1;3] - where
1 is *"Low"*, 2 is *"Medium"* and 3 is *"High"* - were used to describe the population
density and network coverage levels of the city according to daily time slots and
OpenSignal[6] data respectively. A grid on the map was created by storing in

---

[1] http://ardupilot.org/dev/docs/sitl-simulator-software-in-the-loop.html.
[2] https://px4.io.
[3] https://gazebosim.org.
[4] https://www.ros.org.
[5] https://wiki.ros.org/rosbridge_suite.
[6] https://opensignal.com.

each cell the population density and coverage values described above in order to calculate the bandwidth in the considered area. The resulting transmission rate for each cell was computed according to a linear polynomial function y of the above values as follow:

$$Bandwidth = \begin{cases} High & if & y < 0.5 \\ Medium & if\, 0.5 \geq y < 1.5 \\ Low & if & y \geq 1.5 \end{cases}$$

As illustrated in Fig. 1, the three different calculated bandwidth levels (later abbreviated n) are sent to the Adjustable Autonomy Module in order to determine the transmission rate around the drone's position on the map.

3.4   Adjustable Autonomy Control Tower

The Adjustable Autonomy Control Tower consists of two submodules namely: *Alert Module* and *Decision Module*.

The *Alert Module*, as illustrated in Fig. 1, receives data from the *UAVs* and *Bandwidth Simulators* as inputs. Each input is associated to three different variables, namely *"High"*, *"Medium"* and *"Low"* according to Table 1 and each variable is matched with a numeric value in the range [1; 3] - where 1 is *"Low"* and 3 is *"High"*.

Table 1. Drones' information association to variables

Input variables	Description	Variables/numeric values
o	Drone's distance from an obstacle	Low = [5–25] m; Medium = [25–50] m; High = [50–100] m
b	Drone's battery level	Low = [0–20]%; Medium = [21–60]%; High = [61–100]%
n	Transmission rate around drone's position	Output of the bandwidth simulator

The mathematical formula described in (1) was exploited to compute the *Alert*:

$$y = \frac{1}{b-1} * \frac{1}{o-1} * \frac{1}{n-1} \tag{1}$$

where b, o, n, represent the three inputs listed in Table 1 and y represents the drone's level of risk. Thus, the resulting *Alert* was calculated as follows:

$$Alert = \begin{cases} Danger & if & b = 1 & \vee o = 1 \vee n = 1 \\ Warning & if\, 0.15 < y < 1.5 \\ Safe & if & y \geq 1.5 \end{cases}$$

It can be observed in (1) that when one of the input variables value is *"Low"*, the *Alert* assumes the *"Danger"* value. When the input variables values increase, then the *Alert* decreases from *"Danger"* to *"Safe"* through the *"Warning"* level.

The *Decision Module* represents the core of the devised architecture. It is responsible for inferring the appropriate level of autonomy by elaborating both operators' mental workload and mission outcomes via the number of UAVs divided by *"Alert"* state.

A Bayesian Network (BN) classifier, which is a learning probabilistic model from data, was selected for representing both all variables involved in the study and their relationships in order to infer conclusions when some variables are observed. The structure of this model where the estimate LOA of the system is a direct child of the mission outcomes node via workload node is illustrated in Fig. 2. It was considered that the probability of changes in operators' workload is conditioned on changes in the number of drones in *"Alert"* state. Thus, the probability to successfully complete missions is influenced by operators' cognitive workload.

The LOAs proposed in this work, were namely: *"Warning"*, *"Suggestion"* and *"Autonomous"* where the system warns the operator if critical situations occur, suggests feasible actions to him or monitors and performs actions autonomously without any human intervention respectively.

Fig. 2. Bayesian Network model inferring the LOA from drones missions outcomes thus from subjective mental workload features via number of UAVs divided by *"Alert"* state.

4   User Interface

In this section, a user interface showing the 2D map of the city for displaying drones' positions and useful information for the human operator is presented. The devised interface allows the human operator to take control of drones through different flight commands. Depending on the current LOA of the system, the number or type of flight commands displayed dynamically changes thus defining the *"Warning"* or *"Suggestion"* interface.

A wide region of the operator's display is covered with the 2D map of the city in which drones are shown in real time. A colored marker on the map is used to indicate both the drone's GPS position and its current *"Alert"* (Fig. 3a). Three different color are used to depict the drone's level of risk: green (*"Safe"*), yellow

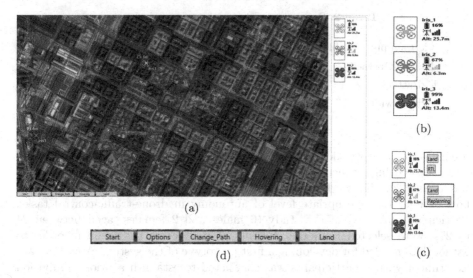

Fig. 3. Warning interface (a), UAVs data summary (b), flight commands in Suggestion interface (c) and control and display information buttons (d). (Color figure online)

(*"Warning"*) and red (*"Danger"*). Drone's marker color changes from green to red according to the linear interpolation described in (1). An extensive visual summary of data about each drone is shown on the panel in the right side of the interface (Fig. 3b). For each drone is reported its unique name, its battery level, the bandwidth coverage of the area around its location and its flying altitude. Right below the map are five controls buttons by which the operator can either issue flight commands or show information about the map or UAVs are placed (Fig. 3d). The *"Start"* button is used to run the UAVs simulation, whereas the *"Options"* button is used to show or hide the bandwidth coverage grid of the city and the drones' paths. The other three buttons namely, *"Land"*, *"Hovering"*, and *"Change_Path"* are only available in the *"Warning"* interface and are used by the human operator to take direct control of the drone. In this modality, the UAV controller can land, hover or change the drone's assigned path by defining the next waypoint with respect to the drone's current position. On the contrary, in the *"Suggestion"* interface, the operator can only select actions among those suggested from the system in the summary panel on the right of the interface (Fig. 3c), according to Table 2. The replanning action implemented in this work provides an alternative path from the actual position of the drone to its target location by exploiting the Bing Map REST API[7] with a route planning request.

5   Experimental Results

As anticipated, the goal of this paper is to build an adjustable autonomy system exploiting decision-making capabilities able to assist control tower operator by

---

[7] https://msdn.microsoft.com/it-it/library/ff701713.aspx.

Table 2. System suggested actions for each drone.

Alert's input variables	Variables values	Feasible actions
distanceObstacle	$Medium \lor Low$	Hovering, Replanning, Land
levBattery	$Medium \lor Low$	Land, Return to Launch (RTL)
levBandwidth	$Medium \lor Low$	Replanning, Land

predicting mental workload changes or overload when the number of UAVs to be monitored highly increases. To this aim, a BN probabilistic model classifier was defined in this work to learn from data collected through a user study, how to infer the appropriate level of autonomy in drone-traffic-control tasks. Participants involved in the study (6 males and 2 females, aged between 24 to 27), were selected from the students of Politecnico di Torino in order to gather data needed for developing a first prototype of the system. A preliminary experiment with 4 participants was conducted to establish a prior subdivision of the number of drones in three different ranges, namely: "*Low*", "*Medium*", and "*High*". In order to do this, participants were invited to monitor from 1 to 6 UAVs characterized by a level of risk linearly proportional to the number of drones. Results obtained showed that a number of drones in "*Low*", "*Medium*" and "*High*" ranges consists in 1, 2 and from 3 up UAVs respectively.

Afterwards, a brief training phase was performed to instruct participants to act as a real UAVs controller by performing some supervision and monitoring tasks of a growing number of drones. They were invited to monitor and eventually intervene on drones' behavior by exploiting flight commands showed in the user interface when critical conditions were warned by the UAVs through an alert.

The experiment was organized in six sessions (1 practice and 5 tests) of two trials, one in "*Warning*" mode and the other in "*Suggestion*" mode by exploiting the related interface. The above modalities were chosen in a random order so that to limit the effect of learning. Each trial lasted approximately 4 min.

The first test (labeled T1), consisted of a single flying drone whose path was designed for avoiding obstacles on its route. The other two tests T2 and T3 were meant to evaluate the operator's performance in monitoring two drones flying in a medium bandwidth zone and at risk of colliding, respectively. The fourth test (labeled T4) consisted of three drones, two of which at high risk of colliding and one with a medium battery level. The other test T5 consisted of five drones, three of which at high risk of colliding. Lastly, T6 consisted of six drones, each of which required operator's interventions to successfully complete the mission. The outcome of each test may be "*successfully completed*" - if all drones land correctly in the intended positions - or "*failed*" - if at least one drone crashes. Such tasks have been specifically designed to test the operator's performance in the possible scenarios he could be involved into in air-traffic management.

During each trial, quantitative data about number of unmanaged drones thus the outcome of each mission as well as information about the "*Alert*" status of each drone were recorded. At the end of each trial, participants were asked to fill a NASA Task Load Index (TLX) questionnaire [18] for each action performed on the drones. This questionnaire was exploited to evaluate operators' self-assessed workload on a six-dimensions scale regarding: *mental demand, physical demand, temporal demand, performance, effort,* and *frustration,* with a score from 0 to 100. A global score is then calculated by a weighting procedure to combine the six individual scale ratings. At the end of each session (after two trials), participants were also asked to indicate which LOA of the system they preferred in performing the test. For each participant, the execution of the tests and the compilation of the questionnaires took about 2 h.

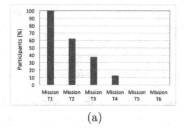 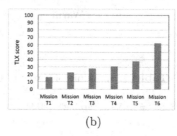

(a)   (b)

Fig. 4. Results in terms of (a) percentage of participants able to succeed missions and (b) NASA-TLX average score in the considered missions.

Results obtained in terms of number of completed missions as well as percentage of participants able to complete such missions are reported in Fig. 4a. Whereas results concerning average values of the operators' perceived workload scores are illustrated in Fig. 4b. It can be observed that the percentage of participants able to complete mission T1 is significantly greater compared to the missions T5 and T6. Concerning operators' self-assessed mental workload, the NASA-TLX average score of mission T6 appeared to be considerably higher than the others. Moving from these findings, operators' mental workload score in managing 1, 2 or more than 3 UAVs may be labeled as *"Low"*, *"Medium"* and *"High"* workload respectively. These findings corroborate the preliminary results obtained above by confirming the previous subdivision into three ranges according to the number of drones.

Results obtained were then exploited to train the Bayesian Network classifier to learn how to determine the appropriate level of autonomy for the system. Evaluation from the point of view of accuracy was then performed. For this purpose, a cross validation technique was used to test the classification model performance and its ability to predict LOAs on unseen data. According to this validation methodology, data collected were divided into two different groups, namely *training set* - for training the BN - and *validation set* - for accuracy validation - as follows: 80% and 20% of the data respectively. Overall data set contains as many rows as the actions carried out by participants on drones. Each row consists of the number of UAVs in the three *"Alert"* states, the operator's mental workload level, the outcome of the mission and his/her preferred LOA in that situation. An example of a test result is shown in Table 3. Then the corresponding line for building both *training* and *validation sets* is shown in Table 4. The Bayesian Network training phase was performed by exploiting the Netica Software[8] then the validation methodology was performed by obtaining a classification LOA accuracy equal to 83.44%. Table 5 shows the confusion matrix for each level of autonomy considered in this study.

Table 3. Example of a test result with 3 UAVs.

Drone 1	Drone 2	Drone 3	Workload	MissionOutcome	Decision
Safe	Safe	Warning	15.36	Success	Warning

Table 4. Example of a row in the *training* or *validation set*.

#UAVs "Safe"	#UAVs "Warning"	#UAVs "Danger"	Workload	MissionOutcome	Decision
Medium	Low	Null	Low	Success	Warning

Table 5. Confusion matrix

	TrueWarning	TrueSuggestion	TrueAutonomous	ClassPrecision
Pred. warning	15	1	0	93.75%
Pred. suggestion	1	30	7	78.95%
Pred. autonomous	0	4	19	82.61%
Class recall	93.75%	85.71%	73.08%	

6   Conclusions and Future Work

In this work, an adjustable autonomy system exploiting decision-making capabilities was developed to assist UAV operators by predicting the appropriate LOA relying on operators' mental workload measurements in drone monitoring scenarios. A Bayesian Network (BN) classifier was exploited as learning probabilistic model and the NASA-TLX questionnaire as subjective workload assessment technique. Obtained results show the proposed model is able to predict the appropriate LOA with an accuracy of 83.44%. Future work will focus on alternative workload assessment techniques, such as physiological measurements, to capture cognitive information in real-time and continually with higher reliability in the measurements.

---

[8] https://www.norsys.com.

References

1. Chen, H., Wang, X.m., Li, Y.: A survey of autonomous control for UAV. In: International Conference on Artificial Intelligence and Computational Intelligence, AICI 2009, vol. 2, pp. 267–271. IEEE (2009)
2. Chen, J.Y., Barnes, M.J., Harper-Sciarini, M.: Supervisory control of unmanned vehicles. Technical report, DTIC Document (2010)
3. Kopeikin, A., Clare, A., Toupet, O., How, J., Cummings, M.: Flight testing a heterogeneous multi-UAV system with human supervision. In: AIAA Guidance, Navigation, and Control Conference, p. 4825 (2012)
4. Jacobs, B., De Visser, E., Freedy, A., Scerri, P.: Application of intelligent aiding to enable single operator multiple uav supervisory control. Association for the Advancement of Artificial Intelligence, Palo Alto (2010)
5. Squire, P., Parasuraman, R.: Effects of automation and task load on task switching during human supervision of multiple semi-autonomous robots in a dynamic environment. Ergonomics $53(8)$, 951–961 (2010)
6. Holsapple, R., Baker, J., Chandler, P., Girard, A., Pachter, M.: Autonomous decision making with uncertainty for an urban intelligence, surveillance and reconnaissance (ISR) scenario. In: AIAA Guidance, Navigation and Control Conference and Exhibit, p. 6310 (2008)
7. Cain, B.: A review of the mental workload literature. Technical report, DTIC Document (2007)
8. Besson, P., Dousset, E., Bourdin, C., Bringoux, L., Marqueste, T., Mestre, D., Vercher, J.L.: Bayesian network classifiers inferring workload from physiological features: compared performance. In: 2012 IEEE Intelligent Vehicles Symposium (IV), pp. 282–287. IEEE (2012)
9. Bennett, K.B., Cress, J.D., Hettinger, L.J., Stautberg, D., Haas, M.W.: A theoretical analysis and preliminary investigation of dynamically adaptive interfaces. Int. J. Aviat. Psychol. $11(2)$, 169–195 (2001)
10. Kaber, D.B., Riley, J.M.: Adaptive automation of a dynamic control task based on secondary task workload measurement. Int. J. Cogn. Ergon. $3(3)$, 169–187 (1999)
11. Miller, S.: Workload measures. National Advanced Driving Simulator, Iowa City (2001)
12. Mark W, S., Frederick G, F., Raja, P., Francesco Di, N., Lawrence J Prinzel, I.: The efficacy of psychophysiological measures for implementing adaptive technology (2001)
13. Wilson, G.F., Monett, C.T., Russell, C.A.: Operator functional state classification during a simulated ATC task using EEG. In: Proceedings of the Human Factors and Ergonomics Society Annual Meeting, vol. 41, p. 1382. Sage Publications, Los Angeles (1997)
14. Magnusson, S.: Similarities and differences in psychophysiological reactions between simulated and real air-to-ground missions. Int. J. Aviat. Psychol. $12(1)$, 49–61 (2002)
15. Wilson, G., Harris, D.: Real-time adaptive aiding using psychological operator state assessment. In: Engineering Psychology and Cognitive Ergonomics. Ashgate, Aldershot (2001)
16. Kaber, D.B., Perry, C.M., Segall, N., Sheik-Nainar, M.A.: Workload state classification with automation during simulated air traffic control. Int. J. Aviat. Psychol. $17(4)$, 371–390 (2007)

17. Di Nocera, F., Camilli, M., Terenzi, M.: Using the distribution of eye fixations to assess pilots' mental workload. In: Proceedings of the Human Factors and Ergonomics Society Annual Meeting, vol. 50, pp. 63–65. Sage Publications Sage, Los Angeles (2006)
18. Rubio, S., Díaz, E., Martín, J., Puente, J.M.: Evaluation of subjective mental workload: a comparison of SWAT, NASA-TLX, and workload profile methods. Appl. Psychol. **53**(1), 61–86 (2004)

Open Access This chapter is licensed under the terms of the Creative Commons Attribution 4.0 International License (http://creativecommons.org/licenses/by/4.0/), which permits use, sharing, adaptation, distribution and reproduction in any medium or format, as long as you give appropriate credit to the original author(s) and the source, provide a link to the Creative Commons license and indicate if changes were made.

The images or other third party material in this chapter are included in the chapter's Creative Commons license, unless indicated otherwise in a credit line to the material. If material is not included in the chapter's Creative Commons license and your intended use is not permitted by statutory regulation or exceeds the permitted use, you will need to obtain permission directly from the copyright holder.

Brain Computer Interfaces

Classification of Motor Imagery Based EEG Signals Using Sparsity Approach

S. R. Sreeja[1](✉), Joytirmoy Rabha[1], Debasis Samanta[1], Pabitra Mitra[1], and Monalisa Sarma[2]

[1] Department of Computer Science and Engineering, Indian Institute of Technology Kharagpur, Kharagpur, West Bengal, India
sreejasr@iitkgp.ac.in, joydan4123@gmail.com,
dsamanta@sit.iitkgp.ernet.in, pabitra@cse.iitkgp.ernet.in
[2] Subir Chowdhury School of Quality and Reliability, Indian Institute of Technology Kharagpur, Kharagpur, West Bengal, India
monalisa@iitkgp.ac.in

Abstract. The advancement in brain-computer interface systems (BCIs) gives a new hope to people with special needs in restoring their independence. Since, BCIs using motor imagery (MI) rhythms provides high degree of freedom, it is been used for many real-time applications, especially for locked-in people. The available BCIs using MI-based EEG signals usually makes use of spatial filtering and powerful classification methods to attain better accuracy and performance. Inter-subject variability and speed of the classifier is still a issue in MI-based BCIs. To address the aforementioned issues, in this work, we propose a new classification method, spatial filtering based sparsity (SFS) approach for MI-based BCIs. The proposed method makes use of common spatial pattern (CSP) to spatially filter the MI signals. Then frequency bandpower and wavelet features from the spatially filtered signals are used to bulid two different over-complete dictionary matrix. This dictionary matrix helps to overcome the issue of inter-subject variability. Later, sparse representation based classification is carried out to classify the two-class MI signals. We analysed the performance of the proposed approach using publicly available MI dataset IVa from BCI competition III. The proposed SFS method provides better classification accuracy and runtime than the well-known support vector machine (SVM) and logistic regression (LR) classification methods. This SFS method can be further used to develop a real-time application for people with special needs.

Keywords: Electroencephalography (EEG)
Brain computer interface (BCI) · Motor imagery (MI)
Sparisty based classification · BCI for motor impaired users

1 Introduction

Brain-Computer Interface systems (BCIs) provides a direct connection between the human brain and a computer [20]. BCIs capture neural activities associated

© The Author(s) 2017
P. Horain et al. (Eds.): IHCI 2017, LNCS 10688, pp. 47–59, 2017.
https://doi.org/10.1007/978-3-319-72038-8_5

with an external stimuli or mental tasks, without any involvement of nerves and muscles and provides an alternative non-muscular communication [21]. The interpreted brain activities are directly translated into sequence of commands to carry out specific tasks such as controlling wheel chairs, home appliances, robotic arms, speech synthesizer, computers and gaming applications. Although, brain activities can be measured through non-invasive devices such as functional magnetic response imaging (fMRI) or magnetoencephalogram (MEG), most common BCI are based on Electroencephalogram (EEG). EEG-based BCIs facilitates many real-time applications due to its affordable cost and ease of use [18].

EEG-based BCI systems are mostly build using visually evoked potentials (VEPs), event-related potentials (ERPs), slow cortical potentials (SCPs) and sensorimotor rhythms (SMR). Out of these potentials SMR based BCI provides high degrees of freedom in association with real and imaginary movements of hands, arms, feet and tongue [10]. The neural activities associated with SMR based motor imagery (MI) BCI are the so-called mu (7–13 Hz) and $beta$ (13–30 Hz) rhythms [16]. These rhythms are readily measurable in both healthy and disabled people with neuromuscular injuries. Upon executing real or imaginary motor movements, it causes amplitude supression or enhancement of mu rhythm and these phenomena are called event-related desynchronization (ERD) and event-related synchronization (ERS), respectively [16].

The available MI-based BCI systems makes use of spatial filtering and a powerful classification methods such as support vector machine (SVM) [17,18], logistic regression (LR) [13], linear discriminant analysis (LDA) [3] to attain good accuracy. These classifiers are computationally expensive and makes the BCI system delay. For real-time BCI applications, the ongoing MI events have to be detected and classified continuously into control commands as accurately and quickly. Otherwise, the BCI user especially motor impaired people may get irritated and bored. Moreover, for the same user, the observed MI patterns differ from one day to another, or from session to session [15]. This inter-personal variability of EEG signals also results in degraded performance of the classifier. The above issues motivates us to design a MI-based BCI system with enhanced accuracy, speed and no inter-subject variations for people with special needs.

With this purpose in hand, we propose a new spatial filtering based sparsity (SFS) approach in this paper to classify MI-based EEG signals for BCIs. In recent years, sparsity based classification has received a great deal of attention in image recognition [22] and speech recognition [9] field. In compressive sensing (CS), this sparsity idea was used and according to CS theory, any natural signal can be epitomized sparsely on definite constraints [5,8]. If the signal and an over-complete dictionary matrix is given, then the objective of the sparse representation is to compute the sparse coefficients, so that the signal can be represented as a sparse linear combination of atoms (columns) in dictionary [14]. If the dictionary matrix is designed from the best extracted feature of MI signal, it helps to overcome the issue of inter-personal and intra-personal variability, also enhances the processing speed and accuracy of the classifier.

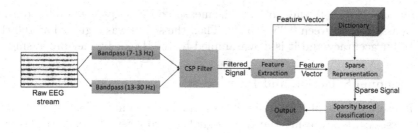

Fig. 1. Framework of the proposed SFS system.

The framework of the proposed system is shown in Fig. 1. In our proposed method, from 10–20 international system of EEG electrode placement, we considered only few channels located over motor areas for further processing. Later, the selected channels of EEG data are passed through a band-pass filter between 7–13 Hz and 13–30 Hz, as it is known from literature that most of MI signals lie within that frequency range. Then CSP is applied to spatially filter the signals and the features obtained from the filtered signals are used to build the columns (atoms) of dictionary matrix. This is an important phase in the proposed approach which is responsible for removing inter-personal variability and enhancement of classification accuracy. Later, sparsity based classification is carried out to discriminate the patterns of two-class MI signals. Furthermore, SFS method provides better accuracy and speed than the conventional support vector machine (SVM) and logistic regression (LR) classifier models.

Our paper is organised as follows. In Sect. 2, we present description of the data and the proposed technique in details. In Sect. 3, the experimental results and performance evaluation are presented. Finally, conclusions and future work are outlined in Sect. 4.

2   Data and Method

This section will describe the MI data used in this research and then the pipeline followed in the proposed method, that is, channel selection, pre-processing and spatial filtering based sparsity (SFS) classification of EEG-based MI data is discussed in detail.

2.1   Dataset Description

We used the publicly available dataset IVa from BCI competition III[1] to validate the proposed approach. The dataset consists of EEG recorded data from five healthy subjects (aa, al, av, aw, ay) who performed right-hand and right-foot MI tasks during each trial. According to the international 10–20 system, MI signals were recorded from 118 channels. For each subject, there were 140 trials for each

---

[1] http://www.bbci.de/competition/iii.

task, and therefore 280 trials totally. The measured EEG signal was filtered using a bandpass filter between 0.05–200 Hz. Then the signal was digitized at 1000 Hz with 16 bit accuracy and it is downsampled to 100 Hz for further processing.

2.2   Channel Selection and Preprocessing

The dataset consists of EEG recordings from 118 channels which is very large to process. As we are using the EEG signal of two class MI tasks (right-hand and right-foot), we extract the needed information from premotor cortex, supplementary motor cortex and primary motor cortex [11]. Therefore, from the 118 channels of EEG recording, 30 channels present over the motor cortex are considered for further processing. Moreover, removal of irrelevant channels helps to increase the robustness of classification system [19]. The selected channels are FC2, FC4, FC6, CFC2, CFC4, CFC6, C2, C4, C6, CCP2, CCP4, CCP6, CP2, CP4, CP6, FC5, FC3, FC1, CFC5, CFC3, CFC1, C5, C3, C1, CCP5, CCP3, CCP1, CP5, CP3 and CP1. The motor cortex and the areas of motor functions, the standard 10 ± 20 system of electrode placement of 128 channel EEG system and the electrodes selected for processing is shown in Fig. 2. The green and red circle indicates the selected channels and the red circle indicates the C3 and C4 channels on the left and right side of the scalp respectively.

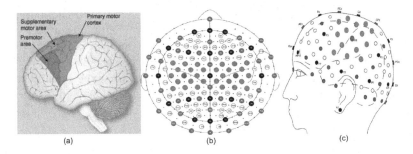

Fig. 2. (a) Motor cortex of the brain (b) Standard 10 ± 20 system of electrode placement for 128 channel EEG system. The electrodes in green and red colour are selected for processing (c) The anterior view of the scalp and the selected channels. (Color figure online)

From domain knowledge we know that, most brain activities related to motor imagery are within the frequency band of 7–30 Hz [16]. Bandpass filter can be used to extract the particular frequency band and also helps to filter out most of the high frequency noise. The bandpass filter can have as many sub-bands as one needed [12]. We have experimented with two sub-bands of 7–13 Hz and 13–30 Hz in the two-class MI signal classification problem. The choice of two sub-bands is due to the fact that mu (μ), beta (β) rhythms reside within those frequency bands. Then data segmentation is done where we used two second samples after the display of cue of each trial. Each segmentation is called as an *epoch*.

2.3   Proposed Spatial Filtering Based Sparsity Approach

The proposed spatial filtering based sparsity (SFS) approach follows three steps such as CSP filtering, design of dictionary matrix and sparsity based classification. A detailed explanation of each of these steps are given below.

CSP Filtering: Generally, for binary classification problems, CSP has been applied widely as it increases the variance of one class while it reduces the variance for the other class [1]. In this paper, how CSP filtering is applied for the given two-class MI-based EEG dataset is explained briefly. Let X_1 and X_2 be the two epochs of a multivariate signal related to right-hand and right-foot MI classes, respectively. They are both of size $(c \times n)$ where c is the number of channels (30) and n is the number of samples (100×2). We denote the CSP filter by

$$X_i^{CSP} = W^T X_i \tag{1}$$

where i is the number of MI classes, X_i^{CSP} is the spatially filtered signal, W is the spatial filter matrix and $X_i \in \mathbb{R}^{c \times n}$ is the input signal to the spatial filter. The objective of the CSP algorithm is to estimate the filter matrix W. This can be achieved by finding the vector w, the component of the spatial filter W, by satisfying the following optimization problem:

$$\max_{w} \left(\frac{w^T C_1 w}{w^T C_2 w} \right) \tag{2}$$

where $C_1 = X_1 X_1^T$ and $C_2 = X_2 X_2^T$. In order to make the computation easier to find w, we computed X_1 and X_2 by taking the average of all epochs of each class. Solving the above equation using Lagrangian method, we finally have the resulting equation as:

$$C_1 w = \lambda C_2 w \tag{3}$$

Thus Eq. (2) becomes **eigenvalue decomposition problem**, where λ is the eigenvalue corresponds to the eigenvector w. Here, w maximizes the variance of right-hand class, while minimizing the variance of right-foot class. The eigenvectors with the largest eigenvalues for C_1 have the smallest eigenvalues for C_2. Since we used 30 EEG channels, we will have 30 eigenvalues and eigenvectors. Therefore, CSP spatial filter W will have 30 column vectors. From that, we select the first m and last m columns to use it as $2m$ CSP filter of W_{CSP}.

$$W_{CSP} = [w_1, w_2, ..., w_m, w_{c-m+1}, ..., w_c] \in \mathbb{R}^{2m \times c} \tag{4}$$

Therefore, for the given two-class epochs of MI data, the CSP filtered signals are defined as follows:

$$X_1^{CSP} \in \mathbb{R}^{2m \times n} := W_{CSP}^T X_1$$
$$X_2^{CSP} \in \mathbb{R}^{2m \times n} := W_{CSP}^T X_2 \tag{5}$$

The above CSP filtering is simultaneously done for the filtered signals under the sub-bands of 7–13 Hz and 13–30 Hz.

Designing a Dictionary Matrix: The spatially filtered signals $\mathbf{X}_1^{CSP}$ and $\mathbf{X}_2^{CSP}$ are obtained for each epoch and for each sub-band. These spatially filtered signals are considered as the training signals in our experiment. Let the number of total training signals be N, considering each MI class i and each sub-band. Here, $i = 1$ for right-hand and $i = 2$ for right-foot class. The dictionary matrix can be designed with one type of feature or a combination of different features. In this work, we designed two types of dictionary matrix, one using frequency bandpower as feature and the other using wavelet transform energy as feature for each training signal. Initially, we experimented with many features like statistical, frequency-domain, wavelet-domain, entropy, auto-regressive coefficients, etc. But we found that bandpower and wavelet energy produces good differentiable between the two classes when it is plotted over the scalp. Figure 3 shows the spatial representation of bandpower and wavelet energy for two different MI classes. The Fig. 3(a) depicts that the bandpower of right-hand is scattered throughout the scalp while for right-foot the bandpower is high in the frontal region. In the same way, in Fig. 3(b) the wavelet energy is distributed all over the scalp for right-hand and only on a particular region for right-foot. Hence, these features are sufficiently good enough to discriminate the two MI classes.

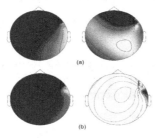

Fig. 3. Scalp plot of (a) bandpower of right-hand and right-foot MI respectively and (b) wavelet energy for right-hand and right-foot MI respectively.

From each row of the training signal, the second moment or the frequency bandpower and the wavelet energy using 'coif1' wavelet is calculated. This feature vector of each training signal forms the dictionary matrix. Concatenating the dictionary matrix of two-classes forms an over-complete dictionary. Since this dictionary matrix includes all the possible characteristics of the MI signals of the subjects, the inter-subject variability can be avoided. Figure 4 shows the dictionary constructed for the proposed approach. Thus, the dictionary matrix is defined as $\mathbf{D} := [\mathbf{D}_1; \mathbf{D}_2]$, where $D_i = [d_{i,1}, d_{i,2}, d_{i,3}, ..., d_{i,N}]$. Each atom or column of the dictionary matrix is defined as $d_{i,j} \in \mathbb{R}^{2m \times 1}$, $j = 1, 2, ..., N$, having $2m$ features. So, the dimension of the dictionary matrix $\mathbf{D}$ using bandpower as feature will be $2m \times 4N$ and it is denoted as $\mathbf{D_{BP}}$ and the same dimension remains on using wavelet energy as feature and it is denoted as $\mathbf{D_{WE}}$.

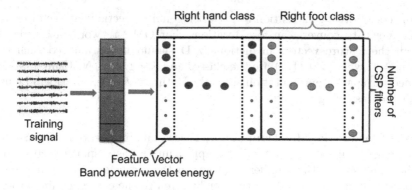

Fig. 4. Two-class dictionary designed for our proposed SFS approach. Each atom in the dictionary is obtained from the training signal of each class and each sub-band.

Sparse Representation: After the construction of dictionary matrix, we have our linear system of equations to get the sparse representation for the input test signal. The test signal is first converted into a feature vector $y \in \mathbb{R}^{m \times 1}$, using the same way as the columns in dictionary $\mathbf{D}$ is generated. So the input vector can be represented as a linear combination of few columns of $\mathbf{D}$ and it is represented as:

$$y = \sum_i s_{i,1}\mathbf{d}_{i,1} + s_{i,2}\mathbf{d}_{i,2} + ... + s_{i,N}\mathbf{d}_{i,N} \tag{6}$$

where $s_{i,j} \in \mathbb{R}, j = 1, 2, ..., N$ are the sparse coefficients and $i = (1,2)$ for the two-class MI signals. In matrix form it can be represented as:

$$y = \mathbf{D}s \tag{7}$$

where $s = [s_{i,1}, s_{i,2}..., s_{i,N}]^T$. The objective of the sparse representation is to estimate the scalar coefficients, so that we can sparsely represent the test signal as a linear combination of few atoms of dictionary $\mathbf{D}$ [14]. The sparse representation of an input signal y can be obtained by performing l_0 norm minimization as follows:

$$\min_s \|s\|_0 \quad subject\ to \quad y = \mathbf{D}s \tag{8}$$

l_0 norm optimization gives us the sparse representation but it is an NP-hard problem [2]. Therefore, a good alternative is the l_1 norm which can also be used to obtain sparsity. Recent development tells us that the representation obtained by l_1 norm optimization problem achieves the condition of sparsity and it can be solved in polynomial time [6,7]. Thus the optimization problem in Eq. (8) becomes:

$$\min_s \|s\|_1 \quad subject\ to \quad y = \mathbf{D}s \tag{9}$$

The orthogonal matching pursuit (OMP) is a greedy algorithm used to obtain sparse representation and is one of the oldest greedy algorithms [4]. It employs the concept of orthogonalization to get orthogonal projections at each iteration and is known to converge in few iterations. For OMP to work in the desired way, all the feature vectors in dictionary $\mathbf{D}$ should be normalized such that $\|\mathbf{D}_i(j)\| = 1$, where $i = (1, 2)$ are the classes and $j = 1, 2, ..., N$. Using OMP we obtained the sparse representation $\mathbf{s}$, for the feature vector $\mathbf{y}$, which will be used further for classifying MI signals.

Sparsity Based Classification: After a successful minimization of sparse representation, the input vector $\mathbf{y}$ will be approximated as a sparse vector which has the same size as the number of atoms in the dictionary $\mathbf{D}$. Each value of the sparse vector corresponds to the weight given to the corresponding atom of the dictionary. The dictionary is made of equal number of atoms for each class. If for example, there are 1400 atoms in the dictionary for a two-class MI, the first 700 values of the sparse signal tells us the linear relationship between the input vector and the first class i.e. right-hand MI class and so on. Hence, the results of the sparse representation can be used for classification by implying some simple classification rules in the sparse vector $\mathbf{s}$. In this work, we make use of two classification rules and it is termed as $classifier_1$ and $classifier_2$. Mathematically, it is defined as follows:

$$Classifier_1(\mathbf{y}) = \underset{i=1,2}{argmax}\ max\left(Var\left(\mathbf{s_i}\right)\right) \tag{10}$$

$$Classifier_2(\mathbf{y}) = \underset{i=1,2}{argmax}\ max\left(nonzero\left(\mathbf{s_i}\right)\right) \tag{11}$$

where $max()$ is a function that returns the maximum value of a vector, the function $Var()$ is used to find the variance of data and $nonzero()$ is used to find the number of sparse (non-zero) elements in a vector. The class i is determined, if it has maximum variance or maximum number of non-zero elements.

3   Experimental Results

The performance of the model in our experiment depends on the prediction performance of the classifier. A k-fold cross validation was performed on the dataset to split the entire data into k folds, from which $k - 1$ folds were used to build the dictionary and *one* fold for testing the model. Each fold was used for testing iteratively and the accuracies were calculated. Two different dictionaries were built: one with bandpower features $\mathbf{D_{BP}}$ and the other with energies of a wavelet transform $\mathbf{D_{WE}}$. Accuracy of a model based on training and testing test, is a good metric by itself to calculate the performance of the classifier.

3.1   Results of Sparsity Based Classification

We had right-hand and right-foot MI signals that needed to be classified. To illustrate how sparsity plays an important role in our classification, Fig. 5 shows

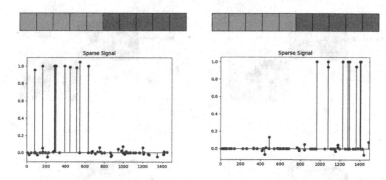

Fig. 5. Sparse representation **s** obtained for the two sample test signals. Here, the left figure represents the sparse signal of right-hand class and the right figure for the right-foot class.

the sparse representation of two sample test signals belonging to two different classes using $\mathbf{D_{BP}}$ as dictionary matrix. Here there are around 1400 atoms in the dictionary and so the first 700 elements corresponds to the first class and the rest for the second class. We can clearly see that the sparse representation is classifying the input signal with high accuracies. Table 1 shows the accuracies of each of the two classifiers in k-fold cross validation using the dictionaries $\mathbf{D_{BP}}$ and $\mathbf{D_{WE}}$, respectively. The result shows that $classifier_1$ performs better than $classifier_2$. It also shows us that the sparsity based classification using the dictionary $\mathbf{D_{WE}}$ outperforms the band-power dictionary $\mathbf{D_{BP}}$. The normalized and non-normalized confusion matrices of each of the classifiers using dictionary $\mathbf{D_{WE}}$ is given in the Fig. 6.

Table 1. k-fold cross validation accuracies for the classifiers using $\mathbf{D_{BP}}$ and $\mathbf{D_{WE}}$ dictionary.

k-folds		$k=1$	$k=2$	$k=3$	$k=4$	$k=5$	$k=6$	$k=7$	$k=8$	$k=9$	$k=10$	Average
$Classifier_1$	$\mathbf{D_{BP}}$	94.64	94.64	96.42	90.47	94.64	91.66	92.85	92.85	93.45	92.26	93.38
	$\mathbf{D_{WE}}$	98.80	97.02	98.21	94.04	98.80	94.64	94.64	96.42	98.21	95.23	96.60
$Classifier_2$	$\mathbf{D_{BP}}$	94.64	95.83	92.26	91.07	93.45	89.88	93.45	91.07	95.64	89.28	92.65
	$\mathbf{D_{WE}}$	98.21	97.02	96.42	94.04	98.62	93.20	94.64	97.82	97.21	96.20	96.33

3.2 Comparison with SVM and LR

To evaluate the proposed SFS method, we compared our method using $\mathbf{D_{WE}}$ as dictionary with the conventional SVM [17,18] and LR [13] methods. As $classifier_1$ gives better accuracy than $classifier_2$, it is used for comparison with the conventional methods. For real-time BCI applications, speed of the classifier is an important issue. Hence, CPU execution time is estimated for all the methods. All the classifier algorithms were performed using the same computer

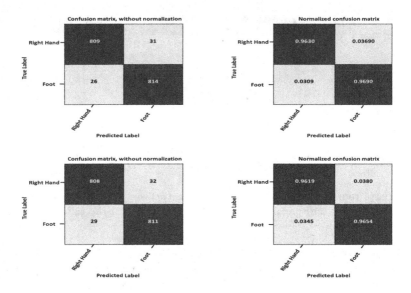

Fig. 6. Confusion matrix of $classifier_1$ and $classifier_2$ using the dictionary $\mathbf{D_{WE}}$.

and same software Python 2.7, making use of Scikit Learn[2] machine learning package. The accuracies and the CPU execution time obtained for different folds for the proposed SFS method using $classifier_1$ and $\mathbf{D_{WE}}$ as dictionary, and the

Table 2. Comparison of k-fold cross-validation accuracy and CPU execution time of various folds for the proposed SFS approach, and the conventional SVM and LR classifier methods.

folds	k-fold cross-validation Accuracy (%)			CPU execution time (Seconds)		
	Proposed SFS	SVM	LR	Proposed SFS	SVM	LR
$k=1$	98.80	94.22	93.74	24.02	30.62	31.00
$k=2$	97.02	93.10	92.88	25.42	29.99	29.34
$k=3$	98.21	93.46	91.79	23.00	28.23	29.21
$k=4$	94.04	92.78	91.86	24.50	29.29	30.19
$k=5$	98.80	94.60	94.44	24.32	30.83	28.00
$k=6$	94.64	91.78	91.32	23.36	29.00	29.75
$k=7$	94.64	91.90	91.46	24.17	29.35	28.86
$k=8$	96.42	92.45	91.98	24.56	29.43	29.94
$k=9$	98.21	93.62	92.85	23.32	29.29	30.32
$k=10$	95.23	92.88	92.52	23.96	28.00	29.76
Average	**96.60**	**93.08**	**92.48**	**24.06**	**29.40**	**29.64**

---

[2] http://scikit-learn.org.

conventional SVM and LR are listed in Table 2. The average values obtained indicates that the proposed SFS method delivers high average classification accuracy and lesser execution time than the SVM and LR methods. Since the proposed method executes in lesser time with higher accuracy, it can be further used to build real-time MI-based BCI applications for motor disabled people.

4   Conclusion

In this work, we used a new spatial filtering based sparsity (SFS) approach to classify two-class MI-based EEG signals for BCI applications. Firstly, the EEG signal with 118 channels are of high-dimension. To reduce the computational complexity, constraints are applied on selecting channels. Secondly, to better discriminate the MI classes, two sub-bands of band-pass filter between 7–13 Hz and 13–30 Hz are applied to the selected number of channels followed by CSP filtering. Thirdly, it is important to note that EEG signals produce variations among users at different sessions. As SFS method requires a dictionary matrix, it is designed using the bandpower and wavelet features obtained from the spatially filtered signals. This dictionary matrix helps us to overcome the inter-subject variability problem. This method also reduces the computational complexity significantly and increases the speed and accuracy of the BCI system. Hence, the proposed SFS approach can be served to design a more robust and reliable MI-based real-time BCI applications like text-entry system, gaming, wheel-chair control, etc., for motor impaired people. Future work will focus on extending the sparsity approach for classifying multi-class MI tasks which can be further used for communication purpose.

References

1. Aghaei, A.S., Mahanta, M.S., Plataniotis, K.N.: Separable common spatio-spectral patterns for motor imagery BCI systems. IEEE Trans. Biomed. Eng. **63**(1), 15–29 (2016)
2. Baraniuk, R.G.: Compressive sensing [lecture notes]. IEEE Signal Process. Mag. **24**(4), 118–121 (2007)
3. Blankertz, B., Tomioka, R., Lemm, S., Kawanabe, M., Muller, K.R.: Optimizing spatial filters for robust EEG single-trial analysis. IEEE Signal Process. Mag. **25**(1), 41–56 (2008)
4. Cai, T.T., Wang, L.: Orthogonal matching pursuit for sparse signal recovery with noise. IEEE Trans. Inf. Theory **57**(7), 4680–4688 (2011)
5. Candès, E.J., Wakin, M.B.: An introduction to compressive sampling. IEEE Signal Process. Mag. **25**(2), 21–30 (2008)
6. Candes, E.J., Wakin, M.B., Boyd, S.P.: Enhancing sparsity by reweighted L1 minimization. J. Fourier Anal. Appl. **14**(5), 877–905 (2008)
7. Donoho, D.L.: For most large underdetermined systems of linear equations the minimal L1-norm solution is also the sparsest solution. Commun. Pure Appl. Math. **59**(6), 797–829 (2006)

8. Donoho, D.L., Tsaig, Y., Drori, I., Starck, J.L.: Sparse solution of underdetermined systems of linear equations by stagewise orthogonal matching pursuit. IEEE Trans. Inf. Theory **58**(2), 1094–1121 (2012)

9. Gemmeke, J.F., Virtanen, T., Hurmalainen, A.: Exemplar-based sparse representations for noise robust automatic speech recognition. IEEE Trans. Audio Speech Lang. Process. **19**(7), 2067–2080 (2011)

10. He, B., Baxter, B., Edelman, B.J., Cline, C.C., Wenjing, W.Y.: Noninvasive brain-computer interfaces based on sensorimotor rhythms. Proc. IEEE **103**(6), 907–925 (2015)

11. He, L., Hu, D., Wan, M., Wen, Y., von Deneen, K.M., Zhou, M.: Common bayesian network for classification of EEG-based multiclass motor imagery BCI. IEEE Trans. Syst. Man Cybern. Syst. **46**(6), 843–854 (2016)

12. Higashi, H., Tanaka, T.: Simultaneous design of FIR filter banks and spatial patterns for EEG signal classification. IEEE Trans. Biomed. Eng. **60**(4), 1100–1110 (2013)

13. Li, Y., Wen, P.P., et al.: Modified CC-LR algorithm with three diverse feature sets for motor imagery tasks classification in EEG based brain-computer interface. Comput. Methods Programs Biomed. **113**(3), 767–780 (2014)

14. Li, Y., Yu, Z.L., Bi, N., Xu, Y., Gu, Z., Amari, S.: Sparse representation for brain signal processing: a tutorial on methods and applications. IEEE Signal Process. Mag. **31**(3), 96–106 (2014)

15. Nicolas-Alonso, L.F., Corralejo, R., Gomez-Pilar, J., Álvarez, D., Hornero, R.: Adaptive stacked generalization for multiclass motor imagery-based brain computer interfaces. IEEE Trans. Neural Syst. Rehabil. Eng. **23**(4), 702–712 (2015)

16. Pfurtscheller, G., Neuper, C.: Motor imagery and direct brain-computer communication. Proc. IEEE **89**(7), 1123–1134 (2001)

17. Siuly, S., Li, Y.: Improving the separability of motor imagery EEG signals using a cross correlation-based least square support vector machine for brain-computer interface. IEEE Trans. Neural Syst. Rehabil. Eng. **20**(4), 526–538 (2012)

18. Sreeja, S., Joshi, V., Samima, S., Saha, A., Rabha, J., Cheema, B.S., Samanta, D., Mitra, P.: BCI augmented text entry mechanism for people with special needs. In: Basu, A., Das, S., Horain, P., Bhattacharya, S. (eds.) IHCI 2016. LNCS, vol. 10127, pp. 81–93. Springer, Cham (2017). https://doi.org/10.1007/978-3-319-52503-7_7

19. Tam, W.K., Tong, K., Meng, F., Gao, S.: A minimal set of electrodes for motor imagery BCI to control an assistive device in chronic stroke subjects a multi-session study. IEEE Trans. Neural Syst. Rehabil. Eng. **19**(6), 617–627 (2011)

20. Wolpaw, J., Wolpaw, E.W.: Brain-Computer Interfaces: Principles and Practice. Oxford University Press, Oxford (2012)

21. Wolpaw, J.R., Birbaumer, N., McFarland, D.J., Pfurtscheller, G., Vaughan, T.M.: Brain-computer interfaces for communication and control. Clin. Neurophysiol. **113**(6), 767–791 (2002)

22. Wright, J., Yang, A.Y., Ganesh, A., Sastry, S.S., Ma, Y.: Robust face recognition via sparse representation. IEEE Trans. Pattern Anal. Mach. Intell. **31**(2), 210–227 (2009)

Open Access This chapter is licensed under the terms of the Creative Commons Attribution 4.0 International License (http://creativecommons.org/licenses/by/4.0/), which permits use, sharing, adaptation, distribution and reproduction in any medium or format, as long as you give appropriate credit to the original author(s) and the source, provide a link to the Creative Commons license and indicate if changes were made.

The images or other third party material in this chapter are included in the chapter's Creative Commons license, unless indicated otherwise in a credit line to the material. If material is not included in the chapter's Creative Commons license and your intended use is not permitted by statutory regulation or exceeds the permitted use, you will need to obtain permission directly from the copyright holder.

Mental Workload Assessment for UAV Traffic Control Using Consumer-Grade BCI Equipment

Federica Bazzano$^{(\boxtimes)}$, Paolo Montuschi, Fabrizio Lamberti, Gianluca Paravati, Silvia Casola, Gabriel Ceròn, Jaime Londoño, and Flavio Tanese

Dip. di Automatica e Informatica, Politecnico di Torino,
Corso Duca degli Abruzzi, 24, 10129 Turin, Italy
{federica.bazzano,paolo.montuschi,fabrizio.lamberti,gianluca.paravati,
silvia.casola,gabriel.ceron,jaime.londono,flavio.tanese}@polito.it

Abstract. The increasing popularity of unmanned aerial vehicles (UAVs) in critical applications makes supervisory systems based on the presence of human in the control loop of crucial importance. In UAV-traffic monitoring scenarios, where human operators are responsible for managing drones, systems flexibly supporting different levels of autonomy are needed to assist them when critical conditions occur. The assessment of UAV controllers' performance thus their mental workload may be used to discriminate the level and type of automation required. The aim of this paper is to build a mental-workload prediction model based on UAV operators' cognitive demand to support the design of an adjustable autonomy supervisory system. A classification and validation procedure was performed to both categorize the cognitive workload measured by ElectroEncephaloGram signals and evaluate the obtained patterns from the point of view of accuracy. Then, a user study was carried out to identify critical workload conditions by evaluating operators' performance in accomplishing the assigned tasks. Results obtained in this study provided precious indications for guiding next developments in the field.

Keywords: Adjustable autonomy · Mental workload
Supervisory control · Learning model

1 Introduction

In recent years, the unmanned aerial vehicle (UAV) applications domain has seen a rapid growing interest in the development of systems able to assist human beings in critical operations [1–3]. Examples of such applications include security and surveillance, monitoring, search and rescue, disaster management, etc. [4].

Systems able to flexibly support different levels of autonomy (LOAs) according to both humans' cognitive resources and their performance in accomplishing

Work reported has been partially funded by TIM JOL Connected Robotics Applications LaB (CRAB).

© The Author(s) 2017
P. Horain et al. (Eds.): IHCI 2017, LNCS 10688, pp. 60–72, 2017.
https://doi.org/10.1007/978-3-319-72038-8_6

critical tasks, may be exploited to determine situations in which system intervention may be required [5–7]. The human's cognitive resources and the ability of the system to dynamically change the LOA according to the considered context are generally termed as *"cognitive or mental workload"* [8] and *"adjustable or sliding autonomy"* [9], respectively.

In literature, several criteria have been investigated to evaluate human's cognitive load. The main measurement techniques have been historically classified into three categories: physiological, subjective, and performance-based [10]. Physiological measurements are cognitive load assessment techniques based on the physical response of the body. Subjective measurements are used to evaluate humans' perceived mental workload by exploiting rankings or scales. Performance or objective measurements are used to evaluate humans' ability to perform a given task.

By moving from the above considerations, the aim of this paper is to build a classification and prediction model of UAV operators' mental workload to support the design of an adaptive autonomy system able to adjust its level of autonomy accordingly. An ElectroEncephaloGram (EEG) signals was used as physiological technique for assessing operators' mental workload and a Support Vector Machine (SVM) was leveraged as learning and classification model [11–13].

A 3D simulation framework was exploited in this work to both experiment different flying scenarios of a swarm of autonomous drones flying in an urban environment and test the operator's performance in UAV-traffic management. A user interface was also used to show the 2D visualization of experimented environment and allow human operators to interact with UAVs by issuing flight commands.

A user study was carried out with several volunteers to both evaluate operators' performance in accomplishing supervision tasks of a growing number of drones and gather different workload measurements under critical conditions.

The rest of the paper is organized as follows. In Sect. 2, relevant works concerning workload measurements are reviewed. In Sect. 3, the device exploited in the study is described. Sections 4 and 5 provide an overview of the overall simulation framework and report details of the user interface considered in this work, respectively. Sections 6 and 7 introduce the methodology that has been adopted to perform the experimental tests and discuss data analysis and the classification procedure. Lastly, Sect. 8 discusses obtained results and concludes the paper by providing possible directions for future research activities in this field.

2   Related Work

Many studies have investigated the relationship between tasks performed by an individual and its cognitive load. In literature, different techniques have been proposed for mental workload assessment [10].

For instance, concerning subjective measurements techniques, [14,15] have exploited the NASA-TLX questionnaire to evaluate users' perceived workload in gaze-writing and robotic manipulation tasks, respectively. Similarly, Squire et al. [16] have investigated the impact of self-assessed mental workload in simulated game activities.

Despite, these measurements have been proved to be a reliable way to assess humans' mental workload [17], they often require annoying or repetitive interactions to the users by asking them to fill different rankings or scales.

In parallel to these studies, other works have evaluated physiological measurements as mental workload assessment techniques. As a matter of example, Wilson et al. [18] exploited EEG channels, electrocardiographic (ECG), electrooculographic (EOG), and respiration inputs as cognitive workload evaluation in air traffic control tasks. Functional Near-Infrared Spectroscopy (fNIRS) and Heart Rate Variability (HRV) techniques were exploited in [19] and [20] to assess the human's mental workload in n-back working memory tasks and ship simulators, respectively. Besserve et al. [21] studied the relation between EEG data and reaction time (RT) to characterize the level of performance during a cognitive task, in order to anticipate human mistakes.

Although these studies have provided evidences to improve accuracy in workload measurements, they traditionally exploit bulky and expensive equipment virtually uncomfortable to use in real application scenarios [22]. Data about suitability of alternative devices in physiological measurements are actually required in order to properly support next advancements in the field. Some activities in this direction have been already carried out. For instance, Wang et al. [12] have proved that a small device, as a 14-channel EMOTIV®Headset, can be successful used to characterize the mental workload in a simple memory n-back task.

The goal of the present paper is to study on results reported in [12] a different application scenario exploiting EEG signals to build a UAV operators' mental workload prediction model in drones monitoring tasks.

3   Emotiv Epoc Headset

This section briefly describes the brain wearables devise EMOTIV Epoc+®[1] considered in this study by illustrating its hardware and software features. More specifically, the EMOTIV Epoc+ (Fig. 1a) is a wireless Brain Computer Interface (BCI) device manufactured by Emotiv. The headset consists of 14 wireless EEG signal acquisition channels at 128 samples/s (Fig. 1b). The recorded EEG signal is transmitted to an USB dongle for delivering the collected information to the host workstation. A subscription software, named Pure·EEG is provided by Emotiv to gather both the raw EEG data and the dense spatial resolution array containing data at each sampling interval.

4   Simulation Framework

The basic idea inspiring the design of the present framework is to test different UAV flying scenarios in an urban environment. Such scenarios simulate

---

[1] https://www.emotiv.com/epoc/.

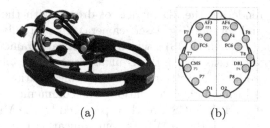

(a)   (b)

Fig. 1. Emotiv EPOC headset (a) and its 14 recorder positions (b).

potentially critical situations in which drones could be involved in. The logical components that were assembled to implement the proposed framework are illustrated in Fig. 2. By digging more in details, the *UAVs Simulator* is the module responsible for simulating swarm of autonomous drones flying in the 3D virtual environment. It consists of three different modules, namely: *Autopilot*, *Physics Simulation* and *Ground Control Station (GCS)*.

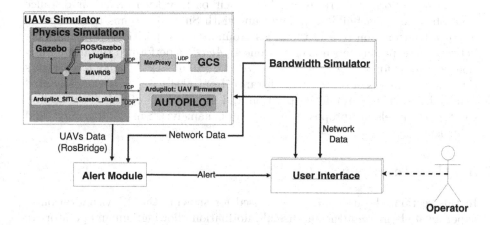

Fig. 2. Logical components of the simulation framework.

The *Autopilot* module is responsible for running drones flight stability software without any specific hardware. More specifically, it exploits the Software-In-The-Loop (SITL)[2] simulator to run the PX4 Autopilot Flightcode[3] - an open source UAV firmware of a wide range of vehicle types. The *Physics Simulation* module is the block devoted to load the 3D urban environment and execute the drone flight simulation in it. Gazebo[4] physics engine was exploited in this block

---

[2] http://ardupilot.org/dev/docs/sitl-simulator-software-in-the-loop.html.
[3] https://px4.io.
[4] https://gazebosim.org.

for modeling and rendering the 3D models of drones with their physic properties, constraints and sensors (e.g. laser, camera). In particular, Gazebo runs on Robot Operating System (ROS)[5], which is a software framework developed for performing robotics tasks. Then, the *Ground Control Station (GCS)* module contains the software used for setting drones' starting locations, planning missions and getting real-time flight information. The communication between the Autopilot Flightcode and the GCS module is provided by the Micro Air Vehicle ROS (MAVROS) node with the MAVLink communication protocol (Fig. 2).

Since drones communicate or transmit information through the network, low bandwidth coverage areas could lead to loss of communication and thus to potentially critical conditions. Hence, a *Bandwidth Simulator* is developed to estimate, in the experimented city, the maximum amount of data the network can transmit in the unit of time. The network transmission rate is assumed to depend on population density of the city sites (parks, stadiums, schools, etc.) and the network coverage.

Lastly, the *Alert Module* is the block devoted to determine the level of risk (later referred to as *"Alert"*) of each drone by gathering data from both UAVs and Bandwidth Simulators. Specifically, as in [23,24], the UAVs Simulator provides drone information regarding both their battery level and their distance from obstacles (e.g. buildings). The Bandwidth Simulator sends the estimated network transmission rate in the areas around drones' positions. The mapping between these parameters and each drone's *"Alert"* is performed through a function defined as follows: $y = (b-1)^{-1} * (o-1)^{-1} * (n-1)^{-1}$, where b represents the drone's battery level, o is its distance from obstacles, n is the estimated bandwidth coverage around its position and y is its level of risk. Three different *"Alert"* levels are proposed in this work, namely: *"Safe"*, *"Warning"* and *"Danger"*.

5   User Interface

In this section, the user interface devised for showing the 2D visualization of experimented environment and useful information allowing human operators to interact with UAVs is presented.

As illustrated in Fig. 3a, a wide region of the operator's display is covered with the 2D map of the city in which the real-time drones' locations are shown. A colored marker is used to depict the drone's GPS position as well as its current status. Three different colors are used to illustrate the drone's level of risk: green (*"Safe"*), yellow (*"Warning"*) and red (*"Danger"*). On the right side of the interface an extensive visual summary for each drone regarding its unique name, its battery level, the bandwidth coverage of the area around its location and its flying altitude, is shown (Fig. 3b). Right below the map five buttons allowing operators to issue flight commands or show general information about the map or drones are placed (Fig. 3c). More specifically, the *"Start"* button is used to run the 3D simulation, whereas the *"Options"* button to show or

---

[5] https://www.ros.org.

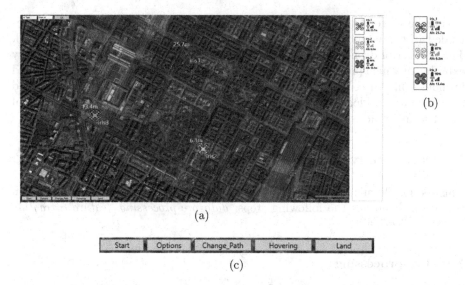

Fig. 3. Monitoring interface (a), UAVs summary (b) and control buttons (c). (Color figure online)

hide the bandwidth coverage of the city and the drones' paths. The other three buttons are used by the human operator to land, hover or change the drone's path, respectively. In this scenario, it is worth observing that EEG signals could be affected by the movement of human operators for pressing the above buttons. Thus, an artifact removal stage is needed in order to remove all undesired signals as detailed in Sect. 7.1.

6   User Tasks

The goal of this paper is to exploit EEG signals to build a prediction model of the UAV operators' mental workload in order to train a system able to autonomously predict operators' performance in UAVs monitoring operations. To this aim, an SVM classification algorithm was exploited to learn the ability of operators to carry out assigned drone-traffic-control tasks in different flying scenarios. Four monitoring tasks were experimented in this work, namely: *M1*, *M2*, *M3* and *M4*. In particular, *M1* consisted of a single flying drone whose path was designed for avoiding obstacles on its route. No operator's action was necessary to successfully complete the mission. *M2* was meant to evaluate the operator's performance in monitoring two drones at risk of colliding. Collisions were specifically designed distant over time in order to allow the operator to be virtually able to deal with them by keeping the effort to complete the mission relatively low. Mission *M3* consisted of five drones, three of which at high risk of colliding. This mission was intentionally created to be very difficult to complete even though theoretically still manageable. Lastly, *M4* consisted of six drones, each of which required operator's interventions to successfully complete the mission. It was devised to be hardly to complete.

Furthermore, a mission is considered *"successfully completed"* when all drones landed in the intended positions or *"failed"* when at least one drone crashed. The number of drones in each mission was also defined relying on a preliminary experiment which proved no significance difference in operators' mental workload in monitoring three or four UAV. Data collected during mission M1 were used as a mental workload baseline whereas those recorded in M4 as high mental workload reference.

7   Data Analysis and Classification

This section details the data analysis and classification procedure performed in this work. It entails the following steps: *data pre-processing, feature extraction* and *classification*.

7.1   Pre-processing

The EEG consists of recording electric signals produced by the activation of thousands of neurons in the brain. These signals are gathered by electrodes located over the scalp of a person. However, some spurious signals may affect the EEG data due the presence of noise or artifacts. In particular, the artifacts which are signals with no cerebral origin can be divided in two groups. The first group is related to physiological sources such as eye blinking, ocular movement and heart beating. The second group consists of mechanical artifacts, such as the movement of electrodes or cables during data collection [25]. Thus, a pre-processing stage is needed to remove all undesired signals and noise. It consists of three different phases, namely: *filtering, offset removal* and *artifact removal*. The EEGlab toolbox under the Matlab environment [26] was exploited in this phase.

Since the EEG signals frequencies are within 0.5 and 45 Hz, the *filtering* phase implements a Finite Impulse Response (FIR) passband filter to remove signals with high frequencies and increase signal to noise ratio. The *offset removal* phase eliminates potential offset residues after the filtering phase. The last stage exploits the Artifact Subspace Reconstruction (ASR) algorithm for artifact removal [27].

7.2   Feature Extraction

Given the preprocessed data, relevant features have to be extracted to train the classification model. For this purpose, temporal ranges of the signals containing relevant events to be analyzed are defined. In this work, the signal was split in different time windows as follows: 15 s after the start of the EEG recording and 15 s before the first failure, divided in 5 s windows. Data recorded during the idle drone's takeoff phase was ignored to avoid exploiting related mental workload measurements as baseline reference in the UAV monitoring experiment. Data in the range just before and after the first failure were not recorded since they may be affected of biases due to the operator's frustration for failing the assigned task. For each window the following features were calculated channel by channel: Power Spectral Density, Mean, Variance, Skewness, Kurtosis, Curve length, Average non-linear energy and Number of peaks [12]. These features were then concatenated in order to make each window corresponds to a row of features appearing in order of channel. Each row was then assigned to a label that states whether the operator failed or not the task for that particular mission.

7.3   Classification

The aim of this step is to train the classification system considered in this study with the operators' mental workload for predicting their performance in UAVs monitoring operations. Three different models were exploited in this work: two classifiers for predicting the outcome of each mission for each single subject; in the third one, overall data gathered from all operators were used, in order to understand whether a generalized model may be also employed.

A procedure dealing with *feature scaling*, *hyperparameter optimization*, *results validation* and *learning model design*, was proposed in order to judge the model considered from the point of view of accuracy.

Feature Scaling. An important issue in signal processing field, and in particular with the EEG data is the high variability of the features extracted from each subject thus their different ranges. An appropriate scaling method is needed in order to normalize all data into the same range. A *z-score* scaler was used as normalization method for subtracting mean values from all measured signals and then dividing the difference by the population standard deviation [28].

Hyperparameter Optimization and Validation Methodology. Since the aim of the classification methodology is to have a good accuracy on unseen data, an appropriate validation method becomes necessary in order to measure the generalization error of the implemented model. For this purpose, a k-fold cross validation technique was used to both find the best model with the optimal parameters and test its performance on new unseen data. It consists of samples subdivision in k folds, where k − 1 are used in each iteration to train the model, and the remaining one is used to evaluate the results.

According to this validation methodology, data were divided into three different groups, namely *training set*, *validation set*, and *test set* as follows: 20% as *test set*, and the other 80% as *training* and *validation sets*. A ten-fold cross validation is then performed on *training* and *validation sets* as follows: samples are divided in ten folds, nine of which are used in each iteration to train the model, and the other one is used to evaluate the results. This procedure is then iterated until all folds are used one time as *validation set*. The training accuracy is then evaluated as the mean of all the obtained results in the different iterations. The parameters leading to the best model performance called "*Hyperparameters*" are then selected [29]. Lastly, the model is evaluated using the *test set*.

Learning Model. A Support Vector Machine (SVM), which is a learning model able to infer a function from labeled training data, is exploited in this phase to deduce from the operator's EEG workload his ability to succeed or not a mission. It is implemented with two different kernels: linear and Radial Basis Function (RBF). The former is used to find the best hyperplane separation in binary classification problems by tuning the regularization parameter C. The latter is generally used in problems that are not linearly separable and require to find also the best value of the γ parameter [13].

The C parameter is used to regularize and control the bias variance trade-off. The γ parameter is used to define the variance of the Radial Basis Function (RBF). A grid search using powers of ten from 10^{-2} to 10^2 was used to tune the C parameter through the cross-validation phase. For the γ parameter, powers of ten from 10^{-4} to 10 were used by considering that bigger values lead to adjust better the model to the training set but bring possible problems of variance or over-fitting. Smaller values may bring bias or under-fitting problems.

8   Results and Discussion

As anticipated, the goal of this paper is to build a UAV operators' mental work-load prediction model in order to train a system able to autonomously predict operators' performance in UAVs monitoring operations. To this aim, mental workload data have been collected through a user study.

The study involved 10 participants (8 males and 2 females, aged between 19 to 24), selected from the students of Politecnico di Torino. After a brief training, participants were invited to perform the four tasks M1, M2, M3 and M4 in sequence through the user interface. Such tasks have been specifically designed to test operators' performance in UAVs monitoring operations with an increasing drones' level of risk. Each task, whose length was strictly depending on the operator's piloting choices, took from 2 to 7 min. During each experiment (i.e., all tasks performed), physiological measurements gathered by the EEG signal through the EMOTIV Epoc+®Headset were recorded. The EEG signal was split in different time windows as detailed in Sect. 7.2. For each window, the following features were calculated: Power Spectral Density, Mean, Variance, Skewness, Kurtosis, Curve length, Average non-linear energy and Number of peaks. These features were then concatenated in order to make each window correspond to a row of features appearing in order of channel. Each row was then assigned to a label that states whether the operator failed or not the task for that particular mission. This procedure was performed to generate an heterogeneous population in order to build a classifier able to autonomously predict the label from operators' mental workload measured by EEG signals.

Results obtained in terms of classification algorithm accuracy are reported in Table 1 specifying the hyperparameters used to train each single model. The first ten rows of the table represent the obtained results in the individual model trained using single subject data. The last row shows the overall results using all the collected data. By digging more in details, as shown in Table 1, the fifth and

Table 1. Results concerning the accuracy of the classification algorithm for the individual and overall models.

Participant ID	Model						
	SVM - linear kernel			SVM - RBF kernel			
	C	Accuracy (validation set)	Accuracy (test set)	C	γ	Accuracy (validation set)	Accuracy (test set)
1	0.01	0.949	0.933	100	0.0001	0.949	0.933
2	100	0.923	0.973	100	0.0001	0.934	0.973
3	0.01	0.965	1	100	0.0001	0.965	1
4	0.01	0.851	0.965	10	0.0001	0.851	0.93
5	*	*	*	*	*	*	*
6	0.1	0.885	0.895	10	0.001	0.899	0.864
7	*	*	*	*	*	*	*
8	0.01	0.944	0.969	100	0.0001	0.936	0.969
9	0.01	0.986	0.927	10	0.001	0.897	0.864
10	0.01	0.995	1	10	0.001	0.995	1
Overall	0.1	0.852	0.839	10	0.001	0.872	0.856

seventh rows present corrupted data that have been discarded for the validation purpose. In those cases, participants only completed one mission successfully, making it very difficult to train the model due to class skewness. As a result, no individual model was trained using those data. However, they were used in the overall model.

The accuracy scores obtained with the ten-fold cross-validation phase (Sect. 7.3) are reported in Table 1 as "Accuracy (Validation set)". The obtained accuracy with new unseen data is reported as "Accuracy (Test set)". It is worth observing that the accuracy scores in these two columns for the same row are not largely different. This observation allows to conclude, that the proposed model is not affected by problems of variance thus performs well if tested with other participants under the same conditions.

Results regarding the accuracy of the test sets show that the linear kernel always perform better or equal than the RBF kernel for individual models. On the contrary, the RBF kernel performs better than linear kernel for the overall model. Specifically, the SVM with the linear kernel is able to predict the operator's performance outcomes thus the level of his/her mental workload with an average accuracy equal to 95.8% and 83.9% when the model is trained on a single user and on all collected data, respectively. Whereas, an accuracy equal to 94.1% and 85.6% is reached with the SVM - RBF kernel when the model is trained using the single user and overall data, respectively. This may be reasonably due to the fact that individual models trained using single subject data are simpler classification problems than those with all collected data.

In this work, the data analysis and classification procedure was performed offline on the data collected through the user study. Future works will be aimed to address alternative procedures in order to allow online evaluation of the data.

References

1. Kopeikin, A., Clare, A., Toupet, O., How, J., Cummings, M.: Flight testing a heterogeneous multi-UAV system with human supervision. In: AIAA Guidance, Navigation, and Control Conference, p. 4825 (2012)
2. Parasuraman, R., Miller, C.: Delegation interfaces for human supervision of multiple unmanned vehicles: theory, experiments, and practical applications. In: Cooke, N.J., Pringle, H.L., Pedersen, H.K., Connor, O. (eds.) Human Factors of Remotely Operated Vehicles, pp. 251–266. Emerald Group Publishing Limited, Bingley (2006)
3. Wickens, C.D., Dixon, S.: Workload demands of remotely piloted vehicle supervision and control: (1) single vehicle performance. Technical report, DTIC Document (2002)
4. Sarris, Z., Atlas, S.: Survey of UAV applications in civil markets. In: Proceedings of the 9th Mediterranean Conference on Control and Automation, pp. 1–11 (2001)
5. Freedy, A., Sert, O., Freedy, E., McDonough, J., Weltman, G., Tambe, M., Gupta, T., Grayson, W., Cabrera, P.: Multiagent adjustable autonomy framework (MAAF) for multi-robot, multi-human teams. In: International Symposium on Collaborative Technologies and Systems, CTS 2008, pp. 498–505. IEEE (2008)
6. Côté, N., Canu, A., Bouzid, M., Mouaddib, A.I.: Humans-robots sliding collaboration control in complex environments with adjustable autonomy. In: Proceedings of the 2012 IEEE/WIC/ACM International Joint Conferences on Web Intelligence and Intelligent Agent Technology, vol. 2, pp. 146–153. IEEE Computer Society (2012)
7. Heger, F.W., Singh, S.: Sliding autonomy for complex coordinated multi-robot tasks: analysis & experiments (2006)
8. Cain, B.: A review of the mental workload literature. Technical report, DTIC Document (2007)
9. Goodrich, M.A., Schultz, A.C.: Human-robot interaction: a survey. Found. Trends Hum. Comput. Interact. $1(3)$, 203–275 (2007)
10. Miller, S.: Workload measures. National Advanced Driving Simulator, Iowa City, USA (2001)
11. Lim, W.L., Sourina, O., Liu, Y., Wang, L.: EEG-based mental workload recognition related to multitasking. In: 2015 10th International Conference on Information, Communications and Signal Processing (ICICS), pp. 1–4. IEEE (2015)
12. Wang, S., Gwizdka, J., Chaovalitwongse, W.A.: Using wireless eeg signals to assess memory workload in the n-back task. IEEE Trans. Hum. Mach. Syst. $46(3)$, 424–435 (2016)
13. Walter, C., Schmidt, S., Rosenstiel, W., Gerjets, P., Bogdan, M.: Using cross-task classification for classifying workload levels in complex learning tasks. In: 2013 Humaine Association Conference on Affective Computing and Intelligent Interaction (ACII), pp. 876–881. IEEE (2013)
14. Hayashi, T., Kishi, R.: Utilization of NASA-TLX for workload evaluation of gaze-writing systems. In: 2014 IEEE International Symposium on Multimedia (ISM), pp. 271–272. IEEE (2014)

15. Cannon, D., Siegel, M.: Perceived mental workload and operator performance of dexterous manipulators under time delay with master-slave interfaces. In: 2015 IEEE International Conference on Computational Intelligence and Virtual Environments for Measurement Systems and Applications (CIVEMSA), pp. 1–6. IEEE (2015)
16. Squire, P., Parasuraman, R.: Effects of automation and task load on task switching during human supervision of multiple semi-autonomous robots in a dynamic environment. Ergonomics **53**(8), 951–961 (2010)
17. Hart, S.G., Staveland, L.E.: Development of NASA-TLX (task load index): results of empirical and theoretical research. Adv. Psychol. **52**, 139–183 (1988)
18. Wilson, G.F., Monett, C.T., Russell, C.A.: Operator functional state classification during a simulated ATC task using EEG. In: Proceedings of the Human Factors and Ergonomics Society Annual Meeting, vol. 41, p. 1382. Sage Publications, Los Angeles (1997)
19. Berivanlou, N.H., Setarehdan, S.K., Noubari, H.A.: Quantifying mental workload of operators performing n-back working memory task: toward fNIRS based passive BCI system. In: 2016 23rd Iranian Conference on Biomedical Engineering and 2016 1st International Iranian Conference on Biomedical Engineering (ICBME), pp. 140–145. IEEE (2016)
20. Sugimoto, I., Kitamura, K., Murai, K., Wang, Y., Wang, J.: Study on relation between operator and trainee's mental workload for ship maneuvering simulator exercise using heart rate variability. In: 2016 IEEE International Conference on Systems, Man, and Cybernetics (SMC). IEEE (2016). ISSN 000768–000772
21. Besserve, M., Philippe, M., Florence, G., Laurent, F., Garnero, L., Martinerie, J.: Prediction of performance level during a cognitive task from ongoing eeg oscillatory activities. Clin. Neurophysiol. **119**(4), 897–908 (2008)
22. Lin, C.T., Ko, L.W., Chang, M.H., Duann, J.R., Chen, J.Y., Su, T.P., Jung, T.P.: Review of wireless and wearable electroencephalogram systems and brain-computer interfaces-a mini-review. Gerontology **56**(1), 112–119 (2010)
23. Madgwick, S., Turner, C., Harwin, W.: Adaptation of an commercially available stabilised R/C helicopter to a fully autonomous surveillance UAV. In: Bristol International Unmanned Air Vehicle Systems (U4 JS) Conference (2009)
24. Gageik, N., Müller, T., Montenegro, S.: Obstacle detection and collision avoidance using ultrasonic distance sensors for an autonomous quadrocopter. University of Würzburg, Aerospace Information Technology, Würzburg, Germany, September 2012
25. Bulea, T.C., Kilicarslan, A., Ozdemir, R., Paloski, W.H., Contreras-Vidal, J.L.: Simultaneous scalp electroencephalography (EEG), electromyography (EMG), and whole-body segmental inertial recording for multi-modal neural decoding. JoVE (J. Visual. Exp.) **26**(77), e50602 (2013)
26. Delorme, A., Makeig, S.: EEGLAB: an open source toolbox for analysis of single-trial EEG dynamics including independent component analysis. J. Neurosci. Methods **134**(1), 9–21 (2004)
27. Kothe, C.: The artifact subspace reconstruction method (2013)
28. Kawintiranon, K., Buatong, Y., Vateekul, P.: Online music emotion prediction on multiple sessions of EEG data using SVM. In: 2016 13th International Joint Conference on Computer Science and Software Engineering (JCSSE), pp. 1–6. IEEE (2016)
29. James, G., Witten, D., Hastie, T.: An Introduction to Statistical Learning: With Applications in R. Springer, New York (2014). https://doi.org/10.1007/978-1-4614-7138-7

Open Access This chapter is licensed under the terms of the Creative Commons Attribution 4.0 International License (http://creativecommons.org/licenses/by/4.0/), which permits use, sharing, adaptation, distribution and reproduction in any medium or format, as long as you give appropriate credit to the original author(s) and the source, provide a link to the Creative Commons license and indicate if changes were made.

The images or other third party material in this chapter are included in the chapter's Creative Commons license, unless indicated otherwise in a credit line to the material. If material is not included in the chapter's Creative Commons license and your intended use is not permitted by statutory regulation or exceeds the permitted use, you will need to obtain permission directly from the copyright holder.

Improving Classification Performance by Combining Feature Vectors with a Boosting Approach for Brain Computer Interface (BCI)

Rachel Rajan[✉] and Sunny Thekkan Devassy

GEC, Thrissur, Kerala, India
rachelrajan13@gmail.com, sunnythekkan@rediffmail.com

Abstract. In the classification of multichannel electroencephalograph (EEG) based BCI studies, the spatial and spectral information related to brain activities associated with BCI paradigms are usually pre-determined as default without speculation, which can lead to loses effects in practical applications due to individual variability across different subjects. Recent studies have shown that feature combination of each specifically tailored for different physiological phenomena such as Readiness Potential (RP) and Event Related Desynchronization (ERD) might benefit BCI making it robust against artifacts. Hence, the objective is to design a CSSBP with combined feature vectors, where the signal is divided into several sub bands using a band pass filter, and this channel and frequency configurations are then modeled as preconditions before learning base learners and introducing a new heuristic of stochastic gradient boost for training the base learners under these preconditions. Results showed that Boosting approach using feature combination clearly outperformed the state-of-the-art algorithms, and improved the classification performance, resulting in increased robustness.

Keywords: Brain computer interface · Motor imagery · Feature combination
Spatial-spectral precondition · Stochastic gradient boosting
Rehabilitation training

1 Introduction

Brain-computer interfaces (BCIs) provide a communication channel for a user to control an external device using only one's brain neural activity. They can be used as a rehabilitation tool for patients with severe neuromuscular disabilities [7], and also a range of other applications including neural prosthesis, Virtual Reality (VR), internet access etc. Among different types of neuroimaging techniques, electroencephalogram (EEG) is among one of the non-invasive methods exploited mostly in BCI experiments. And, among them event related desynchronization (ERD), visually evoked potential (VEP), slow cortical potential (SCP), and P300 evoked potentials are widely used for BCI studies.

Rachel Rajan M. Tech student; S. Thekkan Devassy Asst. Professor.

© The Author(s) 2017
P. Horain et al. (Eds.): IHCI 2017, LNCS 10688, pp. 73–85, 2017.
https://doi.org/10.1007/978-3-319-72038-8_7

In accordance with the topographic patterns of brain rhythm modulations, feature extraction using Common Spatial Patterns (CSP) algorithm [17] provides subject-specific and discriminant spatial filters. However, CSP has some limitations, as it is sensitive to frequency bands related to neural activity, because of that the frequency band are manually selected or set to a broad band filter. Apart from that, it also results in overfitting problem when dealt with large number of channels. Hence, the problem of overfitting the classifier and spatial filter rises due to trivial channel configuration. Henceforth, a simultaneous optimization of spatial and spectral filter is highly desirable in BCI studies.

Recent years, motor imagery (MI) based BCI has proven to be an independent system with high classification accuracy. Most of the MI based BCI use brain oscillations at mu (8–12 Hz) and beta (13–26 Hz) rhythms, which displays particular areas of event related desynchronization (ERD) [16] each corresponding to respective MI states (such as right hand or right foot motion). Apart from that, Readiness-potential (RP) [18] which is a slow negative event-related potential that appears before a movement is initiated can also be used as input to BCI to predict future movements. RP is mainly divided into early RP and late RP. Early RP is slow negative potential that begins 1.5 s before action, which is immediately followed by late RP that occurs 500 ms before the movement. In MI based BCI, combining of features vectors [5] i.e., ERD and RP have shown a significant boost in the classification performance.

In the literature, several number of sophisticated CSP based algorithms have been witnessed especially in the BCI study. A brief review has been presented here. Taking into account of avoid overfitting and selection of optimal frequency bands for CSP algorithm, various methods were proposed. To avoid overfitting problem, Regularized CSP (RCSP) [13] was proposed, in which the regularization information was added into the CSP learning procedure. The Common Spatio-Spectral Pattern (CSSP) [11] is an extension of CSP algorithm with time delayed sample. However, due to flexibility issues the Common Sparse Spectral-Spatial Pattern (CSSSP) [6] was presented, where its FIR filter consists of single time delay parameter. Since, these methods were computationally expensive, a Spectrally-weighted Common Spatial Pattern (SPEC-CSP) [19] was designed which alternatively optimizes the temporal filter in frequency domain and then the spatial filter in the iteration process. To improve the performance of SPEC-CSP, Iterative Spatio-Spectral Pattern Learning (ISSPL) [22] was proposed which does not rely on statistical assumptions and optimizes all temporal filters under a common optimization framework.

Despite of various studies and advanced algorithm, it is still a challenge to extract optimal spatial spectral filters for BCI studies, so as to be used as a rehabilitation tool especially for disabled subjects. The spatial and spectral information related to brain activities associated with BCI paradigms are usually pre-determined as default in EEG analysis without speculation, which can lead to loses effects in practical applications due to individual variability across different subjects. Hence, to solve this issue, a CSSBP [12] with combined feature vectors is designed for BCI based paradigms, since the combination of features each corresponding to different physiological phenomena such as Readiness Potential (RP) and Event Related Desynchronization (ERD) can benefit BCI making it more robust against artifacts from non-Central Nervous System (CNS) activity such as eye blinks (EOG) and muscle movements (EMG) [5]. At first, the EEG signal is first divided into several sub bands using a band pass filter, then the channel and frequency bands are modeled as preconditions before classifying and a heuristic of stochastic gradient boost is used to train the base learners under these preconditions. The effectiveness and robustness of the designed algorithm along with feature combination is evaluated on widely used benchmark dataset BCI competition IV (IIa). The remaining part of the paper is organized as follows; a detailed design of proposed Boosting Algorithm is given in Sect. 2, performance comparison results shown in Sect. 3. Finally, conclusion is given in Sect. 4.

2 Proposed Algorithm

Under this section, a combination model of CSSBP (common spatial spectral boosting pattern) with feature combination is given in detail; it includes modeling the problem, and learning algorithm for the model. The model consists of five stages, data preprocessing which includes multiple spectral filtering by decomposing the signal into several sub bands using a band pass filter and spatial filtering, feature extraction using common spatial pattern (CSP), feature combination, training the weak classifiers, and pattern recognition with the help of a combinational model. The architecture of the designed

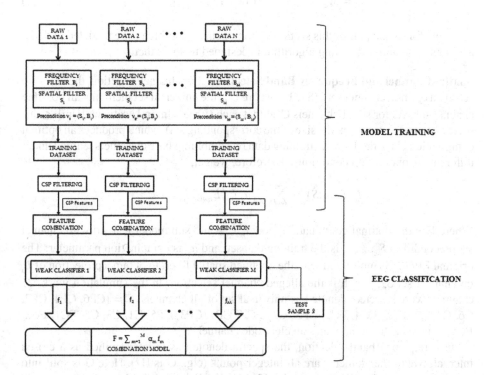

Fig. 1. Block diagram of proposed boosting pattern

algorithm is shown in Fig. 1. The EEG data is firstly spatial filtered and band pass filtered under multiple spatial-spectral preconditions.

Afterwards, the CSP algorithm is applied to extract features of the EEG training dataset and combine these feature vectors, then the weak classifiers $\{f_m\}_{m=1}^M$, are trained and combined to a weighted combination model. Lastly, a new test sample $\hat{x}$ is classified using this combination model.

2.1 Problem Design

During BCI studies, the two main concerns are the channel configuration and frequency band, which are predefined as default for implementing EEG analysis. But, predefining these conditions without deliberations leads to poor performance while executing it in a real scenario due to subject variability in EEG patterns. Hence, an efficient and robust configuration is desirable in case of practical applications.

To model this problem, let us denote the training dataset as $E_{train} = (x_i, y_i)_{i=1}^N$, where E_i is the ith sample and y_i is its corresponding label. The main aim is to find a subset $\omega \subset \nu$, by using a set of all probable preconditions ν, which generates a combination model F by incorporating all sub models trained under condition W_M ($W_M \in \omega$) and reducing the misclassification rate on the train dataset E_{train}, given by,

$$\omega = \arg min_\omega \frac{1}{N} \left| Ei : F(x_i, \omega) \neq y_{i=1}^N \right| \tag{1}$$

In the following part of this section, 2 homogeneous problems are modeled in detail and then an adaptive boosting algorithm is designed to solve them.

Spatial Channel and Frequency Band Selection. For channel selection, the aim is to select an optimal channel set S(S $\subset$ U), where U is the universal set including all possible channel subsets for set of channels C so that each subset Um in U satisfies $|Um| \leq |C|$ (here I.I is used to represent the size of the corresponding set), which produces an optimal combination classifier F on the training data by combining base classifiers learned under different channel set preconditions. Therefore, we get,

$$F(E_{train}; S) = \sum_{S_m \in S} \alpha_m f_m(E_{train}; S_m) \tag{2}$$

Where F is the optimal combination model, f_m is mth sub model learned with channel set precondition S_m, E_{train} is the training dataset, and α_m is combination parameter. The original EEG E_i is multiplied with the obtained spatial filter, to obtain a projection of E_i on channel set S_m, which is the alleged channel selection. In the simulation work, 21 channels were selected, denoted as universal set of all channels, C = (CP6, CP4, CP2, C6, C4, C2, FC6, FC4, FC2, CPZ, CZ, FCZ, CP1, CP3, CP5, C1, C3, C5, FC1, FC3, FC5), where each one indicates an electrode channel.

For frequency band selection, the spectra denoted as G is simplified as a closed interval, where the elements are all integer points (e.g., G is Hz). Here G is split into various sub-bands B and D as given in [12, 14], which denotes a universal set composed of all possible sub-bands. While selection of optimal frequency band, the objective is to obtain an optimal band set B (B $\subset$ D), so that an optimal combination classifier on the training data is produced.

$$F\left(E_{train};B\right) = \sum\nolimits_{B_m \in B} \alpha_m f_m\left(E_{train};B_m\right) \qquad (3)$$

Where f_m is m^{th} weak classifier learned by sub-band B_m. In the simulation study, a fifth order zero phase forward/reverse FIR filter was used to filter the raw EEG signal E_i into sub bands B_m.

2.2 Model Learning Algorithm

Here, the models of channel selection and frequency selection are combined to form a two-tuple, $\vartheta_m = (S_m, B_m)$, it is used to denote a spatial-spectral precondition, and v is represented as a universal set including all these spatial-spectral preconditions. Lastly, the combination function can be computed as

$$F\left(E_{train};\vartheta\right) = \sum\nolimits_{\vartheta_m \in \vartheta} \alpha_m f_m\left(E_{train};\vartheta_m\right) \qquad (4)$$

Hence, for each spatial-spectral precondition $\vartheta_m \in \vartheta$, the training dataset E_{train} is filtered under ϑ_m. The CSP features are obtained by the filtered training dataset E_{train} and these features of individual physiological nature were combined using PROB method [1]. Let us denote the N features by random variables X_i, $i = 1, \ldots, N$ having class labels as $Y \in \{\pm 1\}$. An optimal classifier f_i is defined for each feature i on the single feature space D_i hence reducing the misclassification rate. Let $g_{i,y}$ denote the density of $f_i\left(X_i|Y = y\right)$ for each i and labels say y = +1 or -1. Then f is the optimal classifier on the combined feature space D = $(D_1, D_2, \ldots, D_N)$, and X is the combined random variable X = $(X_1, X_2, \ldots, X_N)$, densities of f (X |Y = y) is given by g_y, hence under the assumption of equal class prior for x = $(x_1, x_2, \ldots, x_N) \in$ D,

$$f_i\left(x_i;\gamma(\vartheta_i)\right) = 1 \leftrightarrow \hat{f}_i\left(x_i,\gamma(\vartheta_i)\right) := \log\left(\frac{g_{i,1}\left(x_i\right)}{g_{i,-1}\left(x_i\right)}\right) > 0 \qquad (5)$$

Where γ is the model parameter determined by ϑ_i and E_{train}, and incorporating independence between the features to the above equation results in an optimal decision function given by,

$$f(x;\gamma(\vartheta)) = 1 \leftrightarrow \hat{f}(x;\gamma(\vartheta)) = \sum\nolimits_{i=1}^{N} \hat{f}_i\left(x_i,\gamma(\vartheta_i)\right) > 0 \qquad (6)$$

In this, the assumption is that, for each class the features are Gaussian distributed with equal covariance, i.e., $X_i|Y = yN\left(\mu_{i,y}, \sum i\right)$, with $w_i := \sum_i^{-1}\left(\mu_{i,1} + \mu_{i,-1}\right)$, then the classifier,

$$f(x;\gamma(\vartheta)) = 1 \leftrightarrow \hat{f}(x;\gamma(\vartheta)) = \sum_{i=1}^{N} [w_i^T x_i - \frac{1}{2}(\mu_{i,1} + \mu_{i,-1})^T w_i] > 0 \qquad (7)$$

Then obtained weak classifier can be rewritten as $f_m(E_{train};\vartheta_m)$, which is trained using the boosting algorithm. Thus, the classification error defined earlier can be formulated as,

$$\{\alpha, \vartheta\}_0^M = min_{\{\alpha,\vartheta\}_0^M} \sum_{i=1}^{N} L\left(y_i, \sum_{m=0}^{M} \alpha_m f_m(x_i;\gamma(\vartheta_m))\right) \qquad (8)$$

A Greedy approach [8] is used to solve (8), which is given in detail below,

$$F(E_{train}, \gamma, \{\alpha, \vartheta\}_0^M) = \sum_{m=0}^{M-1} \alpha_m f_m(E_{train};\gamma(\vartheta_m)) + \alpha_M f_M(E_{train};\gamma(\vartheta_M)) \qquad (9)$$

Transforming the Eq. (9) into a simple recursion formula we get,

$$F_m(E_{train}) = F_{m-1}(E_{train}) + \alpha_m f_m(E_{train};\gamma(\vartheta_m)) \qquad (10)$$

We suppose, $F_{m-1}(E_{train})$ is known, then f_m and α_m can be determined by,

$$F_m(E_{train}) = F_{m-1}(E_{train}) + \arg min_f \sum_{i=1}^{N} L(y_i, [F_{m-1}(x_i) + \alpha_m f_m(x_i;\gamma(\vartheta_m))]) \qquad (11)$$

The problem in (11) is solved by using a steepest gradient descent [9], and the pseudo-residuals are given by,

$$r_{\pi(i)m} = -\nabla_F L\left(y_{\pi(i)}, F(x_{\pi(i)})\right)$$
$$= -[\frac{\partial L\left(y_{\pi(i)}, F(x_{\pi(i)})\right)}{F(x_{\pi(i)})}]_{F(x_{\pi(i)}) = F_{m-1}(x_{\pi(i)})} \qquad (12)$$

Here, the first $\hat{N}$ elements of a random permutation of $\{i\}_{i=1}^{N}$ are given by $\{\pi(i)\}_{i=1}^{\hat{N}}$. Henceforth, a new set $\{(x_{\pi(i)}, r_{\pi(i)m})\}_{i=1}^{N}$, which signifies a stochastically partly best descent step direction, is produced and employed to learn $\gamma(\vartheta_m)$ given by,

$$\gamma(\vartheta_m) = \arg min_{\gamma,\rho} \sum_{i=1}^{\hat{N}} [r_{\pi(i)m} - \rho f(x_{\pi(i)};\gamma_m(\vartheta_m))] \qquad (13)$$

The combination coefficient α_m is obtained with $\gamma_m(\vartheta_m)$ as,

$$\alpha_m = \arg min_\alpha \sum_{i=1}^{N} L(y_i, [F_{m-1}(x_i) + \alpha f_m(x_i;\gamma(\vartheta_m))]) \qquad (14)$$

Here, each weak classifier f_m is trained under a random subset $\{\pi(i)\}_{i=1}^{N}$ (without replacement) from the full training data set. This random subset is used instead of the full sample, to fit the base learner as shown in Eq. (13) and the model update is computed using Eq. (14) for the current iteration. During the iteration, a self-adjusted training data pool P is maintained at background, given in detail in Algorithm 1. Then, the number of copies is computed using local classification error and these copies of incorrectly classified samples are then added to the training data pool.

2.3   Algorithm 1: Architecture of Proposed Boosting Algorithm

Input: The EEG training dataset given by $\{x_i, y_i\}_{i=1}^N$, $L(y, x)$ is the squared error loss function, number of weak learners denoted by M, and v is the set of all preconditions.

(1)   Initialize the training data pool $Po = E_{train} = \{x_i, y_i\}_{i=1}^N$,
(2)   for m = 1 to M.
(3)   Generate a random permutation

$$\{\pi(i)\}_{i=1}^{|P_{m-1}|} = randperm(i)_{i=1}^{|P_{m-1}|}$$

(4)   Select the first $\hat{N}$ elements $\{\pi(i)\}_{i=1}^{\hat{N}}$ as $(x_i, y_i)_{i=1}^{\hat{N}}$, from Po.

(5)   Use this $\{\pi(i)\}_{i=1}^{\hat{N}}$ elements to optimize new learner f_m and its related parameters is obtained in output as,

   Output: F is the optimal combination classifier, weak learners obtained as $\{f_m\}_{m=1}^M$, where $\{\alpha_m\}_{m=1}^M$ is the weights of weak learners and $\{\vartheta_m\}_{m=1}^M$ is the preconditions under which these weak learners are learned.

(6)   Input $(x_i, y_i)_{i=1}^N$, and ϑ into a classifier using CSP, extract features and combine these feature vectors to generate family of weak learners.

(7)   Initialize P, $F_0(E_{train}) = arg\ min_\alpha \sum_{i=1}^N L(y_i, \alpha)$
(8)   Optimize $f_m\ (E_{train}; \gamma(\vartheta_m))$ as defined in Eq. (10).
(9)   Optimize α_m as defined in Eq. (11).
(10)   Update Pm using the following steps,

A.   Use current local optimal classifier F_m to split the original training set $E_{train} = (x_i, y_i)_{i=1}^N$ into two parts $T_{True} = \{x_i, y_i\}_{i:y_i} = F_m(x_i)$, and $T_{False} = \{x_i, y_i\}_{i:y_i} \neq F_m(x_i)$

   Re-adjust the training data pool:

B.   For each $(x_i, y_i) \in T_{False}$ do.
C.   Select out all $(x_i, y_i) \in P_{m-1}$ as $\{x_{n(k)}, y_{n(k)}\}_{k=1}^K$.
D.   Copy $\{x_{n(k)}, y_{n(k)}\}_{k=1}^K$ with $d(d \geq 1)$ times so that we get total $(d + 1)K$ duplicated samples.
E.   Return these $(d + 1)$ K samples into P_{m-1} and we get a new adjusted pool P_m. And

$$F_m(E_{train}) = F_{m-1}(E_{train}) + \alpha_m f_m (E_{train}; \gamma(\vartheta_m))$$

F.   end for.
(11)   end for.

(12) for each $f_m\left(E_{train};\gamma(\vartheta_m)\right)$, use mapping $F \leftrightarrow \vartheta$, to obtain its corresponding precondition ϑ_m.

(13) Return F, $\left\{f_m\right\}_{m=1}^M$, $\left\{\alpha_m\right\}_{m=1}^M$, and $\left\{\vartheta_m\right\}_{m=1}^M$.

With the help of Early stopping strategy [23], the iteration time M is determined to avoid overfitting, using $\hat{N} = N$, doesn't introduce randomness, hence smaller $\dfrac{\hat{N}}{N}$ fraction, incorporates more overall randomness into the process. In this work, $\dfrac{\hat{N}}{N} = 0.9$ and a comparably satisfactory performance is obtained for the above approximation. While adjusting P, the copies of incorrectly classified samples, d is computed by the local classification error, $e = \dfrac{|T_{False}|}{N}$ is given by,

$$d = \max\left(1, \left\lfloor \frac{1-e}{e+\in} \right\rfloor\right) \tag{15}$$

Here, the parameter $\in$ is called as accommodation coefficient, and e is always less than 0.5, and decreases during the iterations, so that large weights on samples will be given which were incorrectly classified by strong learners.

3   Result

The robustness of the designed algorithm was assessed on dataset obtained from BCI competition IV (IIa) dataset [2]. In order to remove artifacts obtained from eye and muscle movements, FastICA was employed [15]. For comparing the performance and efficiency of the designed algorithm, Regularized CSP (RCSP) [13] was used for feature extraction. In this, model parameter λ for RCSP, were chosen on the training set using a Hold Out validation procedure. In case of the four-class motor imagery classification task for dataset II, one-versus-rest (OVR) [21] strategy was employed for CSP. PROB method [1] was utilized for feature combination which incorporates independence between ERD and LRP features. Feature selection was done to select relevant features, since as more features cannot improve the training accuracy. Here feature selection was done using Fisher score (a variant, $J = \dfrac{\|\mu_+ - \mu_-\|^2}{\sigma_+ + \sigma_-}$) [10], it makes selection by measuring the discrimination of individual feature in the feature vector for classification. Then the features with largest fisher score are selected as most discriminative features. Linear Discriminant Analysis (LDA) [4] which minimizes the expected risk of misclassification rate was utilized for classification.

Here, the most optimal channel using [20] for all four MI movements i.e., left hand, right hand, foot and tongue were CP4, Cz, FC2, and C1. The 2-D topoplot maps of peak amplitudes of boosting based CSSP filtered EEG in each electrode for subject S1 is shown in Fig. 2.

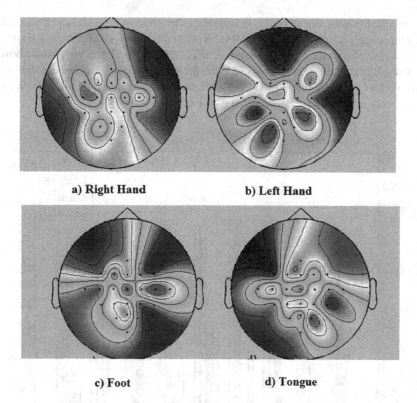

a) Right Hand   **b) Left Hand**

c) Foot   **d) Tongue**

Fig. 2. 2-D topoplot maps of peak amplitude of Boosting based CSSP filtered EEG in each channel for subject S1 in BCI competition IV (II a) dataset.

To compute the spatial weight for each channel, the quantitative vector, $L = \sum_{S_i \in S} \alpha_i S_i$ [17] was used where S_i is the channel sets and α_i are their weights. The spectral weights were computed as given in [12] and then projected onto the frequency bands. In addition, the temporal information were also obtained and visualized. The training dataset are preprocessed under the spatial-spectral pre-condition $\vartheta_m \in \vartheta$, which results in a new dataset on which spatial filtering is done using CSP to obtain the spatial patterns. Then the first two components obtained by CSP are projected onto the space yielding the CSP filtered signal E_m. The peak amplitude P_{mCi} for E_m and each channel $C_i \in C$. Then the P_{mCi} is averaged over all set of preconditions $\vartheta_m \in \vartheta$, computed as $P_{C_i} = (\frac{1}{|\vartheta|}) \sum_{\vartheta_m \in \vartheta} \alpha_m P_{mC_i}$ where α_m is the corresponding weight for the mth condition, which is then visualized using a 2-D topoplot map. From the topoplot, it can be observed that the left hand and right hand movement resulted in activation over the right and left hemisphere of the brain, the foot movement activated the central cortical area and tongue showed activation in the motor cortex region.

The classification results of the test dataset for the proposed method and the other competing method i.e., Regularized CSP (RCSP) is detailed as follows. In all the subjects the maximum number of iterations, M of the boosting algorithm was set to 180, which was computed using early stopping strategy so as to avoid overfitting, and ϵ was set to 0.05. The cohen's kappa values for all 9 subjects in the BCI IV(IIa) dataset is shown in Fig. 3. In case of dataset 2, the CSSBP outperformed the RCSP algorithm and showed highest average cohen's kappa value [3]. From the kappa values, it can be seen that when feature vectors are combined in RCSP algorithm, there was a significant improvement in kappa values in all subjects (except for subjects S4 and S6).

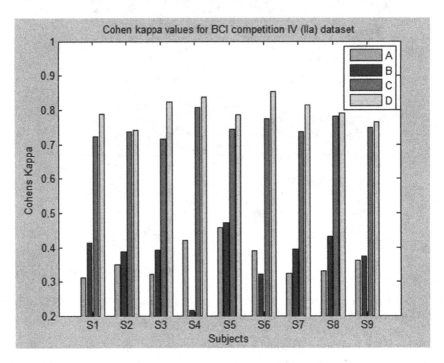

Fig. 3. Cohen's kappa values for all the 9 subjects in BCI IV (II a) dataset, where A is RCSP, B is RCSP with combined feature vectors, C is Boosting based CSSP (CSSBP), and D is Boosting based CSSP (CSSBP) with combined feature vectors.

Whereas the proposed method improved the kappa values compared to the above algorithm and moreover when feature vectors were combined, it outperformed CSSBP with single feature when compared with combined feature vectors. The statistical analysis was done using IBM SPSS ver. 23., it showed significant difference between designed method and the other methods used for comparison in a Mann-Whitney U test. For all the cases, the designed method outperformed for level of significance $p < 0.05$, as shown in Fig. 4.

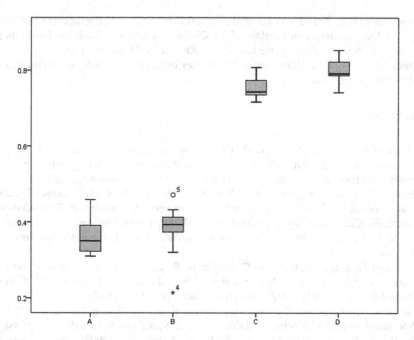

Fig. 4. Boxplots of RCSP and Boosting Approach, where A is RCSP, B is RCSP with combined feature vectors, C is CSSBP, and D is CSSBP with combined feature vectors for BCI IV (IIa) dataset ($p < 0.05$).

4   Conclusion

In this work, a boosting based common spatial-spectral pattern (CSSBP) algorithm with feature combination has been designed for multichannel EEG classification. Here, the channel and frequency configurations are divided into multiple spatial-spectral preconditions by using a sliding window strategy. Under these preconditions, the weak learners are trained using a boosting approach. The motive is to select the most contributed channel groups and frequency bands related to neural activity. From the results, it can be seen that the CSSBP clearly outperformed the other method use for comparison. In addition, combining the widely used feature vectors ERD and readiness potentials (RP) significantly improved the classification performance compared to CSSBP and resulted in increased robustness.

The PROB method was utilized which incorporates independence between ERD and LRP features enhanced the performance. This can also be used to better explore the neurophysiological mechanism of underlying brain activities. Feature combination of different brain tasks in feedback environment, where the subject is trying to adapt with the feedback scenario might cause the learning process complex and time consuming, so for that this process needs to investigate further in future online BCI experiments.

Acknowledgements. The authors would like to thank Fraunhofer First, Intelligent Data Analysis Group, and Campus Benjamin Franklin of the Charite' - University Medicine Berlin (http://www.bbci.de/competition/iii), and the Institute for Knowledge Discovery (Laboratory of Brain-Computer Interfaces), Graz University of Technology (http://www.bbci.de/competition/iv), for providing the dataset online.

References

1. Blankertz, B., Curio, G., Müller, K.-R.: Classifying single trial EEG: towards brain computer interfacing. In: Dietterich, T.G., Becker, S., Ghahramani, Z. (eds.) Advances in Neural Information Processing Systems 14, pp. 157–164. MIT Press, Cambridge (2002)
2. Brunner, C., Leeb, R., Muller-Putz, G., Schlogl, A., Pfurtscheller, G.: BCI competition 2008-Graz data set A, Institute for Knowledge Discovery (Laboratory of Brain-Computer Interfaces), Graz University of Technology (2008). http://www.bbci.de/competition/iv/
3. Cohen, J.: A coefficient of agreement for nominal scales. Educ. Psychol. Measur. **20**(1), 37–46 (1960)
4. Dornhege, G., Blankertz, B., Curio, G., Müller, K.-R.: Boosting bit rates in noninvasive EEG single-trial classifications by feature combination and multiclass paradigms. IEEE Trans. Biomed. Eng. **51**(6), 993–1002 (2004). https://doi.org/10.1109/TBME.2004.827088
5. Dornhege, G., Blankertz, B., Curio, G., Müller, K.-R.: Combining features for BCI. In: Proceedings of the 15th International Conference on Neural Information Processing Systems (NIPS 2002), pp. 1139–1146. MIT Press, Cambridge (2002). http://dl.acm.org/citation.cfm.id=2968618.2968760
6. Dornhege, G., Blankertz, B., Krauledat, M., Losch, F., Curio, G., Müller, K.R.: Combined optimization of spatial and temporal filters for improving brain-computer interfacing. IEEE Trans. Biomed. Eng. **53**(11), 2274–2281 (2006). https://doi.org/10.1109/TBME.2006.883649
7. Jerry, J., et al.: Brain-computer interfaces in medicine. Mayo Clin. Proc. **87**(3), 268–279 (2012). https://doi.org/10.1016/j.mayocp.2011.12.008
8. Friedman, J.H.: Greedy function approximation: a gradient boosting machine. Ann. Stat. **29**(5), 1189–1232 (2001)
9. Friedman, J.H.: Stochastic gradient boosting. Comput. Stat. Data Anal. **38**(4), 367–378 (2002). https://doi.org/10.1016/S0167-9473(01)00065-2
10. Gu, Q., Li, Z., Han, J.: Generalized Fisher Score for Feature Selection. CoRR abs/1202.3725 (2012). http://arxiv.org/abs/1202.3725
11. Lemm, S., Blankertz, B., Curio, G., Müller, K.R.: Spatio-spectral filters for improving the classification of single trial EEG. IEEE Trans. Biomed. Eng. **52**(9), 1541–1548 (2005). https://doi.org/10.1109/TBME.2005.851521
12. Liu, Y., Zhang, H., Chen, M., Zhang, L.: A boosting-based spatial-spectral model for stroke patients; EEG analysis in rehabilitation training. IEEE Trans. Neural Syst. Rehab. Eng. **24**(1), 169–179 (2016). https://doi.org/10.1109/TNSRE.2015.2466079
13. Lotte, F., Guan, C.: Regularizing common spatial patterns to improve BCI designs: unified theory and new algorithms. IEEE Trans. Biomed. Eng. **58**(2), 355–362 (2011). https://doi.org/10.1109/TBME.2010.2082539
14. Novi, Q., Guan, C., Dat, T.H., Xue, P.: Sub-band common spatial pattern (SBCSP) for brain-computer interface. In: 2007 3rd International IEEE/EMBS Conference on Neural Engineering, pp. 204–207 (2007). https://doi.org/10.1109/CNE.2007.369647

15. Mishra, P., Singla, S.: Artifact removal from biosignal using fixed point ICA algorithm for pre-processing in biometric recognition. Measur. Sci. Rev. **13**(1), 7–11 (2013). https://doi.org/10.2478/msr-2013-000

16. Pfurtscheller, G., et al.: Event-related EEG/MEG synchronization and desynchronization: basic principles. Clin. Neurophysiol. **110**(11), 1842–1857 (1999). https://doi.org/10.1016/S1388-2457(99)00141-8

17. Ramoser, H., Muller-Gerking, J., Pfurtscheller, G.: Optimal spatial filtering of single trial EEG during imagined hand movement. IEEE Trans. Rehab. Eng. **8**(4), 441–446 (2000). https://doi.org/10.1109/86.895946

18. Shibasaki, H., Hallett, M.: What is the Bereitschaftspotential? Clin. Neurophysiol. Off. J. Int. Fed. Clin. Neurophysiol. **117**(11), 2341–2356 (2006). https://doi.org/10.1016/j.clinph.2006.04.025

19. Tomioka, R., Dornhege, G., Nolte, G., Blankertz, B., Aihara, K., Müller, K.-R.: Spectrally weighted common spatial pattern algorithm for single trial EEG classification. Mathematical Engineering (Technical reports) (2006)

20. Wang, Y., Gao, S., Gao, X.: Common spatial pattern method for channel selection in motor imagery based brain-computer interface. In: 27th Annual Conference 2005 IEEE Engineering in Medicine and Biology, pp. 5392–5395 (2005). https://doi.org/10.1109/IEMBS.2005.1615701

21. Wu, W., Gao, X., Gao, S.: One-Versus-the-Rest (OVR) algorithm: an extension of common spatial patterns (CSP) algorithm to multi-class case. In: 27th Annual Conference 2005 IEEE Engineering in Medicine and Biology, pp. 2387–2390 (2005). https://doi.org/10.1109/IEMBS.2005.1616947

22. Wu, W., Gao, X., Hong, B., Gao, S.: Classifying single-trial EEG during motor imagery by iterative spatio-spectral patterns learning (ISSPL). IEEE Trans. Biomed. Eng. **55**(6), 1733–1743 (2008)

23. Zhang, T., Yu, B.: Boosting with early stopping: convergence and consistency. Ann. Statist. **33**(4), 1538–1579 (2005)

Open Access This chapter is licensed under the terms of the Creative Commons Attribution 4.0 International License (http://creativecommons.org/licenses/by/4.0/), which permits use, sharing, adaptation, distribution and reproduction in any medium or format, as long as you give appropriate credit to the original author(s) and the source, provide a link to the Creative Commons license and indicate if changes were made.

The images or other third party material in this chapter are included in the chapter's Creative Commons license, unless indicated otherwise in a credit line to the material. If material is not included in the chapter's Creative Commons license and your intended use is not permitted by statutory regulation or exceeds the permitted use, you will need to obtain permission directly from the copyright holder.

LINEUp: <u>Li</u>st <u>N</u>avigation Using <u>E</u>dge Men<u>u</u>
Enhancing Touch Based Menus for Mobile Platforms

Rana Mohamed Eisa[1]([✉]), Yassin El-Shanwany[1], Yomna Abdelrahman[2],
and Wael Abouelsadat[1]

[1] German University in Cairo, Cairo, Egypt
{rana.monir,wael.abouelsaadat}@guc.edu.eg,
yassin.el-shanwany@student.guc.edu.eg
[2] University of Stuttgart, Stuttgart, Germany
Yomna.abdelrahman@vis.uni-stuttgart.de

Abstract. Displaying and interacting with Cascaded Menus on mobile phones is challenging due to the limited screen real estate. In this paper, we propose the *Edge Menu* – U-shaped layout displayed along the edges of the screen. Through the use of transparency and minimum screen space, the Edge Menu can be overlaid on top of existing items on the screen. We evaluated the suitability of two versions of the Edge Menu: List and Nested Menus. We compared the performance of the Edge Menu to the traditional Linear Menu. We conducted three studies and revealed that Edge Menu can support the use of single hand and both hands, it outperforms the regular Linear Menu, and is in average 38.5% faster for Single hand usage, and 40% faster for Dual hands usage. Edge Menu using both hands is in average 7.4% faster than Edge Menu using Single hand. Finally, the Edge Menu in Nested Menus shown to be faster than Linear Menus in Nested Menus with 22%–36%.

Keywords: Cell phones · Edge Menus · Linear Menus
Nested Menus · Gestures · Mobile interaction · Menu techniques
Mobile phone menus

1 Introduction

Mobile phones are used today to perform various functions and are not limited to making voice calls only. Users are manipulating images and videos, writing

© The Author(s) 2017
P. Horain et al. (Eds.): IHCI 2017, LNCS 10688, pp. 86–106, 2017.
https://doi.org/10.1007/978-3-319-72038-8_8

documents, broadcasting events, and even creating and editing 3D models on mobile phones. The processing capabilities of some recent mobile phones is similar to that of laptops, which makes them suitable for performing any task. However, the limited screen real estate on mobile presents itself as the biggest obstacle against the utilization of the underlying hardware and sophisticated software applications. There is currently over 1 billion smartphones worldwide [2]. Hence, it is no exaggeration to claim that navigating through lists generally is one of the most frequently performed daily tasks.

In this paper, we describe our work aiming to enhance menu navigation on mobile phones. We conducted three studies. In the first two studies, we explored one of the regularly visited lists, Contacts' List. Since, calling a previously stored phone number in the Contacts' List is one of the most commonly performed daily tasks. Although the current design of the Contacts' List, in Android and in iPhone, seems adequate to most users, yet we believe it will be soon challenged by the rapidly increasing number of entries. As the current trend of merging social contacts with phone contacts in one list continues to spread, the average number of entries is expected to rise rapidly. A typical Internet user has about 600 social ties [16]. In Facebook, the mean number of friends among adult users is 338 and the median comes in at 200 friends [1]. At this rate, Contacts' Lists with several hundred entries, will gradually become the norm. At the moment, finding a contact can be done using speed dial, search by voice, search by typing name and using the menu. Each of these interaction techniques suits a specific context. For instance, while search by voice might be the fastest way to dial a contact, it requires the user to be in a relatively quite environment.

Moreover, many software applications have complex features which are organized into deeply Nested Menu structures. This renders them unusable on mobile screens - where the limited screen size would make the display of such menus impossible.

In our third study, we developed the Edge Menu as a proposed solution to this problem. The Edge Menu displays each level of a Nested Menu on one side of the screen and the user alternates between left and right edges while navigating in the menu using symmetric bi-manual interaction.

In this research, we aim to enhance menu navigation through the following contributions:

- Investigating the Edge Menu - U-shaped menu.
- A comparison is done between different Layout and Interaction techniques; Edge Menu and Linear Menu - Circular and Linear Scrolling.
- We did an extended evaluation for Edge Menus; using Nested Edge Menus.

2   Related Work

Menu Navigation is still an open topic that has many usability issues that need more investigation and research. Our work builds on strands of prior work: (1) Menus Design, (2) List Navigation task, (3) Contacts' List usage and (4) Edge Screen.

2.1 Menus for Mobile

Several researchers have developed menus which attempt to speed up selection in large sets of items presented on a small cellphone screen. Kim et al. [22] developed a 3D Menu which utilizes the depth cue. The researchers' formal evaluation reveals that as the number of items gets larger and the task complexity is increased, the 2D organization of items is better. For a small number of items, the 3D Menu yields a better performance. Foster and Foxcroft [13] developed the Barrel Menu which consists of three horizontally rotating menu levels stacked vertically; the top level represents the main menu items. Selecting an item from a level is achieved by rotating the level left or right, resulting in the child elements of the current item being displayed in the menu level below. Francone et al. [14] developed the Wavelet Menu, which expands upon the initial Marking Menus by Kurtenbach and Buxton [21]. Bonnet and Appert [7] proposed the Swiss Army Menu which merges standard widgets, such as a font dialog, into a Radial Menu layout. Zhao et al. [35] used an Eyes-Free Menu with touch input and reactive auditory feedback.

2.2 List Navigation

Menus used in mobile phones are influenced by Linear Menus which were originally created for desktop graphical user interfaces (**GUI**). Such menus suit desktop environments, where large screen size can accommodate displaying more items. However, Linear Menus are not a good option for a mobile phone interface, as the screen is much smaller. Smartphone users are forced to do excessive scrolling to find an item in a Linear Menu since the screen can only display a handful of items at a time. Almost all menus are formatted in a linear manner, listing entries that are arranged from the top to the bottom of the screen. When presenting a list of items to the user, the available hardware and software have limited the computer system architecture to a linear format. Pull-Down Menus and Pop-Up Menus are a typical example of the linear arrangement. Most of these menus are either static on the screen or are activated from a specific mouse action [9].

2.3 Contacts' List

The Contacts' List has been the focus of several research works. Oulasvirta et al. [26] recommended augmenting each entry with contextual cues such as user location, availability of user, time spent in location, frequency of communication and physical proximity. Jung, Anttila and Blom [19] proposed three special category views: communication frequency, birthday date, and new contacts. This is meant to differentiate potentially important contacts from the rest. Bergman et al. [6] modified the Contacts' List to show unused contacts in smaller font at the bottom of the list. Plessas et al. [27] and Stefanis et al. [29] proposed using the call log data and a predictive algorithm for deciding which entries are most likely to be called at any specific time. Campbell et al. [24] utilized an

EEG signal to identify the user choice. Ankolekar et al. [4] created Friendlee, an application which utilized call log and social connections to enable faster access to the sub-social-network reachable via mobile phone, in addition to contacts.

2.4   Utilizing Screen Edge and Bezel

Apple Macintosh was the first to utilize the screen edge by fixating the menu bar at the top edge of the screen. Wobbrock developed the Edge Keyboard [32,34], where the character buttons are placed around the screen's perimeter, and could be stroked over or tapped like ordinary soft buttons. More recently, screen edge and bezel have attracted the attention of researchers to enable richer interactions on mobile. Li and Fu [23] developed the BezelCursor which is activated by performing a swipe from the bezel to the on-screen target. The BezelCusor supports swiping for command invocation as well as virtual pointing for target selection in one fluid action. Roth and Turner [28] utilized the iPhone bezel to create the Bezel Swipe. Crossing a specific area in the screen edge towards the inside activates a particular functionality. The user continues with the gesture to complete the desired operation. Chen et al. [10] utilized the bezel to enhance copy and paste. Based on Fitts' Law, nearer bigger targets are faster to reach to, compared to farther smaller ones. Thus, the target's size is an important parameter to take into consideration, because the larger the target is; the faster, easier and more efficient the target's selection is [11]. Jain and Balakrishnan [18] have proven the utility of bezel gestures in terms of efficiency and learnability. Hossain et al. [17] utilized the screen edges to display proxies of off-screen objects to facilitate their selection. Recently Samsung provided *Samsung Galaxy Edge* series, a mobile phone with a 3D melted glass that covered the curves of the mobile phone [3]. This design has a huge potential, which supports our research even more; seeking to prove that the Edge Menu Design is more usable than the regular Linear Menu.

In this work, we aim to evaluate the new Edge Menu design to enhance the navigation performance on smartphones. Namely we focus on three main research questions (**RQ**):

1. Does Edge Menu offer better User Experience than Linear Menu?
2. Does the kind of interaction influence the easiness of navigating through the menu list and reaching the user's target?
3. Will Nested Edge Menus speed up selection process while list navigation?

Menu Design and Interaction

Our main goal was to enable the quick selection of an entry in a list and speed up the navigation in a Nested Menu. While in previous works, researchers redefined the layout of the menu list totally, our strategy is to preserve the linear organization of entries and focus on speeding up the interaction.

To achieve this, we designed three user studies, for the first two studies we conducted two experiments that focus in Contacts' Lists. The main goal of any user is to speed up the selection process of the target name. Thus, selecting the first letter of both the first name and the last name is the most efficient technique to narrow down the Contacts' List as quickly as possible. Although not all users store the first and the last name of a contact, the same technique is applicable to contacts with just a single entry stored. In the latter case, the first two letters of the entry will be utilized in the search - this is further to be utilized in further studies.

Later, for the third study we ran an experiment to enhance the search in Nested Menus same way we aim to enhance One-Level Menus. Although redesigning menus might result in efficient interaction, yet our approach would enable the porting of existing applications to the mobile platforms with less effort. We formulated three guiding design goals;

- Support Dual-hands and Single-hand interaction
- Minimize finger travel distance
- Utilize screen edges

Although users prefer Single-hand interaction [20], two-handed input has proven quicker [22,25]. We anticipate that the overwhelming number of contacts might require the user to utilize two hands to reach the target entry faster. The second design goal was to minimize finger time travel distance on the screen. Fitts' Law teaches that movement time is inversely correlated with distance to target and to width of target [12]. The third design goal was to make use of the screen edges since user's fingers are often located there while holding the phone. Walker and Smelcer [31] and Froehlich et al. [15] have shown that utilizing an edge as a stopping barrier improves target acquisition time.

Our design effort yielded a menu fitted to the edges which makes it easily reachable using single hand and two hands. Two variations were developed to support the design goals. Since performance difference could be attributed to more than one factor, we opted for implementing simpler designs supporting only a single design goal for comparison purposes. In this paper our focus is to investigate if single and multi-level Edge Menu designs will work better than Linear Menu designs, with Single hand and Dual hands.

2.5   Layout Design

Linear Menu. Since Android based phones already have a Linear Menu used in the Contacts' List application, we were interested in using it as a baseline and to investigate the difference in performance between the different designs, (see Fig. 1). We implemented the Linear Menu in our system following the same interaction style as offered by Android OS. To support selecting both the first name and the last name, we extended the selection mechanism to accept two letters instead of one. Thus the user would need to tap twice for the two first letters. It is worth noting that in Android 2.2, the Contacts' List had a feature to select both first and last names. The user would start by selecting the first letter of the first name, then continue by swiping the finger horizontally for

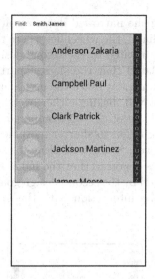

Fig. 1. Linear Menu with flicking support

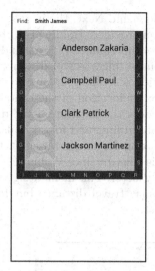

Fig. 2. Edge Menu with flicking support

a short distance and next move vertically - either upward or downward - to select the first letter of the last name. Although this feature was dropped from later versions of Android, we felt it is more appropriate to utilize an interaction mechanism which supports selection of the first two letters to be comparable with our design.

Edge Menu. An Edge Menu consists of a U shaped panel fitted to the left, right and bottom edges of the screen, (see Figs. 2 and 10). For the purpose of the Contacts' List, the menu items are the alphabetical letters and for the purpose of the Nested Menu, the menu items are the default menu icons. We decided not to use the upper edge since it is the furthest away from the user's fingers. For the first study, we decided to use names with first and last names not first names only to make the study consistent, the later case will be supported in future studies. The user taps on the first letter of the first name followed by a tap on the first letter of the last name. This narrows down the choices for the user. Scrolling through the results is done by flicking up and down. This menu design was motivated by the first design goal which is to support both two handed and single handed interaction, and the third which is to use screen edges.

2.6 Interaction Design

Linear Menu with Wheel. This menu consists of two components: a linear list of alphabet letters placed in the right edge of the screen and a wheel for scrolling at the bottom (see Fig. 3). To select an entry, the user starts by choosing the first letter of the first name and next select the first letter of the second name from the menu. Next, the user scrolls through the narrowed down results using the wheel provided. Holding the phone in one hand, the wheel lies where the user would rest his thumb. This menu design was motivated by the second design goal to minimize finger travel distance. We speculated that the slowest part of the interaction is scrolling up and down to locate an entry. Since the user is unaware of the exact location of the contact, the employed flicking either overshoots or undershoots the location of the desired entry. Tu et al. [30] compared flicking to radial scrolling and found that radial scrolling led to shorter movement time than flicking for larger target distance. However, it was not clear if using the thumb is efficient since Wobbrock et al. [33] has reported that the index finger is generally faster. This menu design was motivated by the second design goal which is minimize travel distance but focused on the interaction with the narrowed down list.

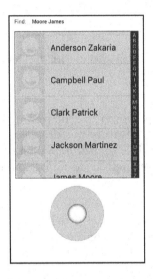

Fig. 3. Linear Menu with radial control for scrolling

Fig. 4. Edge Menu with radial control for scrolling

Edge Menu with Wheel. This design is similar to the Edge Menu but augmented with a wheel for scrolling through the results list (see Fig. 4). After choosing the first letter, a wheel is displayed in proximity to the last position of the user's finger. The user scrolls through the list of contacts by moving the finger in a circular motion on the wheel - following the same interaction style as in the Linear Menu with wheel. Clockwise movement causes scrolling down and anti-clockwise movement signals scrolling up. The speed of the rotation governs how fast the scrolling of names occurs. The user does not have to maintain his finger within the wheel border as any radial movement above or close to it, activates the scrolling. Finally, the user taps on the desired contact. This menu design attempts to support the three stated design goals.

2.7   Pre Study: Observing Mobile Holding Position

We observed people in public areas, while holding their mobile phones, to observe the most common, comfortable position to hold their mobile phones. After observing many samples of people, almost all people grabbed their phones in a position where the phone's back rests on the users' palms (see Fig. 5).

Fig. 5. Most habitual holding position of a cellphone

3   Study I: Evaluating Edge Menus Layout and Interaction Techniques

To answer **RQ** and to test our hypothesis of whether using Edge Menu instead of Linear Menu improves the user's performance or not? We started 3 studies sequentially.

Our goal with the evaluation was to find which menu is most efficient while working with a large-size list. A secondary goal was to understand the importance of our design goals and decide which is most relevant for future design efforts.

3.1   Design

We applied a repeated-measures design, where all participants were exposed to all conditions. An application displaying the menus and measuring user performance was implemented. The study has two independent variables, specifically the menu type with four levels; *Linear Menu, Edge Menu, Linear Menu with Wheel* and *Edge Menu with Wheel*, and the list size with three levels; *201 entries, 300 entries* and *600 entries*; and two dependent variables the mean execution time and error rate. The latter is defined as the percentage of trials with an incorrect selection of a target name. The mean execution time, is defined as the time between the display of a target name to the participant and the participant tapping on that name in the Contacts' List. The order of the conditions was counter-balanced to avoid any learning effects. The study time was around 60–120 min plus 3 min for the training trials.

3.2   Apparatus

Our experimental setup consisted of a Samsung S3 device with a 4.8 in. (1280 × 720) display running Android 4.0.

3.3   Participants and Procedure

We recruited 36 participants (18 females) and (18 males) with an average age of 26 years ($SD = 2.27$) using university mailing lists. Four of the participants were left-handed. None of the participants had any previous experience using Edge Menus. After arriving in the lab and welcoming the participants, they signed a consent form and received an explanation of the purpose of the study.

We equally divided the participants to 3 groups each with 12 participants. First group was tested using 201 contacts; we divided them accordingly to 3 blocks, each having 67 trials. Thus each participant performed 804 trials: (4 menus × 67 trials × 3 blocks). The total number of trials in the experiment was *9648* (12 participants × 804 trials).

Second group was tested using 300 contacts; we divided them accordingly to 3 blocks, each having 100 trials. Thus each participant performed 1200 trials: (4 menus × 100 trials × 3 blocks). The total number of trials in the experiment was *14400* (12 participants × 1200 trials).

Finally, the Third group was tested using 600 contacts; we divided them accordingly to 3 blocks, each having 200 trials. Thus each participant performed 2400 trials: (4 menus × 200 trials × 3 blocks). The total number of trials in the experiment was *28800* (12 participants × 2400 trials).

The target names were carefully selected to ensure that the user will need to navigate in the Contacts' List before reaching the required name. The alphabet was divided into 3 sets: the first set contained names starting with letters A to I, second set contained names starting with letters J to Q, and the last set contained names starting with letters R to Z, (see Fig. 6). Each block contained an equal number of names from the three sets. Names were not repeated between blocks to avoid learning effects. In this experiment a large Contact's List size was chosen to evaluate the difference in performance since the user has to scroll through many target names.

In this experiment we asked the participants to use only single hand while performing the experiment. Hence, the user uses only one hand to hold the mobile phone and experiments the Edge Menu and Linear Menu likely.

3.4   Results

We analyzed the Mean Execution Time. Data from the practice trials was not used in the analysis. A univariate repeated measures ANOVA was carried out on the remaining data. Significant main effect was found for menu type. Mauchley's test indicated that the assumption of sphericity had been violated, therefore degrees of freedom were corrected using Greenhouse-Geisser estimates of sphericity $F(2.79, 30.68) = 82.758$. $p < .0001$ Post-hoc analyses were carried out to compare means for menu type. Four statistically significant groups were detected

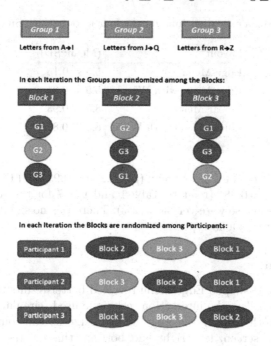

Fig. 6. An explanation of each trial's arrangement

from the analysis, namely: Linear Menu and Linear Menu with wheel, Edge Menu and Edge menu with wheel. Thus, Linear Menu and Linear Menu with Wheel performance was similar, but together they were statistically different from the other three groups. The fastest performance was accomplished using Edge menu ($\mu = 5.5$ s, $\sigma = 0.15$), followed by Edge menu with wheel ($\mu = 5.9$ s,

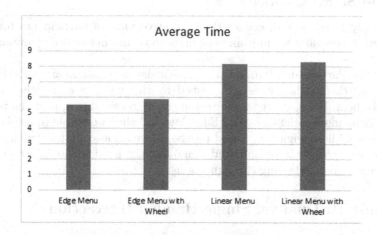

Fig. 7. Study I: mean execution time

Table 1. Mean execution time for the four layouts using Single hand

Layout	(Mean::SD)	
Edge Menu	5.5 s	0.15
Edge Menu with Wheel	5.9 s	0.21
Linear Menu	8.2 s	0.93
Linear Menu with Wheel	8.3 s	0.88

$\sigma = 0.21$). Third came the Linear Menu ($\mu = 8.2$, $\sigma = 0.93$) and Linear Menu with wheel ($\mu = 8.3$ s, $\sigma = 0.88$) (refer to Table 1 and Fig. 7 for the results). Participants' errors in response were very few (2%). There was no significant difference between the different menu types.

3.5   Discussion

In conclusion, the U-shaped Edge Menu revealed better results than the regular Linear Menu; regardless the interaction technique used (circular or linear).

In addition to that, since the Edge Menu design spreads out the letters on three sides of the screen; left, right and bottom, this creates an opportunity for the user to use either one of his hands to interact or his two hands if the first letter of the first name and that of the last name reside in different sides. Although, it is not guaranteed to always have such an allocation. Consequently, half the Contacts' List entries were names whose first letters were residing in the same side and the other half were names whose first letters were residing in different sides. Therefore in Study II we aim to explore dual hand interaction as informed by the subjective measures from the participants (questionnaire).

3.6   Post Study: Questionnaire

It was really important to collect the subjective view of participants towards the design in general after finishing the first study and before doing any further research.

After the Participants finished the Experiment, a questionnaire was distributed among them. They were all satisfied by the experience and the options offered to them. However, the major comment we received was, that the participants will be more satisfied by the Edge Menu, if they were able to use both of their hands while navigating. Based on the information collected by the questionnaire, we carried the second study, enabling the participants to use both of their hands while navigating through the list.

4   Study II: Dual vs. Single Handed Interaction

After proving that the Edge Menu outperforms the Linear Menu, while maintaining the same testing environment and conditions. It was time to prove that the Edge Menu can perform even better when using both hands, since the menu items are distributed along both screen edges (see Fig. 8). In this experiment the user was asked to use both of his hands while trying the new Edge Menu design using linear scrolling only. The circular scrolling technique was eliminated in this study since it wasn't proven that it is better than the normal linear technique. We investigated different lengths of lists - different numbers of contacts - to make sure that our study will almost fit most of the applications. The Experiment Design, Apparatus and Task were similar to that of Study I.

4.1 Design

This study has 2 independent variables, specifically the menu type with two levels; *Linear Menu* and *Edge Menu* and the list size with three levels; *201 entries*, *300 entries* and *600 entries*, and 2 dependent variables the error rate and mean execution time. The distribution of the blocks throughout the trial was same as of the First Study, (see Fig. 6). In each trial, the participant is instructed to locate and press on a specific contact name. Thus, simulating the typical interaction that occurs while calling a number.

4.2 Participants and Procedure

Similar to the first study, We recruited 36 participants (18 females) and (18 males) with an average age of 25 years ($SD = 2.24$) using university mailing lists. Six of the participants were left-handed. None of the participants had any previous experience using Edge Menus. After arriving in the lab and welcoming the participants, they signed a consent form and received an explanation of the purpose of the study.

We equally divided the participants to 3 groups each with 12 participants. First group was tested using 201 contacts; we divided them accordingly to 3 blocks, each having 67 trials. Thus each participant performed 402 trials: (2 menus $\times$ 67 trials $\times$ 3 blocks). The total number of trials in the experiment was *4824* (12 participants $\times$ 402 trials).

Fig. 8. Study setup - user while performing a trial

Second group was tested using 300 contacts; we divided them accordingly to 3 blocks, each having 100 trials. Thus each participant performed 600 trials: (2 menus × 100 trials × 3 blocks). The total number of trials in the experiment was *7200* (12 participants × 600 trials).

Finally, the Third group was tested using 600 contacts; we divided them accordingly to 3 blocks, each having 200 trials. Thus each participant performed 1200 trials: (2 menus × 200 trials × 3 blocks). The total number of trials in the experiment was *14400* (12 participants × 1200 trials).

4.3   Results

A paired samples t-test using the execution time of the Edge Menu and that of Linear Menu for each level of the Contacts' List size (201 - 300 - 600) was performed. The results were very promising. For the 201 Contacts level, The fastest performance was accomplished using Edge Menu, Edge Menu had statistically significant lower execution time (5.15 s) compared to Linear Menu (7.75 s), $t(11) = 4.083$, $p < .05$.

Table 2. Mean execution time for the two layouts using Dual hands

Layout	201 contacts	300 contacts	600 contacts
Edge Menu	5.15 s	5.11 s	5.6 s
Linear Menu	7.75 s	8.5 s	8.7 s

Also, for the 300 contacts, Edge Menu had statistically significant lower execution time (5.11 s) compared to Linear Menu (8.5 s), $t(11) = 6.811$, $p < .05$. Finally, for the 600 Contacts level, the fastest performance was accomplished using Edge Menu, Edge Menu had statistically significant lower execution time (5.6 s) compared to Linear Menu (8.7 s), $t(11) = 6.534$, $p < .05$.

Interestingly, results showed that for the 201 contacts, Edge Menu outperformed Linear Menu with 33.54%. Similarly, for the 300 contacts, Edge Menu outperformed Linear Menu with 39.88%. Finally, for the 600 contacts, Edge Menu outperformed Linear Menu with 35.63%. Impressively, results have shown slight improvement in performance of the users while using the Edge Menu with both hands than Edge Menu with Single hand. The average performance of the 2 menu types with different number of trials (201 - 300 - 600 Contacts) have been recorded (refer to Table 2 and Fig. 9 for the results).

4.4   Discussion

After performing the second study, it was proven that the Edge Menu outperforms Linear Menu, specially the Dual Edge Menu, and is worth for usage and for further research. This was the initial exploration but of course our study is for

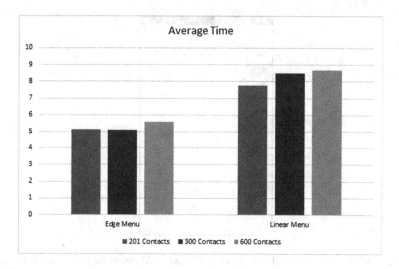

Fig. 9. Study II: mean execution time

limited use case and we envision that this could be extended for wider application than the Contacts' List. Therefor, we investigated the extension of the U-shaped Edge Menu via Nested Menus to allow more content navigation/display.

5 Study III: Evaluating Nested U-Edge Menus

In this Study we extend our design to include Nested Menus. Our goal with the evaluation was to find which menu is most efficient while working with a large-size list. A secondary goal was to understand the importance of our design goals and decide which is most relevant for future design efforts.

5.1 Design

The goal of this study is to compare the performance of the Edge Menu to a standard Linear Menu, on mobile, in the case of navigating a Nested Menu structure. We measured two dependent variables; execution time and error rate. The latter is defined as the percentage of trials with an incorrect selection of an item. The Execution Time is defined as the time between the communication of a menu item to the participant till tapping on that target. There were two independent variables; *Menu-Type* and *Menu-Depth*. *Menu-Type* had two levels; *Linear Menu* and *Edge Menu*. *Menu-Depth* had four levels; *Depth-2*, *Depth-3*, *Depth-4* and *Depth-5* - representing Nested Menus with different depths.

5.2 Apparatus

Our experimental setup consisted of a Samsung S3 device with a 4.8 in. (1280 × 720) display running Android 4.0.

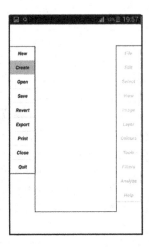

Fig. 10. Nested Edge Menu. Each level of a Nested Menu is displayed on one side of the screen.

5.3   Participants and Procedure

Eleven unpaid university students, six males and five females, performed the experiment (age $\mu = 21.5$).

In each trial, the participant is provided with a target menu item along with the path to follow to reach to that menu item. The participant task is to navigate through the menu, (see Fig. 10) and click on the specified menu item.

At the beginning of the experiment, the task was explained to the participant. Before using each of the two designs, an explanation of the menu and the interaction was provided and some practice trials were executed. We instructed participants to use a specific hand posture with each menu type. In the Edge Menu, the participant was asked to hold the phone using two hands and use the thumbs to select. Meanwhile, in the Linear Menu, the user holds the phone with one hand and uses the thumb of that hand to perform the interaction. The study duration was around 50 min.

The experiment was divided into 3 blocks, each having 20 trials. The total number of trials in the experiment was; (11 Participants $\times$ 2 Menus $\times$ 4 Depths $\times$ 20 Trials $\times$ 3 Blocks = 5,280 trials.

5.4   Results

Error Rate was very small (less than 2%), thus was not included in the analysis. Since we wanted to compare the performance of the Edge Menu to the Linear Menu at every nesting level, we conducted a paired samples t-test using the execution time of the Edge Menu and that of Linear Menu at each Menu-Depth. For Depth-5, Edge Menu had statistically significant lower execution time (3.88 s) compared to Linear Menu (6.1 s), $t(10) = 3.3$, $p < .05$. Similar results were found

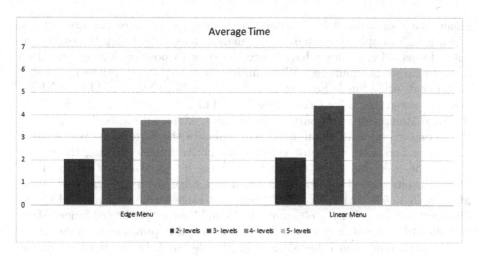

Fig. 11. Study III: mean execution time

Table 3. Mean execution time for the two layouts using Nested Menus

Layout	Depth-2	Depth-3	Depth-4	Depth-5
Edge Menu	3.4 s	3.4 s	3.77 s	3.88 s
Linear Menu	3.5 s	4.42 s	4.95 s	6.1 s

for Depth-4, where Edge Menu mean execution time was (3.77 s) while Linear Menu was (4.95 s), $t(10) = 2.9$, $p < .05$. For Depth-3, Edge Menu mean was (3.4 s) while Linear Menu was (4.42 s), $t(10) = 3.4$, $p < .05$. In Depth-2, there was no statistical significance between the two menus (refer to Table 3 and Fig. 11 for the results).

5.5 Discussion

In this experiment, the enhancement in performance due to Edge Menu was not the same at every menu-depth. In Depth-5, Edge Menu caused a decrease of 36% in execution time, while in Depth-4, it caused a decrease of 24%, and in Depth-3, the decrease was 22.6%. Thus in conclusion, the gain in performance increases as the number of levels in the menu increases. We believe that this is because at the first levels of the menu, the user has almost the same step counts. However, as we go deeper the step counts from the beginning of the trial increases and the user needs to interact more. Therefor, at this point the difference between the Edge Menu results and Linear Menu results are really significant.

6 Summary

In the three studies, our results revealed that Edge Menu is faster, and yields better performance than the Linear Menu. In the two variations of the Edge

Menu, the user utilized both hands to simultaneously enter the first letters, which is an example of a symmetric bi-manual task [5,8]. Using the two hands outperforms using a Single hand since the time to position a Single hand on the next target is eliminated. When unifying the testing conditions in the first experiment, using Single hand while testing both Edge Menu and Linear Menu. Results showed that Edge Menu outperformed Linear Menu by 32.93%. Similarly, the Edge Menu with wheel outperformed Linear Menu with wheel by 28.92%. In the second experiment, in an attempt to enhance the Edge Menu performance even more and meet the most comfortable position while holding the mobile phone, the user was asked to use both of his hands while testing the Edge Menu. Results showed that for the 201 contacts, Edge Menu outperformed Linear Menu with 33.54%. Also, for the 300 contacts, Edge Menu outperformed Linear Menu with 39.88%. For the 600 contacts, Edge Menu outperformed Linear Menu with 35.63%. Interestingly, results have shown slight improvement in Edge Menu using both hands than Edge Menu using Single hand. In the third study, the Edge Menu showed a remarkable decrease in the execution time, 36%, 24% and 22.6% for Depth-5, Depth-4 and Depth-3. We believe that the menu's icons size contributed to the positive results demonstrated by the Edge Menu. Spreading out the menu items, across the edge of the screen gives more space to each item. Each icon activation area along the sides in the Edge Menu was 1.5x as large as the activation area in the Linear Menu. Our results agree with previous works that larger activation areas yields faster performance [11] (Fig. 12 and Table 4).

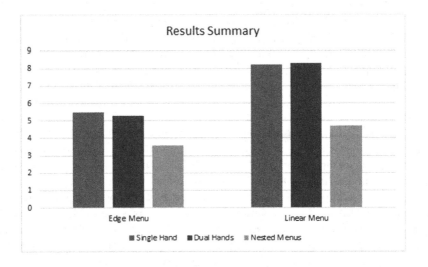

Fig. 12. Average results summary

Table 4. Summary of the 3 studies' results

Layout	Single hand	Dual hands	Nested menus
Edge Menu	5.5 s	5.28 s	3.6 s
Linear Menu	8.2 s	8.3 s (Single)	4.7 s

7 Limitations and Future Work

There were several limitations we explored through designing the 3 studies, most of which have been resolved during performing the experiments. The main challenge was supporting different lists' sizes, this we were able to resolve in the second study by running the experiment on different Contact's List size. Only few of the limitations were left for future research. The main goal would be creating a platform that allows application designers to integrate/convert their work directly with the Edge Menu. We believe that the source code and research done in this paper should be available for other researchers in an open source library, to help out researchers to add their ideas.

8 Conclusion

We developed the Edge Menu which is a U shaped menu fitted to the left, right and bottom edges of a mobile screen. An Edge Menu is superior to a Linear Menu by 23% to 40%. However, further research is required to enable the Edge Menu to support greater set of items - for example, languages with longer alphabet. While our findings suggest that the two variations of the Edge Menu will yield better performance in a larger list, this still needs to be verified using a formal study. The work explored the practicality and feasibility of Edge Menu design. Based on our user studies and experiments, it is proven that the Edge Menu yields better performance than the regular Linear Menu. By these results, encouraging software developers and application designers to start integrating Edge Menu with their designs instead of Linear Menu, and explore the capabilities offered by this relatively new design.

References

1. Six new facts about Facebook (2014). http://www.pewresearch.org/fact-tank/2014/02/03/6-new-facts-about-facebook/
2. Smart phone market share (2016). http://www.idc.com/prodserv/smartphone-market-share.jsp
3. The official samsung galaxy site (2017). http://www.samsung.com/uk/smartphones/galaxy-s7/design/
4. Ankolekar, A., Szabo, G., Luon, Y., Huberman, B.A., Wilkinson, D., Wu, F.: Friendlee: a mobile application for your social life. In: Proceedings of the 11th international Conference on Human-Computer interaction with Mobile Devices and Services, p. 27. ACM (2009)

5. Balakrishnan, R., Hinckley, K.: Symmetric bimanual interaction. In: Proceedings of the SIGCHI Conference on Human Factors in Computing Systems, pp. 33–40. ACM (2000)

6. Bergman, O., Komninos, A., Liarokapis, D., Clarke, J.: You never call: demoting unused contacts on mobile phones using DMTR. Pers. Ubiquit. Comput. **16**(6), 757–766 (2012)

7. Bonnet, D., Appert, C.: SAM: The Swiss Army Menu. In: Proceedings of the 23rd Conference on l'Interaction Homme-Machine, p. 5. ACM (2011)

8. Buxton, W., Myers, B.: A study in two-handed input. ACM SIGCHI Bull. **17**, 321–326 (1986). ACM

9. Callahan, J., Hopkins, D., Weiser, M., Shneiderman, B.: An empirical comparison of pie vs. linear menus. In: Proceedings of the SIGCHI Conference on Human Factors in Computing Systems, pp. 95–100. ACM (1988)

10. Chen, C., Perrault, S.T., Zhao, S., Ooi, W.T.: Bezelcopy: an efficient cross-application copy-paste technique for touchscreen smartphones. In: Proceedings of the 2014 International Working Conference on Advanced Visual Interfaces, pp. 185–192. ACM (2014)

11. Fitts, P.M.: The information capacity of the human motor system in controlling the amplitude of movement. J. Exp. Psychol. **47**(6), 381 (1954)

12. Fitts, P.M.: The information capacity of the human motor system in controlling the amplitude of movement. J. Exp. Psychol. Gen. **121**(3), 262 (1992)

13. Foster, G., Foxcroft, T.: Barrel menu: a new mobile phone menu for feature rich devices. In: Proceedings of the South African Institute of Computer Scientists and Information Technologists Conference on Knowledge, Innovation and Leadership in a Diverse, Multidisciplinary Environment, pp. 97–105. ACM (2011)

14. Francone, J., Bailly, G., Nigay, L., Lecolinet, E.: Wavelet menus: a stacking metaphor for adapting marking menus to mobile devices. In: Proceedings of the 11th International Conference on Human-Computer Interaction with Mobile Devices and Services, p. 49. ACM (2009)

15. Froehlich, J., Wobbrock, J.O., Kane, S.K.: Barrier pointing: using physical edges to assist target acquisition on mobile device touch screens. In: Proceedings of the 9th International ACM SIGACCESS Conference on Computers and Accessibility, pp. 19–26. ACM (2007)

16. Hampton, K., Goulet, L.S., Rainie, L., Purcell, K.: Social networking sites and our lives. Pew Internet & American Life Project, 16 June 2011

17. Hossain, Z., Hasan, K., Liang, H.-N., Irani, P.: Edgesplit: facilitating the selection of off-screen objects. In: Proceedings of the 14th International Conference on Human-Computer Interaction with Mobile Devices and Services, pp. 79–82. ACM (2012)

18. Jain, M., Balakrishnan, R.: User learning and performance with Bezel menus. In: Proceedings of the SIGCHI Conference on Human Factors in Computing Systems, pp. 2221–2230. ACM (2012)

19. Jung, Y., Anttila, A., Blom, J.: Designing for the evolution of mobile contacts application. In: Proceedings of the 10th International Conference on Human Computer Interaction with Mobile Devices and Services, pp. 449–452. ACM (2008)

20. Karlson, A.K., Bederson, B.B., SanGiovanni, J.: Applens and launchtile: two designs for one-handed thumb use on small devices. In: Proceedings of the SIGCHI Conference on Human Factors in Computing Systems, pp. 201–210. ACM (2005)

21. Kurtenbach, G., Buxton, W.: The limits of expert performance using hierarchic marking menus. In: Proceedings of the INTERACT 1993 and CHI 1993 Conference on Human Factors in Computing Systems, pp. 482–487. ACM (1993)

22. Leganchuk, A., Zhai, S., Buxton, W.: Manual and cognitive benefits of two-handed input: an experimental study. ACM Trans. Comput. Hum. Interact. (TOCHI) **5**(4), 326–359 (1998)
23. Li, W.H.A., Fu, H.: BezelCursor: Bezel-initiated cursor for one-handed target acquisition on mobile touch screens. In: SIGGRAPH Asia 2013 Symposium on Mobile Graphics and Interactive Applications, p. 36. ACM (2013)
24. Mukerjee, M.K.: Neurophone: brain-mobile phone interface using a wireless EEG headset. In: MobiHeld (2010)
25. Nicolau, H., Jorge, J.: Touch typing using thumbs: understanding the effect of mobility and hand posture. In: Proceedings of the SIGCHI Conference on Human Factors in Computing Systems, pp. 2683–2686. ACM (2012)
26. Oulasvirta, A., Raento, M., Tiitta, S.: Contextcontacts: re-designing smartphone's contact book to support mobile awareness and collaboration. In: Proceedings of the 7th International Conference on Human Computer Interaction with Mobile Devices & Services, pp. 167–174. ACM (2005)
27. Plessas, A., Stefanis, V., Komninos, A., Garofalakis, J.: Using communication frequency and recency context to facilitate mobile contact list retrieval. Int. J. Handheld Comput. Res. (IJHCR) **4**(4), 52–71 (2013)
28. Roth, V., Turner, T.: Bezel swipe: conflict-free scrolling and multiple selection on mobile touch screen devices. In: Proceedings of the SIGCHI Conference on Human Factors in Computing Systems, pp. 1523–1526. ACM (2009)
29. Stefanis, V., Komninos, A., Plessas, A., Garofalakis, J.: An interface for context-aware retrieval of mobile contacts. In: Proceedings of the 15th International Conference on Human-Computer Interaction with Mobile Devices and Services, pp. 492–497. ACM (2013)
30. Tu, H., Wang, F., Tian, F., Ren, X.: A comparison of flick and ring document scrolling in touch-based mobile phones. In: Proceedings of the 10th Asia Pacific Conference on Computer Human Interaction, pp. 29–34. ACM (2012)
31. Walker, N., Smelcer, J.B.: A comparison of selection time from walking and pull-down menus. In: Proceedings of the SIGCHI Conference on Human Factors in Computing Systems, pp. 221–226. ACM (1990)
32. Wobbrock, J.: The benefits of physical edges in gesture-making: empirical support for an edge-based unistroke alphabet. In: CHI 2003 Extended Abstracts on Human Factors in Computing Systems, pp. 942–943. ACM (2003)
33. Wobbrock, J.O., Myers, B.A., Aung, H.H.: The performance of hand postures in front-and back-of-device interaction for mobile computing. Int. J. Hum. Comput. Stud. **66**(12), 857–875 (2008)
34. Wobbrock, J.O., Myers, B.A., Hudson, S.E.: Exploring edge-based input techniques for handheld text entry. In: 23rd International Conference on Distributed Computing Systems Workshops, Proceedings, pp. 280–282. IEEE (2003)
35. Zhao, S., Dragicevic, P., Chignell, M., Balakrishnan, R., Baudisch, P.: Earpod: eyes-free menu selection using touch input and reactive audio feedback. In: Proceedings of the SIGCHI Conference on Human Factors in Computing Systems, pp. 1395–1404. ACM (2007)

Open Access This chapter is licensed under the terms of the Creative Commons Attribution 4.0 International License (http://creativecommons.org/licenses/by/4.0/), which permits use, sharing, adaptation, distribution and reproduction in any medium or format, as long as you give appropriate credit to the original author(s) and the source, provide a link to the Creative Commons license and indicate if changes were made.

The images or other third party material in this chapter are included in the chapter's Creative Commons license, unless indicated otherwise in a credit line to the material. If material is not included in the chapter's Creative Commons license and your intended use is not permitted by statutory regulation or exceeds the permitted use, you will need to obtain permission directly from the copyright holder.

Applications

Design Considerations for Self Paced Interactive Notes on Video Lectures - A Learner's Perspective and Enhancements of Learning Outcome

Suman Deb[1]([envelope]), Anindya Pal[1], and Paritosh Bhattacharya[2]

[1] Department of CSE, National Institute of Technology Agartala, Jirania, India
sumandeb.cse@nita.ac.in, anindya2674@gmail.com
[2] Department of Mathematics, National Institute of Technology Agartala,
Jirania, India
pari76@rediffmail.com

Abstract. Video lectures form a primary part of MOOC instruction delivery design. They serve as gateways to draw students into the course. In going over these videos accumulating knowledge, there is a high occurrence of cases [1] where the learner forgets about some of the concepts taught and focus more on what is the minimum amount knowledge needed to carry forward to attempt the quizzes and pass. This is a step backward when we are concerned with giving the learner a learning outcome that seems to bridge the gap between what he knew before and after the course to completion. To address this issue, we are proposing an interaction model that enables the learner to promptly take notes as and when the video is being viewed. The work contains a functional prototype of the application for taking personalized notes from MOOC contents. The work [12] is an integration of several world leading MOOC providers content using application program interface(API) and a customize interface module for searching courses from multiple MOOC providers as COURSEEKA and personalised note taking module as MOOKbook. This paper largely focuses on a learner's perspective towards video based lectures and interaction to find the enhancements in interaction with longer retention of MOOC contents.

Keywords: MOOC note · Self pace learning · Personalized learning
MOOCbook · MOOC Video Interaction · Enhanced learning outcome

1 Introduction

A MOOC is a model of delivering education in varying degrees, massive, open, online, and most importantly, a course [13,14]. Most MOOCs have a structure similar to traditional online higher education counterparts in which students watch lectures online and offline, read material assigned to them, participate in online forums and discussions and complete quizzes and tests on the course material. The

© The Author(s) 2017
P. Horain et al. (Eds.): IHCI 2017, LNCS 10688, pp. 109–121, 2017.
https://doi.org/10.1007/978-3-319-72038-8_9

online activities can be supplemented by local meet-ups among students who live near one another (Blended Learning) [3]. The primary form of information delivery in MOOC format is videos. One of the challenges faced by the online learners of today is the need of an interface which enables to take notes from the video lectures [2]. Traditional methods used thus far by the student community are time absorbing and cumbersome in terms of organization. This work is an attempt to address the issue enabling the learner to focus more on the curriculum than on how to compile and access the materials later. As MOOC courses being accessed through out world, beyond any geographical region. Inherently it triggers another level of interaction and understanding difficulty due to cultural, linguistic variation. In addition to that human learning variation takes a great role in graceful MOOC acceptance, learning pleasure and learning outcome.

2   Problem Statement

There is a significant concern over what the learners end up learning as compared to what the MOOC instruction designer intended them to do [4,7]. Many just fall into the trap of knowing just enough to pass the quizzes and course assessments, this neglecting any other concepts that learner may have eventually come across but forgotten about it [8,18]. For the learners who seem to acknowledge this issue on their own, they tend to view the videos again and again until they feel that they have substantial command over the topic being taught in these videos [6,9]. Now, while this may be a good practice, this takes an awful amount of time. Also, watching multiple video lectures on a specific topic may overlap various contents as well tend to forget [15] the previously viewed contents [10,16]. Instead, if there was an interface that lets the learner decide on taking essential parts of the video in a form which can enable them to revise the concepts later and on-demand, it would make sense. This work designs an integrated *MOOC takers note book* that makes an integration of various course providers content on a personalized note interface [11]. This enables cross reference, transcript copy, still frame capture and personalize text note. Taking notes are a manifestation of that conscious effort of peoples natural tendency to forget things with time [19]. Lecture or handouts given in class by the instructor are all the same but people seem to remember more when they are actively taking a record of what is happening, on their own. But there is a flipside to the scenario in digital note taking. People are more reluctant to take notes verbatim, with every word on the document [5]. The trade off between digital and conventional notes are discussed in the experiments presented in [17]. But despite these findings, modern day challenges make to utilize ones time in the best possible way.

3   MOOCbook a Novel Model

Since videos represent the most significant part of MOOCs, it is a mandate that the note taking process will revolve around them. The length of the videos varies from provider to provider, typically ranging from 2–4 min (micro-lectures) to a maximum of 15 min. As a video progresses, there are certain checkpoints that an instructor breaks a topic into and these checkpoints serve as the keynotes for the topic at hand. For example, a video about supervised learning of machine learning would typically discuss about the common examples in which it is used, then explain the algorithm employed, plot the points representing the features and interpret it, differentiate with other machine learning algorithms and finally conclude the scenarios and advantages where the algorithm applies.

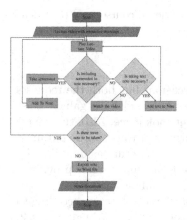

Fig. 1. MOOKBook work flow

These checkpoints, although important to the MOOC taker at that instant, seem to fade away when the next video starts. The MOOC taker is reluctant on obligating to memory rather tend only to remember those parts which are needed to pass the quizzes. To address this issue, we propose a novel model whereby the MOOC taker can take notes on the fly when they are taking the course through watching videos. For the MOOC taker, the parts of the course which they intend to take note, it happens to be certain points in the video. It is assumed that the video is accompanied by an interactive transcript that scrolls and highlights what the instructor is saying at that moment of the video. During the video, there may happen to be equations, diagrams, graphs and example scenarios that explains the topic from various perspectives. To take the corresponding notes by hand, it would take stopping the video, taking the conventional note book up and writing or drawing whats on the video screen at that instant. This would take up the valuable time that the MOOC taker has invested already. The proposed on the go note taking, while the MOOC taker watches the video is a meta description extraction using a client side scripting on the browser that the learner is currently using to access the materials. The parts of the lecture which catches the attention of the learner are simultaneously displayed in the transcript. A recurrence script extracts transcript with the screen and add the portions to the notebook on events initiated by the user. The learner can save a considerable amount of time which they would otherwise be using for taking the notes conventionally. The user can view the updated note in the browser itself so that it gives a better perspective of what has been learnt (Fig. 1).

4   Architectural Design

4.1   Design of COURSESEEKA Module

As a starting point in achieving the goals set forth by, an online interface has been developed where the learners first objective i.e. the need to identify suitable courses that may address his current learning objective, from an array of courses enlisted in various course providers, namely coursera, udacity and udemy. edx

Fig. 2. Fuzzy closeness approximation algorithm in action for filtering a search from multiple MOOC providers simultaneously

Fig. 3. A retrieved course from (a) Udemy (b) Coursera

had also been approached for their API on two occasions but both the requests got rejected. These course providers are fairly popular and have gained trust among the learning masses as the MOOC movement took place. Also, these have well defined APIs which enlist course related information that can be obtained easily. The COURSEEKA interface is based on the architecture as described by Fig. 5. The interface aims to find courses available from three course providers, namely courser.org, udacity.com and udemy.com and combine their results into a single web page where a user can query a course specific search term according to his learning objective, and the courses will then be filtered accordingly (Figs. 2, 3, 4 and 5).

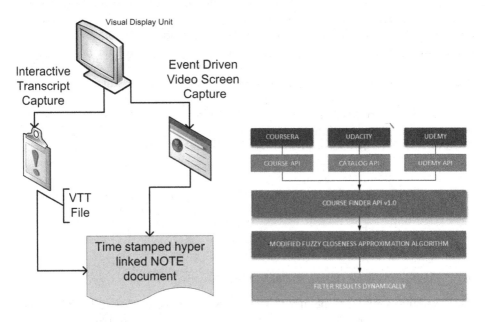

Fig. 4. MOOKBook multi modal note generation

Fig. 5. COURSEEKA API stack

4.2 Modified Fuzzy Closeness Approximation Algorithm

Existing interfaces on course search is based on matching the keywords wholly. While this may seem as a very nave way to get courses recommended to a learner based on his search term, our web application has a learner centric approach to getting the search results that will suit someone who is willing to manage his online MOOC curriculum in a very specific way. His search results are constrained to be from one of the major MOOC providers (as has been told already) existing today. Moreover, the search algorithm is based on a modified fuzzy string closeness approximation algorithm which is clever enough to infer what the MOOC learner is specifically searching for even if he is halfway through or even less than what he intends to type.

5 Implementation

5.1 Prototype Specifications

The prototype is a web application that hosts a video with interactive transcript and has control buttons to preview and append notes. The interface aims to capture portions of the text of the video content i.e. the transcript along with screen captures, preview them and append to the notebook inside the webpage itself. Finally, the user has the option to download the notebook thus formed. All of this happens using client side scripting, which is relevant since time is of the essence when the user is taking the note as the video plays. This eliminates the load off the servers hosting massive amounts of data in the MOOC servers.

5.2 Prototype Demonstration

An initial working prototype has been implemented which uses the three APIs combined and lists all the courses relevant to a learners interest as they types in a search query. The search results are then displayed centrally using a Fuzzy String Closeness Approximation. As an example of working demo, the video course cited is one of the those featured in the first week of the Machine Learning course by Professor Andrew Ng of Stanford university, hosted by coursera.org. The instructor goes about explaining Un-supervised learning in the course. Figure 6 The distinguishable parts of the video are listed as under: 1. Difference between unsupervised learning and supervised learning (two graphs). 2. Applications of Supervised Learning (images depicting them). 3. Tackling a problem (cocktail party problem) using unsupervised learning (image de-picting the scenario). 4. Cocktail party problem algorithm (code in python) 5. A quiz with options to choose from. These distinguishable parts are of concern to the learner when compiling a digital note about the video. The MOOCbook interface is equipped to take snapshots of these parts and scrape the transcripts of the relevant portions as and when the learner deems it necessary. Figure 6 shows a screen of the video captured for preview. The snapshot is taken using the videos and videos interactive transcript JS libraries in tandem. If the preview is deemed good for

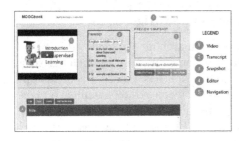

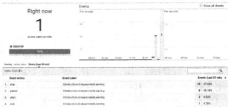

Fig. 6. MOOKBook GUI and interactions   **Fig. 7.** Analytic dashboard

Event Action	Total Events	Unique Events	Event Value	Avg. Value
percent played	18	1	900	50
play	11	1	2,456	223.27
seek end	7	1	3187	455.29
seek start	7	1	2032	290.29
pause	4	1	62	15.5
start	1	1	0	0
end	2	1	0	0
volume change	1	1	0	0
enter fullscreen	1	1	0	0
exit fullscreen	1	1	0	0
	53	8	8637	162.96

Fig. 8. MOOCBook final note in MS word   **Fig. 9.** Example clickstream data collected from google analytics

adding to the note, the user then proceeds accordingly. To capture the lecture discussions relevant to the note being compiled, we have made use of the VTT file available with the video in courser. The VTT file has timestamps along with text content, which is scraped using suitable javascript code, and added to the note. Thus, the cocktail party problem algorithm now has a proposed problem, a solution with code and relevant transcripts, all in one note, viewable in the browser itself where the video is still playing. The note thus far compiled, is now available for download to the client machine using the jquery word export plugin made using JS. The final note file is a MS Word document (Figs. 7, 8 and 9).

6   Synthesis of Experiments and Result

The system developed for taking notes from MOOCs, namely MOOCbook is taken up for testing effectiveness. Pretests were concluded before the actual experiment to establish clear reference point of comparison between treatment group and control group. To investigate whether the proposed system effectively generates a learning outcome that lasts even after the video completes, post tests were conducted between the two groups. The subject matter that is portrayed in the two videos which are featured in the system developed is an introduction to the two major varieties of Machine Learning algorithms. Both the treatment and the control groups have a basic knowledge of what Machine Learning is about.

6.1   Evaluation Criterion

The current MOOC interfaces available on the Internet featured on MOOC platforms like coursera, udacity etc. are designed to deliver content over multiple media formats. The primary format, namely videos are designed to be accompanied by in-video quizzes that assess the learners comprehension with the help of in-video quizzes as well as separate assessments module. But certain parts of the video are overlooked by the learner because he may be impulsively following the video to complete the quizzes and the assessments. For this purpose, it happens that the learner may have peeked into the questions beforehand and accordingly is inclined to get the answers from the video. So, he is skimming portions of the video in order to find the answers and thus is not open to effective learning. The questions to understand how the system enhances the learning outcome of a learner have been identified as under:

- *Question 1:* How much time is spent on viewing the video, including activation of play and pause buttons on the video player?
- *Question 2:* Whether skimming the video helps in understanding the content?
- *Question 3:* Did the users feel the need to seek to certain parts of the video to find answers to questions which are known beforehand the experiment?
- *Question 4:* Does a digital note assistant help in reviewing and recalling portions of the content in a way that saves time and thus increase the effective learning of the MOOC taker?
- *Question 5:* Did the users who were provided with the MOOCbook module actually refer the downloaded note?

6.2   Methodology

The participants of this experiment are 6th Semester Under Graduate Engineering students. There are 84 students in total, divided into two groups, one being a control group and the other being the treatment group. They are shown two videos each on the system developed. The control group gets to see only the videos, while the treatment group sees the MOOCbook interface at play, which enables them to take notes if necessary. Each of the participants are allotted 40 min for viewing the videos. The combined length of the videos is $(12.29 + 14.13) = 26.42$ min. Throughout the duration of the video featured in MOOCbook, all activities of the user are recorded with the help of Google analytics that serve as a gateway to learn key insights into how the users interact with the video player while seeing the videos. The data collected through Google analytics is downloadable and hence form our dataset of study. The data downloaded from Google analytics is in the form of csv files which are obtained individually from all the 84 users of the experiment. The effectiveness of the

MOOCbook interface was tested using independent-samples t-test. It is aimed to compare means between two unrelated groups on the same continuous variable. In this case, it has been used to understand whether the learning outcome undergraduate engineering student is increased on the application of MOOCbook. Thus the independent variable here is "User of MOOCbook or not "(one of the groups being users who had MOOCbook interface at their disposal and the other being who did not use MOOCbook) and the dependent variable is the "learning outcome ".

Assumptions. As requirement of independent t-test, the 6 point compliance of assumptions as detailed under.

1. The dependent variable, namely learning outcome is measurable in a continuous scale.
2. The independent variable i.e. whether MOOCbook user or not, has two possibilities viz. either the user is given the MOOCbook interface or the user is not. Thus there are two categorical, independent groups.
3. There is independence of observations since there is no relationship between the observations in each group or between the groups themselves.
4. There is no significant outliers, meaning there are no values in the dataset that does not follow the usual pattern.
5. The dependent variable which is learning outcome is approximately normally distributed for each group of the independent variable.
6. There is homogeneity of variances.

6.3   Instruments

The various analytical processes aimed at answering the questions identified have been enlisted here. A short demonstration was performed which walked through the MOOCbook interface to the participants before the experiment so that they are familiar with the system. A questionnaire aimed at measuring MOOC awareness among the participants serves as a pretest before the experiment, and two post tests comprising data analysis of clickstream events generated during experiment and a quiz is aimed at testing effectiveness of the MOOCbook interface.

Pretest. The pretest was carried out before the participants were given access to the system. The two groups were surveyed about their MOOC awareness. A questionnaire specific to MOOC awareness was used in this regard.

Post Intervention Tests

1. **Clickstream data analysis** - To address how behavior of participants differ on the provision of the MOOCbook interface in terms of interaction with the video (questions 1–3 of **Evaluation Criteria** section), the data generated through clickstream events of the video on the google analytics server was analyzed.

2. **Learning outcome** - To answer the questions 4 and 5 enlisted in **Evaluation Criteria** section, a quiz was conducted with the participants and the results were evaluated.

Null Hypotheses

- H1: There is no significant difference in terms of MOOC taking experience between the treatment group and the control group.
- H2: There is no significant difference between the participants in terms of the pattern of clickstream events generated for the videos watched.
- H3: There is no significant difference between treatment and the control group in terms of learning outcome generated from the experiment.

Pretest Results. Data in Fig. 10 shows that the treatment group pre-test mean scores was 7.07 (SD = 2.443) while the control group pre-test mean score was 6.88 (SD = 2.098). To ensure the comparison between two groups, a two tailed t-test was done on the sample for 5% level of significance. The findings are shown in Fig. 11. The mean difference between the treatment and the control group in terms of Test Scores is 0.190. The findings (Fig. 11) lead to the conclusion that there is no significant difference between the treatment and control group prior to the experimental study conducted. Both groups were found to have common ground of knowledge when it comes to MOOCs and thus are ideal for the MOOCbook test scenario. Hence hypothesis H1 failed to be rejected (Fig. 12).

Variable	Observations	Minimum	Maximum	Mean	Std. Deviation
Treatment Group	42	3	10	7.07	2.443
Control Group	42	3	10	6.88	2.098

Fig. 10. Pre-test score results of treatment and control group

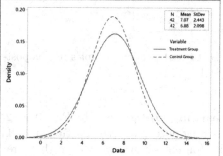

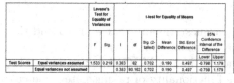

		Levene's Test for Equality of Variances		t-test for Equality of Means					95% Confidence Interval of the Difference	
		F	Sig.	t	df	Sig. (2-tailed)	Mean Difference	Std. Error Difference	Lower	Upper
Test Scores	Equal variances assumed	1.533	0.219	0.383	82	0.702	0.190	0.497	-0.798	1.179
	Equal variances not assumed			0.383	80.162	0.702	0.190	0.497	-0.798	1.179

Fig. 11. Independent samples test as pretest

Fig. 12. Normal distribution for pretest scores

Post Test Results Clickstream Data Analysis. Data in Fig. 13 shows the summary of clickstream data obtained from 84 participants. The control group generated analytics data from only the video player interactions like play, pause, fullscreen etc. while the treatment group was capable of generating note-taking events like Add Text To Note, Add Image To Note etc. in addition to what control group users were allowed. For the purpose of analysis, only the clickstream data with respect to video player interactions is taken up. The note-taking interactions will not be taken in the post test analysis. The normal distribution graph of the post-test-1 scores for the two groups is shown in Fig. 15. To analyze the hypothesis H2, a two tailed t-test was done on the sample for 5 % level of significance. The mean difference between the treatment and the control group in terms of the number of events registered while watching the videos is -32.667. The findings of the Independent Samples Test is depicted in Tabular data Fig. 14. The above findings lead to the conclusion that there is a significant difference between the treatment and control group post the experimental study conducted. Both groups were found to have interacted in a very different way when it came to viewing the videos. The number of clickstream events were far higher for the control group without the notes system than the treatment group with notes enabled. This leads to the conclusion that hypothesis H2 is false and does not hold.

Variable	Observations	Minimum	Maximum	Mean	Std. Deviation
Treatment Group	42	18	63	40.24	14.043
Control Group	42	38	129	72.90	21.354

Fig. 13. Post-test clickstream results of treatment and control group

		Levene's Test for Equality of Variances		t-test for Equality of Means						95% Confidence Interval of the Difference	
		F	Sig	t	df	Sig (2-tailed)	Mean Difference	Std Error Difference		Lower	Upper
Events	Equal variances assumed	4.100	0.046	-8.283	82	0.000	-32.667	3.944		-40.512	-24.821
	Equal variances not assumed			-8.283	70.876	0.000	-32.667	3.944		-40.530	-24.803

Fig. 14. Independent samples test as post-test 1

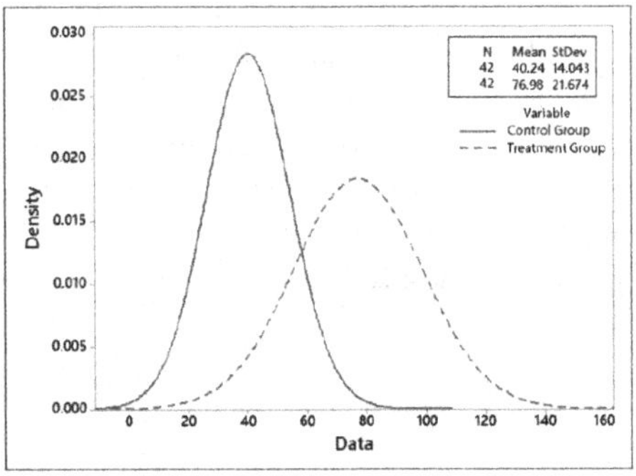

Fig. 15. Normal distribution for post test 1 scores

Learning Outcome. The Post Test 2 is a questionnaire that aims to find the learning outcome of the participants. The questions contained here are set from the content of the two videos that are hosted in the MOOCbook system. The control group once again is devoid of the functionality of taking notes whereas the treatment group is notes module enabled. The results obtained as shown in Fig. 16 will be directly connected with how much of the lessons depicted within the videos are comprehended by the users. Thus the direct measure of how much a knowledge a learner can retain will be obtained. To analyze the hypothesis H2, a two tailed t-test was done on the sample for 5% level of significance. The mean difference between the treatment and the control group in terms of the Qscores (scores obtained by the participants on the questionnaire) is -2.333. The findings of the Independent Samples Test is depicted in Fig. 17. The findings lead to the conclusion that there is a significant difference between the treatment and control

Variable	Observations	Minimum	Maximum	Mean	Std. Deviation
Treatment Group	42	-5	8	40.24	14.043
Control Group	42	-2	10	72.90	21.354

Fig. 16. Post-test 2 results of treatment and control group

| | | Equality of Variances | | t-test for Equality of Means | | | | | 95% Confidence Interval of the Difference | |
		F	Sig.	t	df	Sig. (2-tailed)	Mean Difference	Std. Error Difference	Lower	Upper
QScores	Equal variances assumed	4.915	0.029	-2.951	82	0.004	-2.33333	0.79070	-3.90630	-0.78037
	Equal variances not assumed			-2.951	75.697	0.004	-2.33333	0.79070	-3.90826	-0.75841

Fig. 17. Independent samples test as post-test 2

group post the experimental study conducted. Both groups were found to have had a very different learning outcome in terms of understanding the contents depicted in the videos. The number of correct answers for the quiz questions were far higher for the treatment group with the notes system enabled than the control group with notes disabled. This leads to the conclusion that hypothesis H3 is false and does not hold. Thus the notes module plays a significant part in terms of making the lessons more content aware to the learners. They are able to differentiate key points told by the lecturer and form memory mappings of lesson checkpoints which later help them to retrieve the same, i.e. recall lesson key points.

7 Conclusion

This work is an attempt to address the issues enabling the learner to focus more on the curriculum than on how to compile and access the materials later. A novel model MOOCbook was presented and a working prototype has been demonstrated for this purpose. The results obtained have provided us with some insights to get into what people are looking for in terms of enhancing their learning outcome. One of the major finding was a need of self paced MOOC note. The empirical experiments conducted and anecdotal response have shown significant improvement in engagement to accomplish MOOC course as well enhancement in learning outcome. All the work has been done from a learner's perspective. The inclusion of this tool along with MOOC provider's platforms will pave the way for enhanced digital learning in the future.

References

1. Barba, N., Gluhanich, L.: 4 Pros and 4 Cons of MOOCs: Whether to take study from classroom to online (2014). https://www.geteverwise.com/career-success/4-pros-and-4-cons-of-moocs-whether-to-take-study-from-classroom-to-online/. Retrieved 19 June 2017

2. Giannakos, M.N., Jaccheri, L., Krogstie, J.: Looking at MOOCs rapid growth through the lens of video-based learning research. IJET **9**(1), 35–38 (2014)

3. Davis, K., et al.: The theory of multiple intelligence. In: The Cambridge Handbook of Intelligence, pp. 485–503 (2011)

4. Fleming, N., Baume, D.: Learning Styles Again: VARKing up the right tree!. Educational Developments 7.4 (2006)

5. Barrington, E.: Teaching to student diversity in higher education: How multiple intelligence theory can help. Teaching High. Educ. **9**(4), 421–434 (2004)

6. Redding, S.: Through the Student's Eyes: A Perspective on Personalized Learning and Practice Guide for Teachers. Temple University, Center on Innovations in Learning (2013)

7. Kop, R., Fournier, H., Mak, J.S.F.: A pedagogy of abundance or a pedagogy to support human beings? Participant support on massive open online courses. In: The International Review of Research in Open and Distributed Learning, vol. 12(7), pp. 74–93 (2011)

8. Vivian, R., Falkner, K., Falkner, N.: Addressing the challenges of a new digital technologies curriculum: MOOCs as a scalable solution for teacher professional development. Res. Learn. Technol. 22 (2014)

9. Norton, A., Sonnemann, J., McGannon, C.: The Online Evolution: When Technology Meets Tradition in Higher Education, vol. 48. Grattan Institute, Australia (2013)

10. Kostolnyov, K., Armanov, J.: Use of adaptive study material in education in E-learning environment. Electron. J. e-Learn. **12**(2), 172–182 (2014)

11. Gynther, K.: Design framework for an adaptive MOOC enhanced by blended learning supplementary training and personalized learning for teacher professional development. Electro. J. e-Learn. **14**(1), 15–30 (2016)

12. Deb, S., et al.: Enhancing personalized learning with interactive note taking on video lectures-an analysis of effective HCI design on learning outcome. In: Communications in Computer and Information Science (CCIS). Springer (2017). ISSN No: 1865–0929(2017)

13. IITBombayX: Iitbombayx.in (2017). https://www.iitbombayx.in/dashboard. Retrieved 27 June 2017

14. NMEICT: Nmeict.iitkgp.ernet.in (2017). http://www.nmeict.iitkgp.ernet.in/audio.php. Retrieved 27 June 2017

15. Rubin, D.C., Wenzel, A.E.: One hundred years of forgetting: A quantitative description of retention. Psychol. Rev. **103**(4), 734 (1996)

16. Murre, J.M., Chessa, A.G., Meeter, M.: A mathematical model of forgetting and amnesia. Front. Psychol. **4**, 76 (2013)

17. Mueller, P.A., Oppenheimer, D.M.: The pen is mightier than the keyboard advantages of longhand over laptop note taking. Psychol. Sci. **25**(6), 1159–1168 (2014)

18. Clow, D.: MOOCs and the funnel of participation. In: Proceedings of the Third International Conference on Learning Analytics and Knowledge. ACM (2013)

19. Ros, C.P., et al.: Social factors that contribute to attrition in MOOCs. In: Proceedings of the first ACM Conference on Learning @ Scale Conference. ACM (2014)

Open Access This chapter is licensed under the terms of the Creative Commons Attribution 4.0 International License (http://creativecommons.org/licenses/by/4.0/), which permits use, sharing, adaptation, distribution and reproduction in any medium or format, as long as you give appropriate credit to the original author(s) and the source, provide a link to the Creative Commons license and indicate if changes were made.

The images or other third party material in this chapter are included in the chapter's Creative Commons license, unless indicated otherwise in a credit line to the material. If material is not included in the chapter's Creative Commons license and your intended use is not permitted by statutory regulation or exceeds the permitted use, you will need to obtain permission directly from the copyright holder.

Using Psycholinguistic Features
for the Classification of Comprehenders
from Summary Speech Transcripts

Santosh Kumar Barnwal$^{(\boxtimes)}$ and Uma Shanker Tiwary

Indian Institute of Information Technology, Allahabad, India
`iis2009002@gmail.com`

Abstract. In education, some students lack language comprehension, language production and language acquisition skills. In this paper we extracted several psycholinguistics features broadly grouped into lexical and morphological complexity, syntactic complexity, production units, syntactic pattern density, referential cohesion, connectives, amounts of coordination, amounts of subordination, LSA, word information, and readability from students' summary speech transcripts. Using these Coh-Metrix features, comprehenders are classified into two groups: poor comprehender and proficient comprehender. It is concluded that a computational model can be implemented using a reduced set of features and the results can be used to help poor reading comprehenders for improving their cognitive reading skills.

Keywords: Psycholinguistics · Natural language processing
Machine learning classification

1 Introduction

Reading is a complex cognitive activity where learners read texts to construct a meaningful understanding from the verbal symbols i.e. the words and sentences and the process is called as reading comprehension. In Reading process, the three main factors - the learner's context knowledge, the information aroused by the text, and the reading circumstances together construct a meaningful discourse. Previous researches claim that in academic environment several reading and learning strategies including intensive reading and extensive reading [2], spaced repetition [7] and top-down and bottom-up processes [1] play vital role in students developing comprehension skills.

Intensive Reading: It is the more common approach, in which learners read passages selecting from the same text or various texts about the same subject. Here, content and linguistic forms are repeated themselves, therefore learners get several chances to comprehend the meaning of the textual contents. It is usually classroom based and teacher centric approach where students concentrate on linguistics, grammatical structures and semantic details of the text to retain in

© The Author(s) 2017
P. Horain et al. (Eds.): IHCI 2017, LNCS 10688, pp. 122–136, 2017.
https://doi.org/10.1007/978-3-319-72038-8_10

memory over a long period of time. Students involve themselves in reading passages carefully and thoroughly again and again aiming to be able translating the text in a different language, learning the linguistic details in the text, answering comprehension questions such as objective type and multiple choice, or knowing new vocabulary words. Some disadvantages are - (a) it is slow, (b) needs careful reading of a small amount of difficult text, (c) requires more attention on the language and its structure, including morphology, syntax, phonetics, and semantics rather than the text, (d) text may be bored to students since it was chosen by the teacher, and (e) because exercises and assessments are part of comprehension evaluation, students may involve in reading only for the preparation for a test and not for getting any pleasure.

Extensive Reading: On the other hand, extensive reading provides more enjoyments as students read big quantities of own interest contents; focus on to understand main ideas but not on the language and its structure, skipping unfamiliar and difficult words and reading for summary [12]. The main aim of extensive reading is to learn foreign language through large amounts of reading and thus building student confidence and enjoyment. Several Research works claim that extensive reading facilitating students improving in reading comprehension to increase reading speed, greater understanding of second language grammar conventions, to improve second language writing, and to motivate for reading at higher levels [10].

The findings of previous researches suggest that extensive and intensive reading approaches are beneficial, in one way or another, for improving students' reading comprehension skills.

Psycholinguistic Factors: Psycholinguistics is a branch of cognitive science in which language comprehension, language production and language acquisition are studied. It tries to explain the ways in which language is represented and is processed in the brain; for example, the cognitive processes responsible for generating a grammatical and meaningful sentence based on vocabulary and grammatical structures and the processes which are responsible to comprehend words, sentences etc. Primary concerned linguistic related areas are: Phonology, morphology, syntax, semantics, and pragmatics. In this field, researchers study reader's capability to learn language for example, the different processes required for the extraction of phonological, orthographic, morphological, and semantic information by reading a textual document.

More recent work, Coh-Metrix [5] offers to investigate the cohesion of the explicit text and the coherence of the mental representation of the text. This metrix provides detailed analysis of language and cohesion features that are integral to cognitive reading processes such as decoding, syntactic parsing, and meaning construction.

2 Brief Description of Coh-Metrix Measures

Coh-Metrix is an automatic text analysis tool forwarding traditional theories of reading and comprehension to next higher level and therefore, can plays important role in different disciplines of education such as teaching, readability, learning etc. The tool analyses and measures features of texts written in English language through hundreds of measures, all informed by previous researchers in different disciplines such as computational linguistics, psycholinguistics, discourse processes and cognitive sciences. The tool integrates several computational linguistics components including lexicons, pattern classifiers, part-of-speech taggers, syntactic parsers, semantic interpreters, WordNet, CELEX Corpus etc. Employing these elements, Coh-Metrix can analyze texts on multi levels of cohesion including co-referential cohesion, causal cohesion, density of connectives, latent semantic analysis metrics, and syntactic complexity [5].

All measures of the tool have been categorized into following broad groups:

1. **Descriptive measures:** These measures describe statistical features of text in form of total number of paragraphs, total number of sentences, total number of words, average length of paragraphs with standard deviation, average number of words with standard deviation, mean number of syllables in words with standard deviation etc.

2. **Easability components:** For measuring text easability score, the tool provides several scores including text narrativity, syntactic familiarity, and Word Concreteness.

3. **Referential Cohesion:** It is a linguistic cue that helps readers in making connections between different text units such as clauses, and sentences. It includes Noun overlap (words overlap in terms of noun), and Argument overlap (sentences overlap in terms of nouns and pronouns). Coh-Metrix measures semantically similar pairs such as car/vehicle etc.

4. **Latent Semantic Analysis:** It is used to implement semantic co-referentiality for representing deeper world knowledge based on large corpora of texts.

5. **Lexical Diversity:** It is the variety of unique words (types) in a text in relation to number of words (tokens). It refers to variation of Type-token ratio (TTR).

6. **Connectives:** It provides clues about text organization and aid reader in the creation of cohesive links between ideas and clauses. It measures the cohesive links between different conceptual units using different types of connectives such as causal (because, so), logical (and, or), adversative (whereas), temporal (until) and additive (moreover). In addition to this, there is a difference between positive connectives (moreover) and negative connectives (but).

7. **Situation Model:** It refers to the level of reader's mental representation for a text when a given context is activated.

8. **Syntactic Complexity:** It is measured using NP density, mean number of high-level constituents per word, and the incidence of word classes that indicate analytical difficulty (e.g. and, or, if-then, conditionals).

9. **Syntactic Pattern Density:** It refers to the density of particular syntactic patterns, word types, and phrase types. The relative density of noun phrases, verb phrases, adverbial phrases, and prepositions can affect processing difficulty of text, especially with respect to other features in a text.

10. **Word Information:** It provides density scores for various parts of speech (POS), including pronouns, nouns, verbs, adjectives, adverbs, cardinal numbers, determiners, and possessives.
11. **Readability:** It provides the readability formulas of Flesch Reading Ease and Flesch-Kincaid Grade Level [4,9]. Both are two readability tests designed to indicate how difficult a passage in English is to understand. These tests use word length and sentence length as core measures; however they have different weighting factors.

The aim of present work is to identify the linguistic features that can classify students into two groups - students having proficient comprehension skills and students with poor comprehension skills from their summary speech transcripts.

3 Participants and Method

A brief description of the participants, materials, and procedure that we used in this study are described here.

Participants: Twenty undergraduate students (mean age (SD)- 21.4(0.86)) in information technology major; studied in same batch and performed all academic activities only in English, whereas their primary languages were different; participated in this experimental sessions. Students were told that they would be awarded some course credits for participating in the research. Based on their academic performance in last four semesters, these students were divided into two groups - ten as proficient and others as poor comprehenders.

Materials: The reading materials consisted of two passages. One passage (total sentences- 38, total words- 686, sentence length (mean)- 18.0, Flesch-Kincaid Grade level- 13.3) had been selected from students' course book whereas other was a simple interesting story (total sentences- 42, total words- 716, sentence length (mean)- 17.0, Flesch-Kincaid Grade level- 3.9). Both passages were written in English and were unread until the experiment began. Reading story passage was simulated extensive reading experience and reading course passage was simulated intensive reading experience.

Procedure: All experimental sessions were held in a research lab in a set of 5 students. The experiment consisted of two tests. In each test, student had instructed to read a given passage and then to solve a puzzle and lastly to tell summary as much detail as they can. Both tests were similar except the reading material - the story passage was given in first test and the course passage was given in second test. Students were informed to read the passage on computer screen as they would normally read. The speech were recorded using a digital audio recorder software installed in the computer system. The puzzle task was useful to erase students' short term memory of read text to ensure that the summary would come from their long term memory.

4   Feature Analysis

Feature Extraction: The recorded audio files were transcripted in English where brief pauses were marked with commas, while long pauses were marked with full stops (end of sentence) if their places were according to semantic, syntactic and prosodic features. Repetitions, incomplete words and incomprehensible words were not included in transcription. In the experiment, two sets of transcripts were generated - (a) **story transcripts** had texts of story summary audio files and (b) **course transcripts** had texts of course summary audio files. Both sets had twenty texts, ten of proficient comprehenders' audio files and the other ten of poor comprehenders' audio files.

For analysing the texts of both sets of transcripts, we used the computational tool Coh-Metrix. Coh-Metrix 3.0 (http://cohmetrix.com) provided 106 measures; which were categorized into eleven groups as described in Sect. 2.

Feature Selection: In machine learning classifiers including too many features may lead to overfit the classifier and thus resulting in poor generalization to new data. So, only necessary features should be selected to train classifiers.

We applied two different approaches for the selection of necessary features improving the accuracy of the classifiers.

Approach-1: Coh-Metrix provides more than hundreds of measures of text characteristics and several of them are highly correlated. For example, Pearson correlations demonstrated that *z score of narrativity* was highly correlated ($r = 0.911$, $p < 0.001$) with *percentile of narrativity*. Of 106 measures of the tool, 52 variables were selected on the basis of two criteria. First, all such variables which had high correlations with other variables ($|r| \geq 0.80$) were discarded for handling the problem of collinearity. Remaining measures were grouped in feature sets. Thus, after removing all such redundant variables, the feature set of story transcripts had 65 measures whereas the feature set of course transcripts had 67 measures. In Table 1, superscripts 1, 2 and 3 indicate measures presented in only story transcripts, in only course transcripts and in both transcripts respectively. Therefore, in first step, measures indicated with superscripts 1 and 3 were selected for the classification of story transcripts; whereas measures indicated with superscripts 2 and 3 were selected to classify the course transcripts. In next step, we had selected only those measures which were presented in both feature sets. Therefore, in second step, 52 common measures indicated with superscript 3 in Table 1, were selected for the classifications.

Pairwise Comparisons: Pairwise comparisons were conducted to examine differences between proficient comprehenders' text and poor comprehenders' text of both sets of transcripts (story and course). These results are reported below.

1. Descriptive measures: Co-Metrix provided eleven descriptive measures in which six measures were selected as features. Paragraph count, Paragraph length, Sentence length and Word length had significant difference between

Table 1. A comparison of proficient and poor comprehenders' transcripts features. Values shown are mean (standard deviation).

Description	Story transcript		Course transcript	
	Proficient comprehender	Poor comprehender	Proficient comprehender	Poor comprehender
1. Descriptive				
[3]Paragraph count	19.7(5.47)	10.5(4.03)	10.9(2.64)	6.2(2.09)
[3]Paragraph length (μ)	1.202(0.14)	1.088(0.11)	1.405(0.26)	1.239(0.23)
[3]Sentence length (μ)	20.21(3.76)	16.98(3.05)	22.52(5.19)	17.45(5.10)
[3]Sentence length (SD)	10.84(2.42)	9.461(2.33)	10.79(2.92)	8.443(3.25)
[3]Word length (μ, syllables)	1.215(0.04)	1.196(0.04)	1.596(0.05)	1.568(0.08)
[1]Word length (μ, letters)	3.841(0.13)	3.750(0.12)	4.834(0.17)	4.753(0.24)
2. Text Easability Principle Component Scores				
[3]Narrativity(z score)	1.779(0.59)	1.840(0.50)	−0.00(0.46)	−0.01(0.57)
[3]Syntactic simplicity (z score)	−0.04(0.55)	0.072(0.60)	−0.51(0.83)	−0.55(0.71)
[3]Word concreteness (z score)	0.781(0.82)	0.409(1.14)	−0.26(0.82)	0.118(1.36)
[3]Referential cohesion(z score)	2.452(0.82)	3.274(1.58)	1.146(0.95)	1.316(1.06)
[3]Referential cohesion(percentile)	98.29(1.51)	97.55(4.52)	80.46(12.5)	81.97(14.5)
[3]Deep cohesion (z score)	1.590(1.05)	3.188(2.01)	−0.24(0.70)	1.308(2.38)
[1]Deep cohesion (percentile)	87.49(15.0)	95.00(9.63)	41.24(24.3)	70.75(43.1)
[3]Verb cohesion (z score)	0.225(0.93)	1.066(1.18)	0.714(1.15)	1.582(1.35)
[3]Connectivity (z score)	−4.07(1.79)	−3.81(1.40)	−3.52(0.86)	−3.90(0.53)
[1]Connectivity (percentile)	1.392(3.45)	1.062(2.25)	0.169(0.24)	0.014(0.02)
[3]Temporality (z score)	0.443(0.55)	1.039(0.88)	−0.05(1.30)	0.787(0.90)
3. Referential Cohesion				
[3]Noun overlap, adjacent sent. (μ)	0.555(0.14)	0.509(0.33)	0.535(0.18)	0.557(0.24)
[3]Argument overlap, adj. sent. (μ)	0.681(0.08)	0.653(0.30)	0.727(0.16)	0.686(0.16)

(*continued*)

Table 1. (*continued*)

Description	Story transcript		Course transcript	
	Proficient comprehender	Poor comprehender	Proficient comprehender	Poor comprehender
[2]Noun overlap, all sent. (μ)	0.528(0.13)	0.416(0.29)	0.415(0.14)	0.400(0.15)
[2]Argument overlap, all sent. (μ)	0.681(0.07)	0.566(0.24)	0.583(0.16)	0.488(0.13)
[2]Stem overlap, all sent. (μ)	0.572(0.11)	0.504(0.28)	0.526(0.13)	0.522(0.14)
[2]Word overlap, adjacent sent. (μ)	0.192(0.05)	0.231(0.08)	0.147(0.05)	0.149(0.03)
[3]Word overlap, adjacent sent.(SD)	0.139(0.02)	0.141(0.04)	0.117(0.04)	0.133(0.04)
[2]Word overlap, all sentences (μ)	0.184(0.03)	0.190(0.06)	0.107(0.03)	0.112(0.02)
[3]Word overlap, all sentences (SD)	0.155(0.01)	0.159(0.02)	0.107(0.02)	0.125(0.02)
4. LSA				
[2]LSA overlap, adjacent sent. (μ)	0.356(0.05)	0.382(0.16)	0.282(0.06)	0.261(0.10)
[3]LSA overlap, adjacent sent.(SD)	0.218(0.04)	0.197(0.06)	0.170(0.03)	0.182(0.07)
[3]LSA overlap, all sent. (μ)	0.271(0.14)	0.232(0.21)	0.256(0.15)	0.175(0.19)
[3]LSA overlap, all sent. (SD)	0.180(0.10)	0.066(0.14)	0.168(0.10)	0.103(0.16)
[2]LSA overlap, adj. paragraph (μ)	0.409(0.03)	0.391(0.16)	0.321(0.08)	0.330(0.13)
[2]LSA overlap, adjacent para. (SD)	0.219(0.02)	0.195(0.06)	0.143(0.04)	0.127(0.04)
[3]LSA, sentence (μ)	0.440(0.04)	0.390(0.10)	0.351(0.03)	0.274(0.09)
[1]LSA, sentence (SD)	0.180(0.02)	0.200(0.04)	0.143(0.01)	0.159(0.05)
5. Lexical Diversity				
[3]Lexical diversity (MTLD)	41.25(3.99)	38.53(8.87)	44.70(12.9)	40.63(10.0)
[3]Vocabulary Diversity (VOCD)	44.08(5.99)	30.10(18.9)	55.21(13.2)	35.30(20.5)
6. Connectives				
[1]All connectives	132.8(21.3)	147.8(28.3)	96.39(17.0)	125.0(33.0)
[3]Adversative and contrastive conn.	12.91(8.25)	13.11(8.02)	19.03(7.52)	16.17(10.1)

(continued)

Table 1. (*continued*)

Description	Story transcript		Course transcript	
	Proficient comprehender	Poor comprehender	Proficient comprehender	Poor comprehender
[3]Temporal connectives	34.95(12.3)	42.72(12.9)	13.53(6.16)	18.49(18.1)
[3]Expanded temporal connectives	28.45(9.37)	30.83(15.5)	3.402(4.34)	9.725(12.2)
7. Situation Model				
[3]Causal verb (CV) incidence	19.97(5.74)	24.65(10.8)	24.19(9.96)	27.42(15.0)
[2]Causal particles (CP) incidence	37.38(14.2)	50.65(20.0)	31.42(8.95)	43.08(12.1)
[3]Intentional verbs (IV) incidence	34.20(6.66)	35.94(11.0)	12.43(4.16)	17.94(12.7)
[2]Ratio of CP to CV	0.811(0.52)	1.144(1.30)	0.333(0.28)	0.941(1.80)
[2]Ratio of intentional particle to IV	0.694(0.40)	0.961(0.84)	1.383(0.81)	2.116(2.00)
[3]LSA verb overlap	0.070(0.03)	0.085(0.04)	0.130(0.07)	0.119(0.08)
[3]WordNet verb overlap	0.679(0.05)	0.581(0.17)	0.448(0.11)	0.477(0.24)
8. Syntactic Complexity				
[3]Words before main verb (μ)	3.999(0.94)	3.860(1.06)	4.814(2.26)	3.371(1.87)
[3]Numbers of modifiers (μ)	0.652(0.12)	0.523(0.11)	0.867(0.17)	0.803(0.18)
[3]Sentence syntax similarity (μ)	0.110(0.03)	0.083(0.02)	0.086(0.02)	0.079(0.03)
9. Syntactic Pattern - Phrase Density (PD)				
[3]Noun PD, incidence	318.3(17.5)	354.0(20.9)	377.0(22.0)	366.7(30.7)
[3]Verb PD incidence	258.4(18.9)	249.6(20.3)	194.2(25.0)	204.7(46.8)
[3]Adverbial PD incidence	52.71(19.3)	41.99(15.4)	28.08(11.9)	19.79(13.4)
[3]Preposition PD incidence	92.28(20.2)	87.94(24.3)	115.4(21.1)	122.6(34.3)
[3]Agentless passive voice density	2.972(3.35)	1.96(4.76)	10.06(8.84)	12.08(13.5)
[3]Negation density incidence	19.62(7.96)	26.21(13.6)	11.60(6.82)	9.287(6.47)
[3]Gerund density incidence	17.34(7.35)	13.60(11.6)	9.926(8.20)	15.85(12.3)
[3]Infinitive density, incidence	22.69(9.36)	16.78(12.0)	14.65(6.50)	12.78(12.2)

(*continued*)

Table 1. (*continued*)

Description	Story transcript		Course transcript	
	Proficient comprehender	Poor comprehender	Proficient comprehender	Poor comprehender
10. Word Information				
[3]Noun incidence	194.9(22.8)	211.2(30.5)	262.4(33.9)	268.5(67.1)
[3]Verb incidence	163.1(11.6)	153.7(23.4)	115.1(11.0)	119.2(27.2)
[3]Adjective incidence	27.02(6.50)	21.28(15.5)	70.28(21.2)	56.61(28.9)
[3]Adverb incidence	87.22(20.9)	100.1(14.2)	52.92(23.0)	43.46(19.3)
[1]Pronoun incidence	94.14(23.4)	107.0(23.8)	57.50(17.8)	51.63(28.6)
[1]1st person sing. pronoun in.	3.603(4.20)	4.647(9.26)	0(0)	0(0)
[1]1st person plural pronoun in.	3.250(4.61)	1.817(3.94)	0.808(1.33)	1.612(5.10)
[1]2nd person pronoun incidence	8.069(8.60)	15.82(13.2)	0(0)	0(0)
[2]3rd person singular pronoun in.	62.65(21.5)	59.28(37.2)	14.43(6.86)	15.04(15.7)
[1]3rd person plural pronoun in.	12.19(6.30)	20.25(20.7)	33.11(14.3)	34.98(24.9)
[1]CELEX word frequency (μ)	2.6(0.10)	2.777(0.13)	2.374(0.14)	2.433(0.19)
[3]CELEX Log frequency (μ)	3.319(0.04)	3.349(0.11)	3.155(0.06)	3.212(0.16)
[3]CELEX Log min. frequency (μ)	1.384(0.18)	1.449(0.25)	1.234(0.26)	0.945(0.76)
[3]Age of acquisition for words (μ)	257.6(8.85)	258.7(35.4)	382.9(17.2)	346.7(123.)
[3]Familiarity for words (μ)	569.3(4.59)	572.2(6.70)	574.1(6.57)	577.7(6.66)
[2]Concreteness for words (μ)	395.5(21.7)	383.0(25.0)	362.7(15.0)	356.4(23.8)
[1]Meaningfulness words (μ)	413.2(7.03)	399.4(14.3)	422.7(13.7)	414.2(17.9)
[3]Polysemy for words (μ)	4.563(0.44)	4.610(0.28)	3.887(0.39)	3.980(0.46)
[3]Hypernymy for nouns (μ)	6.562(0.36)	6.842(0.98)	6.003(0.34)	5.350(0.77)
[3]Hypernymy for verbs (μ)	1.927(0.14)	1.837(0.20)	1.607(0.12)	1.676(0.22)
[2]Hyper. for nouns and verbs (μ)	1.589(0.12)	1.705(0.36)	1.788(0.10)	1.610(0.21)
11. Readability				
[2]Flesch reading ease	83.49(6.46)	88.38(5.52)	48.89(7.28)	56.43(6.85)

proficient comprehenders' text and poor comprehenders' text of both sets of transcripts.

2. Easability components: The tool provided sixteen easability measures in which eleven measures were selected as features. Deep cohesion, Verb cohesion, Connectivity and Temporality had significant difference between proficient comprehenders' text and poor comprehenders' text of both sets of transcripts.

3. Referential Cohesion: The tool provided ten referential cohesion measures in which nine measures were selected as features. The findings from different overlap measures demonstrated that proficient comprehenders used more *co-referential nouns, pronouns, or NP phrases* than poor comprehenders.

4. Latent Semantic Analysis: The tool provided eight LSA measures and all were selected as features. LSA overlap measures had significant difference between proficient comprehenders' text and poor comprehenders' text of both sets of transcripts.

5. Lexical Diversity: The tool provided four lexical diversity measures in which two measures were selected as features. MTLD and VOCD had more significant difference between proficient comprehenders' text and poor comprehenders' text of both sets of transcripts.

6. Connectives: The tool provided nine lexical connective measures in which four measures were selected as features. The findings from different connective measures demonstrated that proficient comprehenders used more connectives, such as *in other words, also, however, although* etc. than poor comprehenders; whereas poor comprehenders used comparatively more logical operators such as *and, then* etc. as well as more temporal connectives, such as *when* etc.

7. Situation Model: The tool provided eight situation model measures in which seven measures were selected as features. Causal verb measures had significant difference between proficient comprehenders' text and poor comprehenders' text of both sets of transcripts.

8. Syntactic Complexity: The tool provided seven syntactic complexity measures in which three measures were selected as features. Words before main verb (mean), Number of modifiers per noun phrase (mean), and Sentence syntax similarity (mean) had less significant difference between proficient comprehenders' text and poor comprehenders' text of both sets of transcripts.

9. Syntactic Pattern Density: The tool provided eight syntactic pattern density measures and all were selected as features. Noun phrase density, Verb phrase density, Adverbial phrase density, Preposition phrase density, Agentless passive voice density, Negation density, Gerund density, and Infinitive density had high significant difference between proficient comprehenders' text and poor comprehenders' text of both sets of transcripts.

10. Word Information: The tool provided twenty two word information measures in which twenty one measures were selected as features. Noun incidence, Verb incidence, Adjective incidence, and Adverb incidence were highly

significant. Poor comprehenders' transcripts had a comparatively greater proportion of pronouns compared to that of proficient comprehenders.
11. Readability: The tool provided three readability measures in which one measure was selected as feature. Flesch Reading Ease had significant difference between proficient comprehenders' text and poor comprehenders' text of both sets of transcripts.

Table 2. A comparison of proficient and poor comprehenders' features extracted from story transcripts. Values shown are mean (standard deviation).

Description	Proficient comprehender (Story transcript)	Poor comprehender (Story transcript)	p-value < 0.05
Descriptive			
Number of paragraphs	19.7(5.47)	10.5(4.03)	0.001
Number of sentences	23.1(4.70)	11.7(5.37)	0.00
Number of words	453.6(59.1)	197.8(86.4)	0.00
Number of sentences in a paragraph (SD)	0.383(0.17)	0.203(0.19)	0.041
Deep cohesion (z score)	1.590(1.05)	3.188(2.01)	0.044
Lexical Diversity			
Type-token ratio (all words)	0.318(0.02)	0.422(0.11)	0.022
Lexical diversity	44.08(5.99)	30.10(18.9)	0.049
Connectives			
Logic connectives	52.51(14.8)	81.49(20.8)	0.002
Syntactic Complexity			
Mean number of modifiers per noun-phrase	0.652(0.12)	0.523(0.11)	0.029
Minimum editorial distance score for words	0.758(0.26)	0.433(0.39)	0.049
Minimum editorial distance score for lemmas	0.738(0.26)	0.407(0.37)	0.035
Syntactic Pattern Density			
Noun phrase density	318.3(17.5)	354.0(20.9)	0.001
Word Information			
Average word frequency for content words	2.6(0.10)	2.777(0.13)	0.004
Meaningfulness content words (mean)	413.2(7.03)	399.4(14.3)	0.017
Readability			
Second language readability score	29.53(3.27)	33.88(4.30)	0.021

Approach-2: In this approach, we selected appropriate features from all 106 Coh-Metrix measures by applying Welch's two-tailed, unpaired t-test on each measure of both types of comprehenders' transcripts. All features that were significant at $p < 0.05$ were selected for classification. Thus, the feature set of story transcripts had 15 measures (Table 2) whereas the feature set of course transcripts had 14 measures (Table 3).

Table 3. A comparison of proficient and poor comprehenders' features extracted from course transcripts. Values shown are mean (standard deviation).

Description	Proficient comprehender (Course transcript)	Poor comprehender (Course transcript)	p-value < 0.05
Descriptive			
Number of paragraphs	10.9(2.64)	6.2(2.09)	0.00
Number of sentences	15.5(5.40)	7.7(2.90)	0.001
Number of words	336.9(101.0)	133.3(52.1)	0.00
Sentence length(mean)	22.52(5.19)	17.45(5.10)	0.041
LSA			
Latent Semantic Analysis (mean)	0.351(0.03)	0.274(0.09)	0.028
Lexical Diversity			
Type-token ratio (content word lemmas)	0.618(0.07)	0.741(0.11)	0.009
Type-token ratio (all words)	0.425(0.04)	0.552(0.12)	0.012
Lexical diversity	55.21(13.2)	35.30(20.5)	0.021
Connectives			
All connectives, incidence	96.39(17.0)	125.0(33.0)	0.03
Situation Model			
Causal verbs and causal particles incidence	31.42(8.95)	43.08(12.1)	0.026
Word Information			
Hypernymy for nouns (mean)	6.003(0.34)	5.350(0.77)	0.03
Hypernymy for nouns and verbs (mean)	1.788(0.10)	1.610(0.21)	0.038
Readability			
Flesch reading ease	48.89(7.28)	56.43(6.85)	0.028
Flesch-Kincaid grade Level	12.03(2.19)	9.724(1.81)	0.02

5   Classification

We examined several classification methods such as Decision Trees, Multi-Layer Perceptron, Naïve Bayes, and Logistic Regression using Weka toolkit [6]. 10-fold cross-validation method had been applied to train these classifiers. The results of these classifiers are reported in Table 4 in terms of classification accuracy and root mean square error (RMSE). The classification accuracy refers to the percentage of samples in the test dataset that are correctly classified (true positives plus true negatives). Root-mean-square error (RMSE) is frequently used as measure of the differences between values predicted by a classifier and the values expected. In this experiment, it provided the mean difference between the predicted students' comprehension level and the expected comprehension level. The baseline accuracy represents the accuracies that would be achieved by assigning every sample to the larger training size of the two classes. In this experiment, both classes had 10 training samples, therefore, the baseline accuracy for poor vs. proficient comprehenders' transcripts would be achieved by assigning all the samples in any one group and thus the baseline accuracy of the experiment would be 0.5 (10/20 = 0.5).

6   Result and Discussion

Table 4 shows the accuracies for classifying poor vs. proficient comprehenders' transcripts. The classifier accuracies were not as high for approach-1 compared to approach-2; however, they were above or equal to the baseline for all four classifiers. Also, common features provided better accuracies as compared to first

Table 4. Accuracies for the four classifiers.

Feature sets	# Features	Logistic regression	Naïve Bayes	Decision tree	Multi-layer perceptron
Approach-1:					
First Step-					
Feature set (Story transcript)	65	60% (0.63)	60% (0.6)	90% (0.3)	80% (0.39)
Feature set (Course transcript)	67	65% (0.59)	75% (0.46)	50% (0.62)	65% (0.5)
Second Step-					
Common feature (Story transcript)	52	85% (0.4)	80% (0.44)	90% (0.3)	80% (0.38)
Common feature (course transcript)	52	75% (0.49)	85% (0.4)	65% (0.48)	65% (0.49)
Approach-2:					
Story transcript	15	*100% (0)*	*95% (0.22)*	*100% (0)*	*90% (0.28)*
Course transcript	14	*90% (0.31)*	75% (0.41)	*95% (0.23)*	80% (0.44)

step features (story or course feature set). In this experiment, the reduced set of features applied in approach-2, provided best results for all four classifiers. However it was observed that selection of features using approach-2 were dependent on the participants involved in the experiment as well as the read text; whereas the features of approach-1 were almost robust against these changes. The major findings of this study demonstrate that three cohesion indices- lexical diversity, connectives, and word information, common in both Tables 2 and 3, played a vital role in the classification of both types of the transcripts. The logistic regression classifier classified story transcripts and course transcripts with accuracies 100% and 80% respectively.

Generally in first attempt of reading a new text, science and technology course does not help most students to develop mental model to represent the collective conceptual relations between the scientific concepts, due to lack of their prior domain knowledge. In contrast, story texts carry some general schema such as name, specific place and chronological details of an event; all these schema help students to develop mental model by integrating these specific attributes of the event described in the story [11]. Therefore, students stored the mental model of story text comparatively in more details in their memory compared to that of course text; which was reflected in their transcripts. Proficient and poor both students' story transcripts contained more noun phrases in comparison to course transcripts.

Poor comprehenders may not benefit as much as good comprehenders from reading a complex text because grammatical and lexical linking within the text increases text length, density, and complexity. As a consequence, reading such text involves creation and processing of more complex mental model. Comprehenders with low working-memory capacity experience numerous constraints on the processing of these larger mental models, resulting in lower comprehension and recall performance [8]. As a result poor comprehenders' transcripts consist of comparatively more sentences with mixed content representing their confused state of mental models. Therefore, as shown in Table 1, values of the measures of situation model index were more in poor comprehenders' transcripts in contrast to proficients' transcripts.

The finding in this study also validates a previous study [3], which demonstrated that less-skilled comprehenders produced narratives that were poor in terms of both structural coherence and referential cohesion.

In short, the Coh-Metrix analysis of transcripts provides a number of linguistic properties of comprehenders' narrative speech. Comprehension proficiency were characterized by greater cohesion, shorter sentences, more connectives, greater lexical diversity, and more sophisticated vocabulary. It is observed that lexical diversity, word information, LSA, syntactic pattern, and sentence length provided the most predictive information of proficient or poor comprehenders.

In conclusion, the current study supports to utilize Coh-Metrix features to measure comprehender's ability.

References

1. Angosto, A., Sánchez, P., Álvarez, M., Cuevas, I., León, J.A.: Evidence for top-down processing in reading comprehension of children. Psicología Educativa **19**(2), 83–88 (2013)
2. Attaprechakul, D.: Inference strategies to improve reading comprehension of challenging texts. Engl. Lang. Teach. **6**(3), 82–91 (2013)
3. Cain, K.: Text comprehension and its relation to coherence and cohesion in children's fictional narratives. Br. J. Dev. Psychol. **21**(3), 335–351 (2003)
4. Flesch, R.: A new readability yardstick. J. Appl. Psychol. **32**(3), 221 (1948)
5. Graesser, A.C., McNamara, D.S., Louwerse, M.M., Cai, Z.: Coh-metrix: Analysis of text on cohesion and language. Behav. Res. Methods **36**(2), 193–202 (2004)
6. Hall, M., Frank, E., Holmes, G., Pfahringer, B., Reutemann, P., Witten, I.H.: The weka data mining software: an update. ACM SIGKDD Explor. Newsl. **11**(1), 10–18 (2009)
7. Hunt, A., Beglar, D.: A framework for developing EFL reading vocabulary. Read. Foreign Lang. **17**(1), 23 (2005)
8. Kendeou, P., Broek, P., Helder, A., Karlsson, J.: A cognitive view of reading comprehension: Implications for reading difficulties. Learn. Disabil. Res. Pract. **29**(1), 10–16 (2014)
9. Kincaid, J.P., Fishburne Jr., R.P., Rogers, R.L., Chissom, B.S.: Derivation of new readability formulas (automated readability index, fog count and flesch reading ease formula) for navy enlisted personnel. Technical report, Naval Technical Training Command Millington TN Research Branch (1975)
10. Mason, B., Krashen, S.: Extensive reading in English as a foreign language. System **25**(1), 91–102 (1997)
11. Ozuru, Y., Dempsey, K., McNamara, D.S.: Prior knowledge, reading skill, and text cohesion in the comprehension of science texts. Learn. Instr. **19**(3), 228–242 (2009)
12. Richards, J.C.: Longman Dictionary of Language Teaching and Applied Linguistics (2000)

Open Access This chapter is licensed under the terms of the Creative Commons Attribution 4.0 International License (http://creativecommons.org/licenses/by/4.0/), which permits use, sharing, adaptation, distribution and reproduction in any medium or format, as long as you give appropriate credit to the original author(s) and the source, provide a link to the Creative Commons license and indicate if changes were made.

The images or other third party material in this chapter are included in the chapter's Creative Commons license, unless indicated otherwise in a credit line to the material. If material is not included in the chapter's Creative Commons license and your intended use is not permitted by statutory regulation or exceeds the permitted use, you will need to obtain permission directly from the copyright holder.

LECTOR: Towards Reengaging Students in the Educational Process Inside Smart Classrooms

Maria Korozi[1(✉)], Asterios Leonidis[1], Margherita Antona[1], and Constantine Stephanidis[1,2]

[1] Foundation for Research and Technology – Hellas (FORTH),
Institute of Computer Science (ICS), Heraklion, Greece
{korozi,leonidis,antona,cs}@ics.forth.gr
[2] Department of Computer Science, University of Crete, Heraklion, Greece

Abstract. This paper presents LECTOR, a system that helps educators in understanding when students have stopped paying attention to the educational process and assists them in reengaging the students to the current learning activity. LECTOR aims to take advantage of the ambient facilities that "smart classrooms" have to offer by (i) enabling educators to employ their preferred attention monitoring strategies (including any well-established activity recognition techniques) in order to identify inattentive behaviors and (ii) recommending interventions for motivating distracted students when deemed necessary. Furthermore, LECTOR offers an educator friendly design studio that enables teachers to create or modify the rules that trigger "inattention alarms", as well as tailor the intervention mechanism to the needs of their course by modifying the respective rules. This paper presents the rationale behind the design of LECTOR and outlines its key features and facilities.

Keywords: Smart classroom · Attention monitoring · Ambient intelligence

1 Introduction

In the recent past there has been growing interest in how Information and Communication technologies (ICTs) can improve the efficiency and effectiveness of education; it is acknowledged that when used appropriately, they are potentially powerful tools for advancing or even reshaping the educational process. In more details, ICTs are claimed to help expand access to information and raise educational quality by, among others, helping make learning and teaching a more engaging, active process connected to real life [27]. Learning with the use of ICTs has been strongly related to concepts such as distance learning [4], educational games [7], intelligent tutoring systems and e-learning applications [5]. Additionally, the notion of "smart classrooms", where activities are enhanced and augmented through the use of pervasive and mobile computing, sensor networks, artificial intelligence, etc. [6], has become prevalent in the past decade [30].

However, despite the fact that the educational process is continuously enriched with engaging activities, it is almost inevitable that students will get distracted either by internal stimuli (e.g., thoughts and attempts to retrieve information from memory) or

© The Author(s) 2017
P. Horain et al. (Eds.): IHCI 2017, LNCS 10688, pp. 137–149, 2017.
https://doi.org/10.1007/978-3-319-72038-8_11

external stimuli from the physical (e.g., visuals, sounds) or digital environment (e.g., irrelevant applications); hence, they might not always be "present" to take advantage of all the benefits that a "smart classroom" has to offer. This observation highlights the need for a mechanism that monitors the learners and when necessary, intervenes to appropriately reset attention levels.

The proposed system, named LECTOR, aims to take advantage of the ambient facilities that "smart classrooms" have to offer and enable educators to employ their preferred attention monitoring strategies (including any well-established activity recognition techniques) in order to identify inattentive behaviors and assist the educator in reengaging the students to the current learning activity. In more details, the main contributions of this work are listed below:

- Extensible **mechanism for deploying various attention monitoring strategies** aiming to identify inattentive behaviors
- Extensible **intervention mechanism** for intervening when the students are distracted from the educational process
- Educator-friendly tools for: (i) refining the inattention models and labeling newly discovered student activities, as well as (ii) creating new or modifying existing intervention strategies.

2   Background Theory

Attention is very often considered as a fundamental prerequisite of learning, both within and outside the classroom environment, since it plays a critical role in issues of motivation and engagement [20]. However, as passive listeners, people generally find it difficult to maintain a constant level of attention over extended periods of time, while pedagogical research reveals that attention lapses are inevitable during a lecture. McKeachie [16], suggests that student attention will drift during a passive lecture, unless interactive strategies are used. According to [31], student concentration decays in the same way during a passive lecture as does that of a human operator monitoring automated equipment, with serious implications for learning and performance. Obtaining and maintaining the students' attention is an important task in classroom management, and educators apply various techniques for this purpose, however currently no technological support is available to assist educator in monitoring students' behavior in the classroom and maximizing students' engagement at the task at hand. According to Packard [19], "classroom attention" refers to a complex and fluctuating set of stimulus-response relationships involving curriculum materials, instructions from the teacher and some prerequisite student behaviors (e.g., looking, listening, being quiet, etc.). Such behaviors can be rigorously classified as "appropriate" and "inappropriate" [26]. Appropriate behaviors include attending to the teacher, raising hand and waiting for the teacher to respond, working in seat on a workbook, following text reading, etc., while inappropriate behaviors include (but are not limited to) getting out of seat, tapping feet, rattling papers, carrying on a conversation with other students, singing, laughing, turning head or body toward another person, showing objects or looking at another class mate. Some of the above behaviors would be in fact disruptive to some educational activities.

However, the students should not be forced to spend their whole day not being children, but being quiet, docile, and obedient "young adults" [29]. On the contrary, learning can be more effective if students' curiosity, along with their desire to think or act for themselves, remains intact.

Attention aware systems have much to contribute to educational research and practice. These systems can influence the delivery of instructional materials, the acquisition of such materials from presentations (as a function of focused attention), the evaluation of student performance, and the assessment of learning methodologies (e.g., traditional teaching, active learning techniques, etc.) [20]. However, existing approaches [3, 17, 22, 23, 28] concentrate mainly on computer-driven educational activities. This work broadens the perspective by employing attention monitoring in a real classroom and incorporating a mechanism for suggesting improvements for the learning process; most importantly though, it empowers educators to customize or even create from scratch new inattention detection rules (e.g., *"if the students whisper while the educator is writing to the whiteboard..."*) and intervention strategies.

3   The Smart Classroom Behind LECTOR

LECTOR is employed inside a technologically augmented classroom where educational activities are enhanced with the use of pervasive and mobile computing, sensor networks, artificial intelligence, multimedia computing, middleware and agent-based software [1, 13, 24]. In more details, the hardware infrastructure includes both commercial and custom-made artifacts, which are embedded in traditional classroom equipment and furniture. For example, the classroom contains a commercial touch sensitive interactive whiteboard, technologically augmented student desks [21] that integrates various sensors (e.g., eye-tracker, camera, microphone, etc.), a personal workstation and a smart watch for the teacher, as well as various ambient facilities appropriate for monitoring the overall environment and the learners' actions (e.g., microphones, user-tracking devices, etc.).

The software architecture (Fig. 1b) of the smart Classroom follows a stack-based model where the first layer, namely the AmI-Solertis middleware infrastructure [15], is responsible for (i) the collection, analysis and storage of the metadata regarding the environment's artifacts, (ii) their deployment, execution and monitoring in the AmI-Solertis-enabled systems to formulate a ubiquitous ecosystem. The next three layers, namely the ClassMATE, CognitOS and LECTOR frameworks, expose the core libraries and finally the remaining layer contains the educational applications. Specifically, ClassMATE [14] is an integrated architecture for pervasive computing environments that monitors the ambient environment and makes context-aware decisions; it features a sophisticated, unobtrusive, profiling mechanism in order to provide user related data to the classroom's services and applications. Furthermore, CognitOS [18] delivers a sophisticated environment for educational applications hosting able to present interventions that will be dictated by LECTOR.

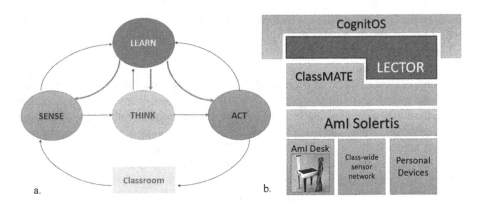

Fig. 1. (a) LECTOR's SENSE-THINK-ACT – LEARN model. (b) The software architecture of the smart classroom

4   LECTOR Approach

LECTOR introduces a non-invasive multimodal solution, which exploits the potential of ambient intelligence technologies to observe student actions (SENSE), provides a framework to employ activity recognition techniques for identifying whether these actions signify inattentive behavior (THINK) and intervenes –when necessary– by suggesting appropriate methods for recapturing attention (ACT). According to cognitive psychology, the sense-think-act cycle stems from the processing nature of human beings that receive input from the environment (perception), process that information (thinking), and act upon the decision reached (behavior). Such pattern became the base for many design principles regarding autonomous agents and traditional AI.

For that to be optimally achieved, the proposed system is able to make informed decisions using volatile information and reliable knowledge regarding the syllabus covered so far, the nature of the current activity, the "expected" behavior of the involved individuals towards it, the behavior of the peers, etc. The aforementioned pieces of information can be classified under the broader term of Context of Use, defined as follows: "Any information that can be used to characterize the situation of entities (i.e., whether a person, place, or object) that are considered relevant to the interaction between a user and an application, including the user and the application themselves. Context is typically the location, identity, and state of people, groups, and computational and physical objects" [8]. Based on the above, the SENSE-THINK-ACT model of LECTOR relies on an extensible modeling component to collect and expose such classroom-specific information.

This work extends the SENSE-THINK-ACT model by introducing the notion of LEARN (Fig. 1a). The fact that the nature of this system enables continuous observation of student activities creates the foundation for a mechanism that provides updated knowledge to the decision-making components. In more details, the LEARN-ing mechanism is able to (i) assess decisions that resulted in negative outcomes in the past (e.g., inattention levels remain high or deteriorate after introducing a mini-quiz intervention during a math course) and (ii) incorporate knowledge provided by the teacher (e.g., disambiguation of student behavior, rejection of suggested intervention during a specific course, etc.).

4.1 Motivating Scenarios

Monitoring the Attention Levels of an Entire Classroom. On Monday morning the history teacher, Mr. James, enters the classroom and announces that the topic of the day will be the "Battle of Gaugamela". During the first 15 min the students pay attention to the teacher who narrates the story; soon enough, the students start losing interest and demonstrate signs of inattentive behavior. In more details, John is browsing through the pages of a different book, Mary and Helen are whispering to each other, Peter stares out the window and Mike struggles to keep his eyes open. When identifying that the entire classroom demonstrates signs of inattention, the system recommends that the lecture should be paused and that a mini quiz game should be started. The teacher finishes up his sentence and decides to accept this intervention. After his confirmation, a set of questions relevant to the current topic is displayed on the classroom board, while their difficulty depends on both the students' prior knowledge and the studied material so far. During use, the system identifies the topics with the lowest scores and notifies the teacher to explain them more thoroughly. As soon as the intervention ends, Mr. James resumes the lecture. At this point, the students' attention is reset and they begin to pay attention to the historical facts. As a result, the quiz not only restored their interest, but also resulted in deeper learning.

Monitoring the Attention Levels of an Individual Student. During the geography class Kate is distracted by a couple of students standing outside the window. The system recognizes that behavior and takes immediate action to attract her interest back on the lecture. To do so, it displays pictures relevant to the current topic on her personal work-station while a discreet nudge attracts her attention. A picture displaying a dolphin with weird colors swimming in the waters of Amazon makes her wondering how it is possible for a dolphin to survive in a river; she patiently waits for the teacher to complete his narration to ask questions about that strange creature. That way, Kate becomes motivated and starts paying attention to the presentation of America's rivers. At the same time, Nick is drawing random pictures on his notebook and seems to not pay attention to the lecture; however, the system already knows that he concentrates more easily when doodling, and decides not to interpret that behavior as inattention.

4.2 Context of Use

LECTOR's decision-mechanisms are heavily dependent on contextual information to (i) identify the actual conditions (student status, lecture progress, task at hand, etc.) that prevail in a smart classroom at any given time and (ii) act accordingly. The term context has been used broadly with a variety of meanings for context-aware applications in pervasive computing [9]. The authors in [10] refer to contexts as any information that can be detected through low-level sensor readings; for instance, in a home environment those reading include the room that the inhabitant is in, the objects that the inhabitant interacts with, whether the inhabitant is currently mobile, the time of the day when an activity is being performed, etc.

However, in a smart classroom contextual awareness goes beyond data collected from sensors. Despite the fact that sensorial readings are important for recognizing student activities, they are inadequate to signify inattention without information regarding the nature of the current course, the task at hand, the characteristics of the learner, etc. This work employs the term Physical Context (PC) to indicate data collected from sensors, while the term Virtual Learning Context (VLC) is used for any static or dynamic information regarding the learning process (e.g., student profile, course related information, etc.) [32].

The exploitation of such contextual information can improve the performance of the THINK component, which employs activity recognition strategies in order to identify student activities and classify them as inattentive or not. Despite the fact that activity recognition mainly relies on sensor readings to detect student activities, the Virtual Learning Context (VLC) is critical to interpret inattention indicators correctly; as an example, in general excess noise indicates that students talk to each other instead of listening to the teacher; however, this is irrelevant during the music class.

Furthermore, VLC is essential for the ACT component; when the system decides to intervene in order to reset students' attention, the selection of the appropriate intervention type depends heavily on the context of use (syllabus covered so far, remaining time, etc.). As an example, if an intervention occurs during the first ten minutes of a lecture, where the main topic has not been thoroughly analyzed by the teacher yet, the system starts a short preview that briefly introduces the lecture's main points using entertaining communication channels (e.g., multimedia content).

4.3 Sensorial Data

LECTOR is deployed in a "smart classroom" that incorporates infrastructure able to monitor the learners' actions and provide the necessary input to the decision-making components for estimating their attention levels. To ensure scalability, this work is not bound to certain technological solutions; it embraces the fundamental concept of Ambient Intelligence that expects environments to be dynamically formed as devices constantly change their availability. As a consequence, a key requirement is to ensure that new sensors and applications can be seamlessly integrated (i.e., extensibility). In order to do so, LECTOR relies on the AmI-Solertis framework, which provides the necessary functionality for the intercommunication and interoperability of heterogeneous services hosted in the smart classroom.

As regards the supported input sources, they range from simple converters (or even chains of converters) that measure physical quantities and convert them to signals, which can be read by electronic instruments, to software components (e.g., a single module, an application, a suite of applications, etc.) that monitor human computer interaction and data exchange. However, a closer look at the sensorial data reveals that it is not the actual value that matters, but rather the meaning of that value. For instance, the attention recognition mechanism does not need to know that a student has turned his head 23° towards south but that he stares out of the window.

Subsequently, LECTOR equips the developers with an authoring tool that enables them to provide the algorithms that translate the raw data into meaningful high-level objects. In more details, through an intuitive wizard (Fig. 2) the developers (i) define the contextual properties (e.g., Speech, Feelings, Posture, etc.) that will be monitored by the system, (ii) specify the attributes of those properties (e.g., level, rate, duration, etc.) and (iii) develop the code that translates the actual values coming directly from the sensors/applications to those attributes. The in-vitro environment where LECTOR is deployed employs the following ambient facilities:

- **Eye-trackers** to observe students' fixations during studying on a personal computer (e.g., reading a passage, solving an exercise) to determine the attention level (e.g., stares at an insignificant area of the screen), the weaknesses (e.g., the student keeps reading the same sentence over and over again), the interests (e.g., fascinated with wild life) and the learning styles (e.g., attempts the easier assignments first) of each student. The same information can be also provided by custom **educational software** (i.e., CognitOS).
- **Sophisticated cameras** (e.g., RGB-D camera such as Microsoft Kinect) that track the head pose of the learner and are used as a surrogate for gaze. The combination of eye-tracking and head pose tracking algorithms offers an accurate overview of what the students are looking at on the computer screen and on whom or what they are focused on (e.g., teacher, class board, etc.). Moreover, the use of cameras is ideal for tracking the body posture and the direction of an individual student, especially when taking into consideration that they constantly move even while seated. Besides learners' orientation, camera input also enables the identification of specific gestures that indicate whether a student is paying attention to the lecture or not (e.g., a student raising his hand). Finally, they can be used to analyze whether the students' capabilities are compromised due to feelings of fatigue (i.e., Drowsiness, Falling Asleep).
- **Microphones** are placed on the teacher's and students' desks to identify who is speaking at any time and the overall noise levels of the classroom, which can reliably indicate inattentive behavior on behalf of the students.
- **Pressure-sensitive sensors** on each learner's chair to identify whether the student is seated or not. This information when combined with data received from strategically placed distance and motion sensors (e.g., near the class board, near the teacher's desk), introduces a primitive localization technique that can be used to estimate the location and the purpose of a "missing" individual (e.g., a student is off the desk but near the board thus solving an exercise).
- **Wearable sensors** that can be used to monitor the students' physiological signals (e.g., heart rate, EDA, etc.).

LECTOR currently uses the aforementioned ambient facilities to monitor some physical characteristics of the students and teachers and translates them, in a context-dependent manner, into specific activities classified under the following categories: Focus, Speech, Location, Posture and Feelings, which are considered appropriate cues that might signify inattention [2, 11, 19, 25].

Fig. 2. Snapshot from the developers' authoring tool, displaying the process of defining the 'SOUND' contextual property.

4.4 Inattention Alarms

LECTOR's THINK component (Fig. 3) is responsible for identifying the students who show signs of inattention. Towards such objective, it constantly monitors their actions in order to detect (sub-) activities that imply distraction and loss of attention. The decision logic that dictates which behaviors signify inattention is expressed via high-level rules in the "Attention rule set", which combines various contextual parameters to define the conditions under which a student is considered distracted. There are two type of rules in the "Attention rule set": (i) rules that denote human activities or sub-activities (e.g., talking, walking, sitting, etc.) and provide input to (ii) rules that signify inattentive behaviors (e.g., disturb, chat, cheat, etc.). Through an educator-friendly authoring tool, namely LECTORstudio [12], the teachers have the opportunity to create or modify the latter, while -due to their complexity- they can only fine-tune the rules that denote human (sub-) activities.

Whenever a stimulus is detected by the SENSE component, the THINK component initiates an exploratory process to determine whether the incoming event indicates that the student(s) has lost interest in the learning process or not. In order to do so, it employs the appropriate attention recognition strategies based on the "Attention rule set". Finally, at the end of the exploratory process, if the result points to inattentive behavior, SENSE appropriately informs the ACT component which undertakes to restore student engagement by selecting an appropriate intervention.

Figure 4 presents the graphical representation of a rule describing the activity "SHOUTING", as created in LECTORstudio. Specifically, the purpose of this rule is to create an exception for the Music course, where students sing, thus raising the noise levels of the classroom higher than usual; in that case, the activity "SHOUTING" should be identified when the sound volume captured through the class microphone exceeds the value of 82 dB.

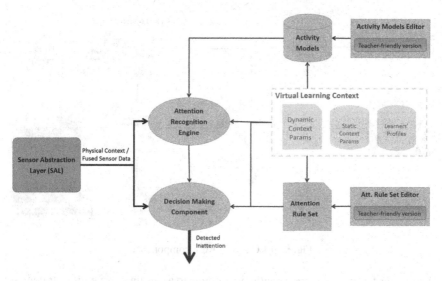

Fig. 3. LECTOR's THINK component.

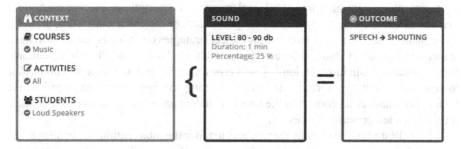

Fig. 4. A rule describing the activity "SHOUTING", as created in LECTORstudio.

4.5 Intervention Rules

As soon as inattentive behavior is detected, the ACT component (Fig. 5) initiates an exploratory process to identify the most appropriate course of action. Evidently, selecting a suitable intervention and its proper presentation (appropriate for the device where it will be delivered) is not a straightforward process, as it requires in-depth analysis of both the learners' profile and the contextual information regarding the current course. The first step is to consult the "Intervention rule set", which, similarly to the "Attention rule set", is comprised of high-level rules describing the conditions under which each intervention should be selected (e.g., if all students are distracted during the math course, recommend an interactive task like a mini-quiz) as well as the appropriate means of presentation (e.g., if a mini-quiz is selected and the intervention is intended for all students, display it to the classroom interactive board).

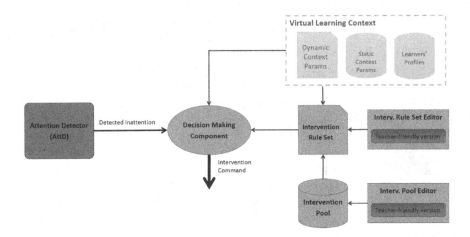

Fig. 5. LECTOR's ACT component.

Each intervention rule, upon evaluation, points to a certain intervention strategy into the "Interventions' Pool" (IP). The IP includes high-level descriptions of the available strategies, along with their low-level implementation descriptions. Furthermore, since inattention can originate either from a single student or the entire classroom, the ACT component should be able to evaluate and select strategies targeting either an individual student or a group of students (even the entire class). To this end, the "Interventions' Pool" should contain interventions of both types, and the decision logic should be able to select the most appropriate one. After selecting the appropriate intervention, the system personalizes its content to the targeted student and converts it to a form suitable for the intended presentation device.

LECTORstudio also permits the teachers to tailor the intervention mechanism to the needs of their course by modifying the "Intervention Rule Set". In more details, a teacher can create custom interventions, customize existing ones in terms of their content, change the conditions under which an intervention is initiated (e.g., the percentage of distracted students), etc.

4.6   Intervention Assessment

Both the THINK and ACT components are able to "learn" from previous poor decisions and refine their logic, while they are open to expert suggestions that can override their defaults. In order to introduce the notion of LEARN, LECTOR provides mechanisms that modify the decision-making processes by correlating knowledge gathered through attention monitoring with student performance and expert input.

To this end, the LEARN component is able to assess the regression of students' attention lapses -through the respective student profile component- with a formerly applied intervention to identify whether it had positive results or it failed to reset attention. In more details, if the system estimates that a particular intervention will reset attention in the context of a specific course and applies it, then after a reasonable amount of time it re-calculates the current attention levels; if it still detects that the students are not committed to the learning process, then the selected recommendation is marked as ineffective in that context. Hence, the ACT component is informed so as to modify its decision logic accordingly, and from that point forward select different interventions for that particular course instead of the one that was proven to be unsuccessful.

On top of the automatic application of active learning interventions, the system also permits additions, modifications, cancellations and ranking of the selected interventions. This allows the teacher to have the final say regarding the lecture format. To this end, the LEARN component takes into consideration the teacher's input and appropriately inform the ACT component so as to refine the intervention rule set and offer more effective alternatives when necessary. In more details, the teacher should be able to: (i) change the recommended intervention with a more appropriate one (e.g., quiz, multimedia presentation, discussion, etc.), (ii) rank the recommendation and (iii) abort the intervention in case it disrupts the flow of the course.

5   Conclusions and Future Work

LECTOR provides a framework and an educator-friendly design studio for the smart classroom in order to improve the educational process. For that to be achieved, it equips the environment with a system that is able to monitor the learners' attention levels depending on rules created by the teachers themselves and intervenes, when necessary, to (i) provide a motivating activity to a distracted student or (ii) suggest an alternative pedagogy that would be beneficial for the entire classroom (e.g., by motivating individuals or suggesting different lecture formats, etc.).

Future work includes full-scale evaluation experiments in order validate the system's efficacy and usability. In particular, two types of user-based experiments will be conducted: (i) Experiments for assessing the usability of the design studio for the teacher's. (ii) Experiments for evaluating the system as a whole. These experiments will be conducted for an extended period of time inside the smart classroom environment, where students and teachers will be engaged with several educational activities while the system will monitor the learners' attention levels throughout the entire process and intervene when necessary. The results of this evaluation will be used to identify whether the system can: (a) appropriately adapt its behavior in order to respect teachers' input, and (b) positively affect –through the delivery of personalized interventions– the students' motivation level and overall performance.

References

1. Antona, M., Leonidis, A., Margetis, G., Korozi, M., Ntoa, S., Stephanidis, C.: A student-centric intelligent classroom. In: Keyson, D.V., Maher, M.L., Streitz, N., Cheok, A., Augusto, J.C., Wichert, R., Englebienne, G., Aghajan, H., Kröse, B.J.A. (eds.) AmI 2011. LNCS, vol. 7040, pp. 248–252. Springer, Heidelberg (2011). https://doi.org/10.1007/978-3-642-25167-2_33
2. Ba, S.O., Odobez, J.-M.: Recognizing visual focus of attention from head pose in natural meetings. IEEE Trans. Syst. Man Cybern. Part B Cybern. 39(1), 16–33 (2009)
3. Barrios, V.M.G., et al.: AdELE: a framework for adaptive e-learning through eye tracking. In: Proceedings of IKNOW, pp. 609–616 (2004)

4. Bates, A.T.: Technology, e-Learning and Distance Education. Routledge, London (2005)
5. Brooks, C., Greer, J., Melis, E., Ullrich, C.: Combining its and e-learning technologies: opportunities and challenges. In: Ikeda, M., Ashley, K.D., Chan, T.-W. (eds.) ITS 2006. LNCS, vol. 4053, pp. 278–287. Springer, Heidelberg (2006). https://doi.org/10.1007/11774303_28
6. Cook, D.J., Das, S.K.: How smart are our environments? An updated look at the state of the art. Pervasive Mob. Comput. **3**(2), 53–73 (2007)
7. Cross, N., Roy, R.: Engineering Design Methods. Wiley, New York (1989)
8. Dey, A.K., et al.: A conceptual framework and a toolkit for supporting the rapid prototyping of context-aware applications. Hum. Comput. Interact. **16**(2), 97–166 (2001)
9. Henricksen, K., Indulska, J.: Developing context-aware pervasive computing applications: models and approach. Pervasive Mob. Comput. **2**(1), 37–64 (2006)
10. Hong, X., et al.: Evidential fusion of sensor data for activity recognition in smart homes. Pervasive Mob. Comput. **5**(3), 236–252 (2009)
11. Hwang, K.-A., Yang, C.-H.: Automated inattention and fatigue detection system in distance education for elementary school students. J. Educ. Technol. Soc. **12**(2), 22–35 (2009)
12. Korozi, M., et al.: LECTORstudio: creating inattention alarms and interventions to reengage the students in the educational process. In: Proceedings of the 10th Annual International Conference of Education, Research and Innovation (2017)
13. Leonidis, A., et al.: A glimpse into the ambient classroom. Bull. IEEE Tech. Comm. Learn. Technol. **14**(4), 3–6 (2012)
14. Leonidis, A., et al.: ClassMATE: enabling ambient intelligence in the classroom. World Acad. Sci. Eng. Technol. **66**, 594–598 (2010)
15. Leonidis, A., et al.: The AmI-Solertis system: creating user experiences in smart environments. In: Proceedings of the 13th IEEE International Conference on Wireless and Mobile Computing, Networking and Communications (2017)
16. McKeachie, W., Svinicki, M.: McKeachie's Teaching Tips. Cengage Learning, Boston (2013)
17. Merten, C., Conati, C.: Eye-tracking to model and adapt to user meta-cognition in intelligent learning environments. In: Proceedings of the 11th International Conference on Intelligent User Interfaces, pp. 39–46. ACM (2006)
18. Ntagianta, A., et al.: CognitOS: a student-centric working environment for an attention-aware intelligent classroom. In: Proceedings of the 20th International Conference on Human-Computer Interaction. Springer, Heidelberg (2017, submitted)
19. Packard, R.G.: The control of "classroom attention": a group contingency for complex behavior. J. Appl. Behav. Anal. **3**(1), 13–28 (1970)
20. Rapp, D.N.: The value of attention aware systems in educational settings. Comput. Hum. Behav. **22**(4), 603–614 (2006)
21. Savvaki, C., Leonidis, A., Paparoulis, G., Antona, M., Stephanidis, C.: designing a technology–augmented school desk for the future classroom. In: Stephanidis, C. (ed.) HCI 2013. CCIS, vol. 374, pp. 681–685. Springer, Heidelberg (2013). https://doi.org/10.1007/978-3-642-39476-8_137
22. Sibert, J.L., et al.: The reading assistant: eye gaze triggered auditory prompting for reading remediation. In: Proceedings of the 13th Annual ACM Symposium on User Interface Software and Technology, pp. 101–107. ACM (2000)
23. Slykhuis, D.A., et al.: Eye-tracking students' attention to PowerPoint photographs in a science education setting. J. Sci. Educ. Technol. **14**(5), 509–520 (2005)
24. Stephanidis, C., et al.: Pervasive computing @ ICS-FORTH. In: Workshop Pervasive Computing @ Home (2008)
25. Sylwester, R.: How emotions affect learning. Educ. Leadersh. **52**(2), 60–65 (1994)

26. Thomas, D.R., et al.: Production and elimination of disruptive classroom behavior by systematically varying teacher's behavior. J. Appl. Behav. Anal. **1**(1), 35–45 (1968)

27. Tinio, V.L.: ICT in Education. e-ASEAN Task Force (2003)

28. Wang, H., et al.: Empathic tutoring software agents using real-time eye tracking. In: Proceedings of the 2006 Symposium on Eye Tracking Research & Applications, pp. 73–78. ACM (2006)

29. Winett, R.A., Winkler, R.C.: Current behavior modification in the classroom: be still, be quiet, be docile. J. Appl. Behav. Anal. **5**(4), 499–504 (1972)

30. Xu, P., Han, G., Li, W., Wu, Z., Zhou, M.: Towards intelligent interaction in classroom. In: Stephanidis, C. (ed.) UAHCI 2009. LNCS, vol. 5616, pp. 150–156. Springer, Heidelberg (2009). https://doi.org/10.1007/978-3-642-02713-0_16

31. Young, M.S., et al.: Students pay attention! Combating the vigilance decrement to improve learning during lectures. Act. Learn. High Educ. **10**(1), 41–55 (2009)

32. Zhang, D., et al.: Survey on context-awareness in ubiquitous media. Multimedia Tools Appl. **67**(1), 179–211 (2013)

Open Access This chapter is licensed under the terms of the Creative Commons Attribution 4.0 International License (http://creativecommons.org/licenses/by/4.0/), which permits use, sharing, adaptation, distribution and reproduction in any medium or format, as long as you give appropriate credit to the original author(s) and the source, provide a link to the Creative Commons license and indicate if changes were made.

The images or other third party material in this chapter are included in the chapter's Creative Commons license, unless indicated otherwise in a credit line to the material. If material is not included in the chapter's Creative Commons license and your intended use is not permitted by statutory regulation or exceeds the permitted use, you will need to obtain permission directly from the copyright holder.

Predicting Driver's Work Performance in Driving Simulator Based on Physiological Indices

Cong Chi Tran[1,2(✉)], Shengyuan Yan[1], Jean Luc Habiyaremye[1], and Yingying Wei[3]

[1] Harbin Engineering University, Harbin 150001, China
[2] Vietnam National University of Forestry, Hanoi 10000, Vietnam
trancongchi_bk@yahoo.com, yanshengyuan@hrbeu.edu.cn,
habijealuc@yahoo.fr
[3] East University of Heilongjiang, Harbin 150086, China
weiyingying2007@126.com

Abstract. Developing an early warning model based on mental workload (MWL) to predict the driver's performance is critical and helpful, especially for new or less experienced drivers. This study aims to investigate the correlation between human's MWL and work performance and develop the predictive model in the driving task using driving simulator. The performance measure (number of errors), subjective rating (NASA Task Load Index) as well as six physiological indices were assessed and measured. Additionally, the group method of data handling (GMDH) was used to establish the work performance model. The results indicate that different complexity levels of driving task have a significant effect on the driver's performance, and the predictive performance model integrates different physiological measures shows the validity of the proposed model is well with $R^2 = 0.781$. The proposed model is expected to provide a reference value of their work performance by giving physiological indices. Based on this model, the driving lesson plans will be proposed to sustain the appropriate MWL as well as improve work performance.

Keywords: Driving simulator · Work performance · Predictive model

1 Introduction

Reducing road accident is an important issue. Contributing factors to crashes are commonly classified as human, vehicle or roadway and environmental [1]. Driving is often heavy mental workload (MWL) tasks, because in order to prevent accidents, drivers of must continually acquire and process much information from their eyes, ears, and other sensory organs. The information includes the movements of other vehicles and pedestrians, road signs and traffic signals, and various situations and changes in the road environment. These incidents require a lot of driver's attention. Human errors such as misperception, information processing errors, and slow decision making are frequently identified as major reasons can cause the accidents [2]. Therefore, improving driver's MWL could be helpful in improving driver performance and reducing the number of accidents.

© The Author(s) 2017
P. Horain et al. (Eds.): IHCI 2017, LNCS 10688, pp. 150–162, 2017.
https://doi.org/10.1007/978-3-319-72038-8_12

For most drivers, both excessive and low MWL could degrade their performance, and furthermore, may affect the safety of the driver and others. Because of when the situation is low-demanding (e.g., in long and boring roads), or conversely when the situation is high demanding (e.g., in the city with much information to process), drivers are overloaded with an increase of workload leading to performance impairments [3, 4]. Only with an appropriate level of MWL, the drivers can perform the right tasks. Therefore, for the purpose of driver's safety, developing an early warning model based on MWL to predict the driver's performance is critical and helpful, especially for new drivers or little experience in driver training.

MWL refers to the portion of operator information processing capacity or resources that is actually required to meet system demands [5]. The MWL is induced not only by cognitive demands of the tasks but also by other factors, such as stress, fatigue and the level of motivation [6, 7]. In many studies of driving task, the MWL was measured by subjective measures, such as NASA task load index (NASA-TLX) [8–10]. However, a major limitation of subjective measures is that they can only assess the overall experience of the workload of driving but cannot reflect changes in workload during the execution of the task. Also, rating scale results also can be affected by characteristics of respondents, like biases, response sets, errors and protest attitudes [11, 12]. Thus, the continuous and objective measures (e.g. physiological signal) to assess the MWL in addition to evaluating the overall workload in driving tasks is necessary [13].

Recently, many driving simulators can measure performance accurately and efficiently, and they are more and more used in driving education tasks. It is commonly accepted that the use of driving simulators presents some advantages over the traditional methods of drive learning because their virtual nature, the risk of damage due to incompetent driving is null [14]. In addition, simulators make it possible to study hazard anticipation and perception by exposing drivers to dangerous driving tasks, which is an ethically challenging endeavor in real vehicles [15], and also offers an opportunity to learn from mistakes in a forgiving environment [16, 17]. In this study, we conducted an experiment to simulate the car driving tasks to assess the relation between work performance, subjective rating, and physiological indices for new drivers. According to these relationships, the study developed a predictive model by using the group method of data handling (GMDH) to integrate all physiological indices into a synthesized index. The physiological indices used in this study were the eye activities (pupil dilation, blink rate, blink duration, fixation duration) and cardiac activities (heart rate, heart rate variability). The performance of the task was measured by the number of errors, and the subjective rating was rated by the NASA-TLX questionnaire.

2 Methodology

2.1 Participants

Twenty-six male engineering students voluntary, age 19.2 ± 1.1 years (mean $\pm$ SD) participated in the experiment. They have very little (less than two months) or no driving experience. They have normal eyesight (normal or corrected to normal vision in both eyes) and good health. For ensuring the objectivity of experimental electrocardiography

(ECG) data, all participants were asked to refrain from caffeine, alcohol, tobacco, and drug six hours before the experiment. All participants completed and signed an informed consent form approved by the university and were compensated with extra credit in extracurricular activities in their course.

2.2 Apparatus

A driving simulator (Keteng steering wheel and City car driving software version 1.4.1) was used in this study. The city car driving is a car simulator, designed to help users feel the car driving in a city or a country in different conditions. Special stress in the City car driving simulator has been laid on the variety of road situations and realistic car driving.

IView X head mounted eye-tracking device (SensoMotoric Instruments) was used to record participants' dominant eye movements. Software configuration has the video recording and the BeGaze version 3.0 eye movement data analysis, sampling rate 50/60 Hz (optional 200 Hz), tracking resolution, pupil/Corneal reflection <0.1° (typical) and gaze position accuracy <0.5°–1.0° (typical). ANSWatch TS0411 was used to measure the heart rate (HR) and HRV (heart rate variability) data.

2.3 Work Performance and Mental Workload Measures

Various MWL measurements have been proposed, and these measurements could be divided into three categories: performance measure, physiological measures and subjective ratings [18]. Performance measures can be classified into many categories such as accuracy, task time, worst-case performance, etc. [19]. In this study, the number of errors of driving task was calculated because of some reasons: (1) driving errors to involve risky behaviors that we need to understand to prevent accidents and fatalities [20]. In addition, many studies had shown that the number of errors has a sensitive to differences in the visual environment [21, 22]. (2) in the City car driving software, all driving errors include such as didn't follow the speed limit, driving on the red light, no turn signal when changing the lane, accident and so forth are displayed when driving and counted after finish the task.

Subjective ratings are designed to collect the opinions from the operators about the MWL they experience using rating scales. With the low cost and the ease of administration, as well as adaptability, have been found highly useful in driving tasks [20, 23]. In this study, subjective ratings NASA-TLX [24] was used to evaluate the driver's MWL because of there are many studies successfully applied to measure MWL in the driving [8, 9]. NASA-TLX is a multi-dimensional rating scale using six dimensions of workload to provide diagnostic information about the nature and relative contribution of each dimension in influencing overall operator workload. Six dimensions to assess MWL including mental demand (MD), physical demand (PD), temporal demand (TD), own performance (OP), effort (EF) and frustration (FR).

Physiological measures can be further divided into central nervous system measures and peripheral nervous system measures [25]. These methods do not require the user to generate overt responses, they allow a direct and continuous measurement of the current workload level, and they have high temporal sensitivity and can thus detect short periods of elevated workload [26]. Although central nervous system measures (i.e. electrocardiogram) has high reliability in measurement of driver's MWL [13], the applicability of these measures is limited due to the expensive instruments so it was not suitable to the conditions of this experiment. Therefore, the central nervous system measures were not used in this study.

Eye activity is a technique that captures eye behavior in response to a visual stimulus, and this technique has become a widely used method to analyze human behavior [27]. Eye response components that have been used as MWL measures include pupil dilation, blink rate, blink duration and fixations. Human pupil dilation may be used as a measure of the psychological load because it is related to the amount of cognitive control, attention, and cognitive processing required for a given task [28]. It also has been previously shown to correlate with the cognitive workload, whereby increased frequency of dilation is associated with increased degree of difficulty of a task [29]. In the driving study, pupil dilation was able to reflect the load required by tasks [30], and it would measure the average arousal underlying the cognitive tasks [31]. The blink of the eye, the rapid closing, and reopening of the eyelid is believed to be an indicator of both fatigue and workload. It is well known that eye blink rate is a good indicator of fatigue. Blink rate has been investigated in a series of driver and workload studies with mixed results attributable to the distinction between mental and visual workload [31]. They suggested that blink rate is affected by both MWL and visual demand, which act in opposition to each other, the former leading to blink rate increase, the latter to blink rate decrease. Besides blink rate, blink duration has been shown to be affected by visual task demand. Blink duration has been shown to decrease with increases in MWL. The studies mentioned in Kramer's review all found shorter blink durations for increasing task demands (both mental and visual) [32]. Some studies show that blink duration is a sensitive and reliable indicator of driver visual workload [8, 33]. Eye fixation duration is also extensively used measures and is believed to increase with increasing mental task demands [34]. Recently, fixation duration and the number of fixations have also been investigated in a series of studies about driver hazard perception and they found that increased fixation durations during hazardous moments, indicating increased MWL [20].

The heart rate (HR) and heart rate variability (HRV) potentially offer objective, continuous, and nonintrusive measures of human operator's MWL [26]. Numerous studies show that HR reflects the interaction of low MWL and fatigue during driving [35, 36]. In addition to basic HR, there has also been growing interest in various measures of HRV. Spectral analysis of HRV enables investigators to decompose HRV into components associated with different biological mechanisms, such as the sympathetic/parasympathetic ratio or the low frequency power/high frequency power (LF/HF) ratio, the mean inter-beat (RR), the standard deviation of normal RR intervals (SDNN), etc. The SDNN reflects the level of sympathetic activity about parasympathetic activity and has been found to increase with an increase in the level of MWL [13, 25].

2.4 Experimental Task

There were three levels of task complexity in this experiment such as high, medium and low. Special stress in the City car driving simulator has been laid on the variety of road situations and realistic car driving. The condition setting of task shown in Table 1.

Table 1. Experiment task setting

Condition setting	Task complexity		
	Low	Medium	High
Type and gears	Manual, 6	Manual, 6	Manual, 6
Steering wheel	Left	Left	Left
Vehicular traffic density	10%	20%	40%
Traffic behavior	Quiet traffic	Usual traffic	Fast-moving traffic
Pedestrian traffic density	20%	20%	40%
Frequency of assignments	medium	medium	medium
Point limit	10	10	10
Sudden change of lane by a car	Rare	Often	Very often
Sudden stop of a car in the traffic	Rare	Often	Very often
Driving out of a car on oncoming lane	Often	Often	Very often
Time and weather	Daytime/clear	Daytime/clear	Nighttime/clear

2.5 Group Method of Data Handling

Actually, there are many methods used to develop the predictive model such as GMDH, Neural Networks, Logistic regression, Naive Bayes, etc. This study used the GMDH method [37] to establish a prediction model of work performance. This is a widely used neural network methodology which requires no assumptions of the relationship between predictors and responses [38]. The GMDH algorithm has been widely used in various fields, e.g. nuclear power plants [25], Stirling engine design [39], education [40]. This study investigated the relationship between seven physiological indices and work performance on different levels of task complexity.

2.6 Procedure

All participants received about two hours of training. During the training, they were taught how to use the eye tracking equipment, complete the NASA-TLX questionnaire and driving simulator. After that, each participant was received about 30 min to practice by himself on the driving simulator. This practice served the purpose of familiarizing subjects with the simulator and the general feel of the pedals and steering. The practice step would end until the participant was sure that he understood all procedures. The experiment was conducted on the next day.

Before the experiment, the participant took a 20 min rest, and then wore the measurement apparatus and proceeded with system adjustment. The initial physiological indices were acquired as a baseline before the experiment. During experiment, the physiological indices were collected during each phase (level of task complexity), and the NASA-TLX questionnaire was conducted after each phase to evaluate the subjective MWL of different levels of task complexity. Each phase lasted for about 20 min and had 5 min break after each phase. The limitation of driving speed limits in this study was required less 45 km/h.

The scenario included a normal driving environment in the city (2 km of city roads with some stop signs or crossing lights). Each participant was made to test the three level of the task in a randomized order (Fig. 1). They were asked to follow speed limits and to comply with traffic laws throughout the course of the experiment. Three level of workload with high, medium and low of task complexity in this experiment shown in Table 1.

Fig. 1. Driving task in the experiment: (A) Low task; (B) Medium task; (C) High task

3   Results

3.1   Sensitivity with the Workload Level

At alpha level of .05, a MANOVA results showed that there are a statistically significant difference in task levels, $F(16, 136) = 3.52$, $p < .0005$; Wilk's $\Lambda = .50$, partial $\eta^2 = .293$ with the high observed power of 99.1%. Descriptive statistics was presented in Table 2. There were significant differences in almost methods between workload levels in this driving task, however; no significant difference was found in pupil dilation ($p = .574$) and fixation duration ($p = .143$). The number of errors in performance measure showed that the high task has significantly higher error than the low task by almost 23.3% (Tukey HSD $p = .036$). However, there was no significant difference between the high task and medium task (Tukey HSD $p = .261$), and medium task and low task (Tukey HSD $p = .561$).

Table 2. Sensitivity with the workload level

Method	Task complexity (mean ± SD)			F statistic	Partial	p-value
	Low	Medium	High			
Number of errors (times)	4.1 ± 1.9	4.5 ± 1.8	5.3 ± 1.6	3.241	.080	.045*
NASA-TLX	37.7 ± 11.8	40.0 ± 11.49	53.1 ± 12.8	12.310	.247	.000**
Pupil dilation (px)	50.6 ± 9.2	49.4 ± 8.8	51.1 ± 9.1	1.299	.033	.574
Blink rate (times/min)	46.9 ± 6.1	45.2 ± 5.9	40.5 ± 5.1	8.689	.188	.000**
Blink duration (ms)	134.8 ± 18.9	145.5 ± 21.4	151.4 ± 23.2	4.085	.098	.021*
Fixation duration (s)	46.1 ± 23.7	47.3 ± 17.3	55.6 ± 13.1	1.998	.051	.143
HR (times/min)	77.3 ± 8.1	81.1 ± 8.2	86.1 ± 7.5	8.122	.178	.001*
SDNN (ms)	47.2 ± 17.0	50.3 ± 13.6	57.3 ± 11.7	3.400	.083	.039*

* $p \leq .05$, ** $p \leq .001$

3.2 Correlation Between the Number of Errors and Other Methods

The analysis of correlation was used to examine the relationship between the number of errors and other methods as shown in Table 3. It indicated that the number of errors and the NASA-TLX was positively correlated with each other. The correlation coefficient of $r = 0.563$ was found to be statistically significant at $p < 0.01$ (two-tailed). Mean of NASA-TLX score and the number of errors of each participant shown in Fig. 2.

Table 3. Correlation between the number of errors and other methods

Number of errors	1							
NASA-TLX	.563**	1						
Pupil dilation	.539**	.508**	1					
Blink rate	−.129	−.287*	.037	1				
Blink duration	.449**	.498**	.577**	−.061	1			
Fixation duration	.402**	.330**	.377**	−.055	.408**	1		
HR	.392**	.357**	.384**	−.250*	.511**	.249*	1	
SDNN	.150	.200	.259*	−.081	.189	.084	.280*	1

** Correlation is significant at the 0.01 level (2-tailed).
* Correlation is significant at the 0.05 level (2-tailed).

The statistic also showed that most physiological measures in this study correlate significantly with the number of errors indicate that physiological measures may assess the work performance by participants in the driving complex task.

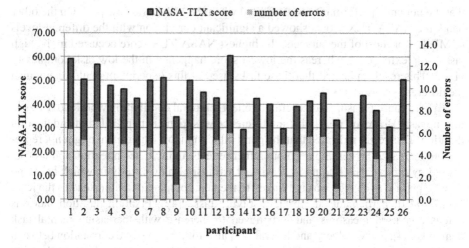

Fig. 2. Mean of the number of errors and NASA-TLX score of each participant in driving task

3.3 Predicting the Number of Errors by Integrating Physiological Measures

Six physiological indices, including pupil dilation (X_1), blink rate (X_2), blink duration (X_3), fixation duration (X_4), HR (X_5) and SDNN (X_6) into a synthesized index and to establish a model of work performance, this study used the GMDH method and the predictive modeling software DTREG version 10.6. The ratio of training and testing in this study was selected as 80%:20% to fit in with the available experimental sample size of 26. Each input variable (X_i) was normalized to a range of 0 and 1 before the training and testing process begins. The network was trained by using a random training data set, and the training data was also never used in the test data.

The results indicated that physiological indices of X_1, X_2, and X_5 were the best significant predictor factors in the performance by the subject. The model is expressed by Eq. (1) with the mean square error was 1.03, and R^2 of the model was 78.1%.

$$\begin{aligned}
Y = {} & 4.816 + 1.152X_5 + 0.588X_2 + 0.233X_1 - 0.477X_5^2 + 0.091X_2^2 + 0.095X_1^2 - 0.433X_5X_2 \\
& - 0.290X_5X_1 - 0.163X_2X_1 + 1.125X_5X_2X_1 - 0.451X_5^3 - 0.276X_2^3 + 0.027X_1^3 - 0.467X_5X_2^2 \\
& - 0.309X_5X_1^2 - 0.844X_2X_5^2 + 0.010X_2X_1^2 + 1.079X_1X_5^2 + 0.217X_1X_2^2
\end{aligned} \tag{1}$$

In the validation data, the result showed that the mean target value for predicted values is 4.62 while mean target value for input data is 4.5 (97.4%). Therefore, this model was suitable to estimate the performance of different MWL based on physiological measures in driving tasks.

4 Discussion

The number of errors was calculated as performance measures for the driving tasks in this study. The evaluation result showed that increasing task complexity makes increase the number of errors. This result is consistent with numerous studies which had found that the human's performance was affected when the MWL was low [41]. On the other hand, the NASA-TLX scores showed a significant correlation with the different levels of MWL. For most of the subjects, the highest NASA-TLX score occurred in the high task complexity phase whereas the lowest score happened in the low task complexity phase. This result indicated that these tasks used in this experiment could distinguish the different levels of MWL.

Eye response measures are useful to reflect temporal distribution workload levels in driving task. However, no significant difference was found in pupil dilation and fixation duration. This result indicated that the pupil dilation in this experiment might not represent an increased processing need but rather reflects an increased attention and arousal caused by errors. This finding is consistent with Bradshaw's study in which he found that the pupil size change was not linked to the task complexity, but instead to the level of arousal of participants in problem-solving tasks [42]. Fixation duration index is extensively used measures and is believed to increase with increasing mental task demands [34], and Goldberg and Kotval [43] also found a negative correlation between fixation time and performance. Although the overall significance in fixation duration between different task levels was not found, there was a significant difference between the high task and low task. This result could be explained that the difference between the task levels (low-medium-high) is small.

Cardiac responses such as HR, HRV were used, and these responses seem more sensitive to the accumulative workload than eye response measures do. The experimental result indicated that mean of participants' HR and HRV components increased when the task complexity increased. These findings were consistent with previous studies [13, 44]. The participants in driving task needed to continuously exert mental effort to keep alert, and fatigue may have reduced the participants' attention. O'Hanlon [45] found that the initial decrease was changed into a gradual increase in HRV in long-time continuous driving and Tripathi, Mukundan and Mathew [46] also found that HRV increased in high-demand vigilance tasks that also require continuous exertion. Another plausible reason is the interaction influence of respiration on HR and HRV. A cognitive load promotes oxygen demand by cells and leads to the production of more cardiac output by increasing HR [47]. During the execution of tasks, participants breathed deep and long, which will increase.

Finally, this study used GMDH method to construct a model to predict the driver's work performance on different workload levels. Although the statistic in table showed that blink rate and HRV measure no correlates with the number of errors significantly at the level of .05, the predictive model that integrates different physiological measures explains 78.1% of the number of errors. With this model, it could provide a reliable reference tool to predict the work performance of drivers.

4.1   Limitations

Some limitations of this study should be mentioned. First, the experiment has used a small sample of a student population to evaluate and predict model; the small sample size reduced the statistical power. These students also do not represent the characteristics of the people who want to learn the driving car. In addition, in the simulation condition, the participants often have psychological comfort because they must suffer the consequences of their mistakes when the operation fails or does not fulfill the requirements of the task. This causes for lack of significant differences among the outcomes and assessment results had limits of reliability. Finally, this result has been not shown the causal relationship between the physiological measures and the error rate but show a correlation between them under certain situations.

5 Conclusions

This paper reports the correlation of human's MWL and work performance in the driving task using driving simulator based on NASA-TLX and six physiological indices. The results show that different complexity levels of the driving task have a significant effect on the new driver's performance. In six physiological indices were used, three indices of pupil dilation, blink duration, and HR were the significant predictor factors, and the validity of this model was very well with $R^2 = 0.78$. Therefore, this model can be used to predict the new driver's work performance and maybe apply for actual. Although the model development process is still in an early phase, it can be used to predict the value of a new driver or little experience driving people on practice phase procedure.

Acknowledgements. The authors would like to thank the reviewers for their valuable remarks and comments. Also, the authors thank the participants who helped conduct this research.

References

1. Knipling, R.R.: Evidence and dimensions of commercial driver differential crash risk. In: Driving Assessment 2005: 3rd International Driving Symposium on Human Factors in Driver Assessment, Training, and Vehicle Design, pp. 2–8 (2005)
2. Todoskoff, A., Dillies, M.-A., Popieul, J.-C., Angue, J.-C.: Characterization of driver's behavior: a joint study in a car driving simulator and in real driving situations. In: Driving Simulation Conference, pp. 295–308 (1999)
3. Meister, D.: Behavioral Foundations of System Development. Wiley, New York (1976)
4. Waard, D.D., Jessurun, M., Steyvers, F.J., Reggatt, P.T., Brookhuis, K.A.: Effect of road layout and road environment on driving performance, drivers' physiology and road appreciation. Ergonomics **38**, 1395–1407 (1995)
5. Eggemeier, F.T., Wilson, G.F.: Performance-based and subjective assessment of workload in multi-task environments. In: Damos, D.L. (ed.) Multiple-task Performance, 217–278. Taylor & Francis, London (1991)
6. Sheridan, T., Stassen, H.: Definitions, models and measures of human workload. In: Moray, N. (ed.) Mental Workload. NATOCS, vol. 8, pp. 219–233. Springer, Boston (1979). https://doi.org/10.1007/978-1-4757-0884-4_12
7. Xie, B., Salvendy, G.: Review and reappraisal of modelling and predicting mental workload in single-and multi-task environments. Work Stress **14**, 74–99 (2000)
8. Benedetto, S., Pedrotti, M., Minin, L., Baccino, T., Re, A., Montanari, R.: Driver workload and eye blink duration. Transp. Res. Part F Traffic Psychol. Behav. **14**, 199–208 (2011)

9. Ryu, K., Myung, R.: Evaluation of mental workload with a combined measure based on physiological indices during a dual task of tracking and mental arithmetic. Int. J. Ind. Ergon. **35**, 991–1009 (2005)

10. Yan, S., Tran, C.C., Wei, Y., Habiyaremye, J.L.: Driver's mental workload prediction model based on physiological indices. Int. J. Occup. Safety Ergon. 1–9 (2017)

11. Dyer, R.F., Matthews, J.J., Wright, C.E., Yudowitch, K.L.: Questionnaire construction manual. DTIC Document (1976)

12. Johnson, A., Widyanti, A.: Cultural influences on the measurement of subjective mental workload. Ergonomics **54**, 509–518 (2011)

13. Heine, T., Lenis, G., Reichensperger, P., Beran, T., Doessel, O., Deml, B.: Electrocardiographic features for the measurement of drivers' mental workload. Appl. Ergon. **61**, 31–43 (2017)

14. Hoeschen, A., Vervey, W., Bekiaris, E., Knoll, C., Widlroiter, H., Ward, D., Uneken, E., Gregersen, N., Falkmer, T., Schelin, H.: Inventory of drivers training needs and major gaps in the relevant training procedures. In: European Commission GROWTH Programme (2001)

15. Underwood, G., Crundall, D., Chapman, P.: Driving simulator validation with hazard perception. Transp. Res. Part F Traffic Psychol. Behav. **14**, 435–446 (2011)

16. Allen, R.W., Park, G.D., Cook, M.L., Fiorentino, D.: The effect of driving simulator fidelity on training effectiveness. DSC 2007 North America (2007)

17. Flach, J.M., Dekker, S., Jan Stappers, P.: Playing twenty questions with nature (the surprise version): reflections on the dynamics of experience. Theor. Issues Ergon. Sci. **9**, 125–154 (2008)

18. Tsang, P.S., Vidulich, M.A.: Mental Workload and Situation Awareness. Wiley, New York (2006)

19. Gawron, V.J.: Human Performance, Workload, and Situational Awareness Measures Handbook. CRC Press, London (2008)

20. Di Stasi, L.L., Álvarez-Valbuena, V., Cañas, J.J., Maldonado, A., Catena, A., Antolí, A., Candido, A.: Risk behaviour and mental workload: multimodal assessment techniques applied to motorbike riding simulation. Transp. Res. Part F Traffic Psychol. Behav. **12**, 361–370 (2009)

21. Baker, C.A., Morris, D.F., Steedman, W.C.: Target recognition on complex displays. Hum. Factors J. Hum. Factors Ergon. Soc. **2**, 51–60 (1960)

22. Downing, J.V., Sanders, M.S.: The effects of panel arrangement and locus of attention on performance. Hum. Factors **29**, 551–562 (1987)

23. Milleville-Pennel, I., Charron, C.: Do mental workload and presence experienced when driving a real car predispose drivers to simulator sickness? An exploratory study. Accid. Anal. Prev. **74**, 192–202 (2015)

24. Hart, S., Staveland, L.: Development of NASA-TLX (Task Load Index): results of empirical and theoretical research. Adv. Psychol. **52**, 139–183 (1988)

25. Gao, Q., Wang, Y., Song, F., Li, Z., Dong, X.: Mental workload measurement for emergency operating procedures in digital nuclear power plants. Ergonomics **56**, 1070–1085 (2013)

26. Wilson, G.F., Eggemeier, F.T.: Psychophysiological assessment of workload in multi-task environments. In: Damos, D.L. (ed.) Multiple-task Performance, 329–360. Taylor & Francis, London (1991)

27. Yan, S., Tran, C.C., Chen, Y., Tan, K., Habiyaremye, J.L.: Effect of user interface layout on the operators' mental workload in emergency operating procedures in nuclear power plants. Nucl. Eng. Des. **322**, 266–276 (2017)

28. Wierda, S.M., van Rijn, H., Taatgen, N.A., Martens, S.: Pupil dilation deconvolution reveals the dynamics of attention at high temporal resolution. Proc. Nat. Acad. Sci. **109**, 8456–8460 (2012)

29. Hampson, R., Opris, I., Deadwyler, S.: Neural correlates of fast pupil dilation in nonhuman primates: relation to behavioral performance and cognitive workload. Behav. Brain Res. **212**, 1–11 (2010)

30. Recarte, M.A., Nunes, L.M.: Mental workload while driving: effects on visual search, discrimination, and decision making. J. Exp. Psychol. Appl. **9**, 119 (2003)

31. Recarte, M.Á., Pérez, E., Conchillo, Á., Nunes, L.M.: Mental workload and visual impairment: differences between pupil, blink, and subjective rating. Span J. Psychol. **11**, 374–385 (2008)

32. Kramer, A.F.: Physiological metrics of mental workload: a review of recent progress. In: Damos, D.L. (ed.) Multiple-task Performance, 279–328. Taylor & Francis, London (1991)

33. Häkkänen, H., Summala, H., Partinen, M., Tiihonen, M., Silvo, J.: Blink duration as an indicator of driver sleepiness in professional bus drivers. Sleep **22**, 798–802 (1999)

34. Recarte, M.A., Nunes, L.M.: Effects of verbal and spatial-imagery tasks on eye fixations while driving. J. Exp. Psychol. Appl. **6**, 31 (2000)

35. Myllylä, T., Korhonen, V., Vihriälä, E., Sorvoja, H., Hiltunen, T., Tervonen, O., Kiviniemi, V.: Human heart pulse wave responses measured simultaneously at several sensor placements by two MR-compatible fibre optic methods. J. Sens. **2012**, 1–8 (2012)

36. Solovey, E.T., Zec, M., Garcia Perez, E.A., Reimer, B., Mehler, B.: Classifying driver workload using physiological and driving performance data: two field studies. In: Proceedings of the 32nd Annual ACM Conference on Human Factors in Computing Systems, pp. 4057–4066. ACM, New York (2014)

37. Ivakhnenko, A.G.: The group method of data handling-a rival of the method of stochastic approximation. Sov. Autom. Control **13**, 43–55 (1968)

38. Stern, H.S.: Neural networks in applied statistics. Technometrics **38**, 205–214 (1996)

39. Ahmadi, M.H., Ahmadi, M.-A., Mehrpooya, M., Rosen, M.A.: Using GMDH neural networks to model the power and torque of a stirling engine. Sustainability **7**, 2243–2255 (2015)

40. Náplava, P., Šnorek, M.: Modelling of students quality by means of GMDH algorithms. Syst. Anal. Model Simul. **43**, 1415–1426 (2003)

41. Wilson, G.F., Russell, C.A.: Real-time assessment of mental workload using psychophysiological measures and artificial neural networks. Hum. Factors **45**, 635–644 (2003)

42. Bradshaw, J.: Pupil size and problem solving. Q. J. Exp. Psychol. **20**, 116–122 (1968)

43. Goldberg, J.H., Kotval, X.P.: Computer interface evaluation using eye movements: methods and constructs. Int. J. Ind. Ergon. **24**, 631–645 (1999)

44. Brookhuis, K.A., de Waard, D.: Monitoring drivers' mental workload in driving simulators using physiological measures. Accid. Anal. Prev. **42**, 898–903 (2010)

45. O'Hanlon, J.F.: Heart Rate Variability: A New Index of Driver Alertness/Fatigue. Automotive Engineering Congress; 0148–7191 (1972)

46. Tripathi, K., Mukundan, C., Mathew, T.L.: Attentional modulation of heart rate variability (HRV) during execution of PC based cognitive tasks. Ind. J. Aerosp. Med. **47**, 1–10 (2003)

47. Brookhuis, K.A., de Waard, D.: Assessment of Drivers' Workload: Performance and Subjective and Physiological Indexes. Stress, Workload and Fatigue. Lawrence Erlbaum Associates Inc., Mahwah (2001)

Open Access This chapter is licensed under the terms of the Creative Commons Attribution 4.0 International License (http://creativecommons.org/licenses/by/4.0/), which permits use, sharing, adaptation, distribution and reproduction in any medium or format, as long as you give appropriate credit to the original author(s) and the source, provide a link to the Creative Commons license and indicate if changes were made.

The images or other third party material in this chapter are included in the chapter's Creative Commons license, unless indicated otherwise in a credit line to the material. If material is not included in the chapter's Creative Commons license and your intended use is not permitted by statutory regulation or exceeds the permitted use, you will need to obtain permission directly from the copyright holder.

Machine Perception of Humans

Exploring the Dynamics of Relationships Between Expressed and Experienced Emotions

Ramya Srinivasan[(✉)], Ajay Chander, and Cathrine L. Dam

Fujitsu Laboratories of America, Sunnyvale, CA, USA
ramya@us.fujitsu.com

Abstract. Conversational user interfaces (CUIs) are rapidly evolving towards being ubiquitous as human-machine interfaces. Often, CUI back-ends are powered by a combination of human and machine intelligence, to address queries efficiently. Depending on the type of conversation issue, human-to-human conversations in CUIs (i.e. a human end-user conversing with the human in the CUI backend) could involve varying amounts of emotional content. While some of these emotions could be expressed through the conversation, others are experienced internally within the individual. Understanding the relationship between these two emotion modalities in the end-user could help to analyze and address the conversation issue better. Towards this, we propose an emotion analytic metric that can estimate experienced emotions based on its knowledge about expressed emotions in a user. Our findings point to the possibility of augmenting CUIs with an algorithmically guided emotional sense, which would help in having more effective conversations with end-users.

Keywords: Conversational user interfaces
Expressed and experienced emotions

1 Introduction

Conversational user interfaces (CUIs) are interactive user interfaces that allow users to express themselves conversationally, and are often powered by a combination of humans and machines at the back end [1]. Across a wide range of applications, from assisting with voice-command texting while driving to sending alerts when household consumables need to be ordered, CUIs have become a part of our everyday lives. In particular, bots within messaging platforms have witnessed rapid consumer proliferation. These platforms cater to a wide spectrum of human queries and messages, both domain-specific as well as general purpose [2].

Depending on the type of issue being discussed, human-to-human conversations in CUIs (i.e., conversations between human in the CUI backend and the human end-user) could involve varying amounts of emotional content. While some of these emotions could be expressed in the conversation, others are felt or experienced internally within the individual [12]. An expressed emotion need

© The Author(s) 2017
P. Horain et al. (Eds.): IHCI 2017, LNCS 10688, pp. 165–177, 2017.
https://doi.org/10.1007/978-3-319-72038-8_13

not always correspond to what the user is actually experiencing internally. For example, one can suppress the internal feelings and express some other emotion in order to be consistent with certain socio-cultural norms [23]. Since experienced emotions are felt internally, they may not be easily perceived by others.

Understanding relationship between expressed and experienced emotions could facilitate better communication between the end-user and human in the CUI backend [7]. Analyzing experienced emotions could also help in uncovering certain aspects of an individual that needs attention and care. For example, a feeling of extreme sadness within an individual could be expressed externally as anger [6]. Employing this type of emotion metric could enhance both the scope and usage of CUIs. In this paper, we propose such an emotion metric by developing a machine learning method to estimate probabilities of experienced emotions based on the expressed emotions of a user.

Problem Setting: We consider the scenario of textual conversations involving individuals needing emotional support. For convenience, we refer to individuals needing support as users. On the other end of the conversation platform are the human listeners (typically counselors). The human listener chats directly with the user using a text-only interface and our algorithm (i.e. the machine) analyzes the texts of the end-user. The machine provides a quantitative assessment of the experienced emotions in the user's text. All assessments are specific to the user under consideration.

The machine first evaluates the conditional probability of experiencing an emotion emo_n internally given that an emotion emo_m is explicitly expressed. In the rest of this paper we represent this conditional probability as $P_t(emo_n|emo_m)$. For example, the probability of experiencing sadness internally given that anger has been expressed, is represented as $P_t(sad|angry)$. From these conditional probabilities, the probabilities of various experienced emotions ($P(emo_n)$) are obtained. A detailed explanation of the procedure is described in Sect. 3.

2   Related Work

CUIs are used for a variety of applications. For example, IBM's Watson technology has been used to create a teaching assistant for a course taught at Georgia Tech [13], Google chatbot, "Danielle", can act like book characters [14], and so on. There are also emotion-based models for chatbots such as [25], wherein the authors propose to model the emotions of a conversational agent.

A summary of affect computing measures is provided in D'Mello et al. [16]. Mower et al. [27] propose an emotion classification paradigm based on emotion profiles. There have been efforts to make machines social and emotionally aware [23]. There are methods to understand sentiments in human-computer dialogues [18], in naturalistic user behavior [24] and even in handwriting [26]. However, we are not aware of any work that estimates the underlying, experienced emotions in text conversations.

Bayesian theory has been used to understand many kinds of relationships in domains such as computer vision, natural language processing, economics, medicine, etc. For example, Ba et al. [15] use Bayesian methods for head and pose estimation. Dang et al. [17] leverage Bayesian framework for metaphor identification. Bayesian inference has been used in recent years to develop algorithms for identifying e-mail spam [28]. More recently, Microsoft Research created a Bayesian network with the goal of accurately modeling the relative skill of players in head-to-head competitions [29]. Our work describes a new application of Bayesian theory, namely, to estimate experienced emotions in text conversations.

3   Method

Let the conditional probability of experiencing an emotion emo_n given that an emotion emo_m is expressed be denoted by $P_t(emo_n|emo_m)$. We evaluate $P_t(emo_n|emo_m)$ using a Bayesian framework. These are then normalized over the space of all expressed emotions emo_m to obtain the probabilities of various experienced emotions emo_n.

First, an emotion recognition algorithm is run on the end-user's texts to determine the probabilities of various expressed emotions. These probabilities serve as priors in the Bayesian framework. Next, we leverage large datasets containing emotional content across many people (such as blogs, etc.) to measure the similarities between words corresponding to a pair of emotions. This information is computed across several people and is reflective of the general relatedness between two emotion-indicating words (for example, between the words "sad" and "angry"). This measure is then normalized (across all possible pairs of emotions considered) to constitute the likelihood probability in the Bayesian framework. The priors and likelihoods are then integrated to obtain $P_t(emo_n|emo_m)$. This conditional probability is specific to the end-user under consideration. This is then normalized over all possible choices of expressed emotions to obtain probabilities of experienced emotions for the end-user under consideration.

While a variety of other approaches could be used for this computation, our choice of the Bayesian framework is motivated by the following facts. First, Bayesian models have been successful in characterizing several aspects of human cognition such as inductive learning, causal inference, language processing, social cognition, reasoning and perception [30]. Second, Bayesian learning incorporates the notion of prior knowledge which is a crucial element in human learning. Finally, these models have been successful in learning from limited data, akin to human inference [31].

3.1   Estimation of Priors

During the course of the user's conversation with a human listener, we perform text analysis at regular time instances to get probabilities of different emotions. These probabilities are determined based on the occurrences of words representative of emotions in user's text. In our setting, we measure the probability of the following emotions—happy, sad, angry, scared, surprised, worried, and troubled. We arrived at these seven emotions by augmenting commonly observed emotions in counseling platforms with those that are widely accepted in psychological research [32]. These probabilities provide some "prior" information about the user's emotions and hence serve as the priors in the Bayesian framework.

Let the prior probability of an emotion i, be denoted by $P_p(emo_i)$. Thus, there are multiple emotion variables, with each of these variables taking a value in the range $[0, 1]$ indicating their probabilities. We leverage word synsets to obtain a rich set of words related to each of the emotions that we want to recognize. Synsets are defined as a set of synonyms for a word. Let the set of synsets across all the emotion categories be referred to as the emotion vocabulary. The words in a user's text are then matched for co-occurrence with the emotion vocabulary and are weighted (normalized) based on their frequency of occurrence to obtain probability of an emotion. We found this simple approach quite reliable for our data. This will give the probabilities for various expressed emotions.

3.2 Estimation of Likelihoods

We estimate similarities between words corresponding to a pair of emotions by training neural word embeddings on large datasets [9]. This similarity gives a measure of relatedness between two emotion-indicating words in a general sense. For example, if the word "sad" has higher similarity with word "anger" than with the word "worry", then we assume that the relatedness between emotions "sad" and "anger" is higher than the relatedness between "sad" and "worry". This may not necessarily be true with respect to every user, but is true in an average sense since the calculation is based on very large datasets of emotional content across several people. Since this measure is data-dependent, we have to choose appropriate datasets containing significant emotional content to get reliable estimates. We then normalize the similarity scores to obtain the likelihood probability. The details are as follows:

Specifically, we train a skip-gram model on a large corpus of news articles (over a million words), blogs and conversations that contain information pertaining to people's emotions, behavior, reactions and opinions. As a result, the model can provide an estimate of relatedness $r_{emo_i-emo_j}$ between two emotions (emo_i and emo_j) leveraging information across a wide set of people and contexts. This quantity is just capturing the relatedness between any two emotions in a general sense, and is not specific to a particular user. We compute likelihood probability of observing emotions emo_j given emo_i, $P_l(emo_j|emo_i)$ based on normalizing the similarities $r_{emo_i-emo_j}$ over the space of all possible emotions under consideration. Thus,

$$P_l(emo_j|emo_i) = \frac{r_{emo_i-emo_j}}{\sum_{all-emo} r_{emo_i-emo_j}} \tag{1}$$

The emotion pairs considered in Eq. (1) do not necessarily represent expressed or experienced emotions; the likelihood probability is just a measure of relatedness between a pair of emotions computed from large datasets.

3.3 Estimating Conditional Probabilities

We employ a Bayesian framework to integrate emotion priors with the likelihood probabilities. Let $P_p(emo_n)$ be the prior probability of an emotion emo_n as obtained from an emotion analysis algorithm, and $P_l(emo_m|emo_n)$, be the likelihood probability of emo_m given emo_n, obtained by using appropriate training dataset. Then, the posterior probability of experiencing an emo_n given an expressed emotion emo_m is given by

$$P_t(emo_n|emo_m) = \frac{P_l(emo_m|emo_n)P_p(emo_n)}{\sum_{all-emo} P_l(emo_m|emo_n)P_p(emo_n)} \qquad (2)$$

The above quantity is specific to the user under consideration.

3.4 Estimating Probabilities of Experienced Emotions

The conditional probabilities computed from Eq. (2) are specific to a user. By normalizing these conditional probabilities across all possible choices of expressed emotions, we obtain the probabilities of various experienced emotions. Specifically,

$$P(emo_b) = \sum_a P_t(emo_b|emo_a)P_p(emo_a) \qquad (3)$$

where in emo_a is an expressed emotion and emo_b is an experienced emotion. The set of expressed and experienced emotions need not be mutually exclusive.

3.5 Dataset

We studied the performance of the algorithm on a dataset consisting of 16 anonymous user conversations with a human listener spanning a total of more than 20 h. Conversations between users and human listener dealt with a variety of topics such as relationship issues, emotional wellbeing, friendship problems, etc. On average, the conversation between a user and the human listener lasted approximately 30 min. Some of these conversations lasted more than an hour (the longest was 70 min) while some lasted only 10 min. We divided the conversations into segments corresponding to the time a user spoke uninterrupted by a human listener. For convenience we refer to each segment as a "transcript". Transcripts numbered A.x are all contiguous parts of the same conversation A. There were over fifty transcripts in the dataset.

4 Results

We illustrate the performance of the proposed method on some user conversations. Users converse with a human listener, henceforth abbreviated as "HL". All results are specific to the user part of the conversation only and apply to the specific time interval only. The identities of the users and the human listener were anonymized by the conversation platform. It is to be noted that an experienced emotion could become expressed at a later time, so the set of expressed and experienced emotions are not mutually exclusive. Also, the algorithm can compute probabilities of experienced emotions only for those emotions for which there is a prior.

4.1   Case Studies

Transcript 1.1 (0th–10th min)

USER: Hi, can you please help me with anxiety.

HL: I'm sorry you're feeling anxious. Can you tell me more about it?

USER: I have no self confidence and have a girlfriend who I really like. I can't cope thinking she is going to find someone better. I am drinking to kill the anxiety.

HL: It sounds like you're feeling really anxious about your girlfriend staying with you. That sounds really difficult.

USER: She is out with work tonight and a colleague who she dated for a bit is there. I don't know how to cope.

HL: It sounds like you're feeling really anxious that she is out with other people including her ex. And you not being there with her is making you feel worse. I'm sorry - that's a really hard feeling.

USER: Can you help?

HL: I can listen to you. And I really am sorry that you're feeling so anxious. Maybe you can tell me more about your relationship and why you are feeling insecure.

USER: I am an insecure person. I am a good looking guy, always get chatted up, but I have no confidence.

Tables 1 and 2 list the expressed and experienced emotions during the first 10 min of the conversation.

Table 1. Expressed emotions for transcript 1.1: 0th–10th min

Expressed emotion	Probabilities
Troubled	.59375
Worried	.40625

Table 2. Experienced emotions for transcript 1.1: 0th–10th min

Experienced emotion	Probabilities
Worried	0.615
Troubled	0.385

Transcript 1.2 (10th–20th min)

USER: I Dont know why I am insecure with her, I just feel inadequate.

HL: You feel insecure and inadequate with her. Have you felt like this with other girlfriends?

USER: Once before but not as bad. She is beautiful.

HL: It sounds like she is really special to you - it's nice that you have a beautiful girlfriend.

USER: She really is. But I Dont think the same the other way.

HL: I'm not sure I understand what you mean. You mentioned that you were also good looking.

USER: I Dont know if she feels the same. Yes I am. Not by my own admission but by what people tell me.

HL: So you think she is beautiful but you're not sure how she feels about you?

USER: I Dont know, I think I might be over eager and care for her too much.

Tables 3 and 4 lists the results of the algorithm.

Table 3. Expressed emotions for transcript 1.2: 10th–20th min

Expressed emotion	Probabilities
Troubled	.703
Worried	.084
Sad	.212

Table 4. Experienced emotions for transcript 1.2: 10th–20th min

Experienced emotion	Probabilities
Worried	0.168
Sad	0.17
Troubled	0.661

Results are listed in Tables 5 and 6. Similar analysis was carried out throughout the conversation. The following is the last transcript of this conversation.

Table 5. Expressed emotions for transcript 1.3: 20th–30th min

Expressed Emotion	Probabilities
Sad	.923
Scared	.068

Table 6. Experienced emotions for transcript 1.3: 20th–30th min

Experienced Emotion	Probabilities
Scared	0.037
Sad	0.9625

Transcript 1.4 (40th–50th min)

USER: I Dont have anyone I can confide in.

HL: That sounds lonely. I think many people feel like that which is why it's nice that we can be there for each other online.

USER: Very lonely. Which is why I'm afraid of losing her. I've told her everything about myself.

HL: it's nice that you've found a confidant in her. and of course now you don't want to loose that connection.

USER: I made it a point to tell her everything, something which I haven't done previous. Its part the reason why in terrified to lose her.

HL: yeah, it sounds like you feel really open but also very vulnerable because of everything you've shared. that's hard.

USER: I'm very vulnerable. Should I go to the doctor?

HL: I'm not sure. If you're thinking about it, it might be a good idea. What kind of advice are you looking for from them?

USER: I Dont know, maybe medication

HL: Ah, I see what you're saying. Medication can help a lot with anxiety for sure. It sounds like you're feeling really bad and anxious and really don't want to feel like this anymore. I think it's always good to find out if a doctor can help with something like that...

Tables 7 and 8 provide the assessment of expressed/experienced emotions.

Table 7. Expressed emotions for transcript 1.4: 40th–40th min

Expressed Emotion	Probabilities
Sad	.286
Scared	.286
Troubled	.214
Worried	.213

Table 8. Experienced emotions for transcript 1.4: 40th–40th min

Experienced emotion	Probabilities
Scared	.1025
Sad	.2995
Troubled	.2414
Worried	.208

We present another case study. For brevity, we omit the conversation excerpts of HL (machine analyzes only user texts) and show results for first part of conversation. Similar analysis was carried for the rest of the conversation.

Transcript 2.1 (0th–10th min)

USER: okay, so I am 18 and my boyfriend is 17. He has BAD anger, it's never been anything physical. but he always gets mad over the littlest things and he always acts like everything bothers him when I say something wrong... but when he does something like that I am supposed to take it as a joke. and then he gets mad and tries to blow it off when I say something as a joke like "yep." "yeah." "nope I am fine." and acts short (Tables 9 and 10).

Table 9. Expressed emotions for transcript 2.1: 0th–10th min

Expressed Emotion	Probabilities
Troubled	.227
Sad	.4228
Angry	.349

Table 10. Experienced emotion for transcript 2.1: 0th–10th min

Experienced emotion	Probabilities
Sad	.486
Troubled	.19
Angry	.322

Transcript 2.2 (10th–20th min)

USER: yeah i just need help getting through that it. yeah... and i'm worried
with me going to college it'll get worse. I guess... it's just hard, not only
that but my mom is freaking out on me and mad at me. all the time when
i haven't done ANYTHING and that is really stressing me out... i don't
know... i really don't she makes me feel lie i am a failure because i don
have a job or anything and it doesn't help that she going through a change
because she is 50... her and my little brother and stepfather constantly gang
up on me. my brother is the worst. My boyfriend says i should leave since i
am 18 but i have no where to go because i do not have a job nor any money
(Tables 11 and 12).

Machine Observations

Table 11. Expressed emotions for transcript 2.2: 10th–20th min

Expressed Emotion	Probabilities
Worried	.2543
Sad	.693
Angry	.052

Table 12. Experienced emotion for transcript 2.2: 10th–20th min

Experienced emotion	Probabilities
Sad	.75
Worried	.2
Angry	.05

4.2   Analysis

Validation with Human Experts: In order to investigate the effectiveness of the
algorithm, we asked human experts to state the top 3 emotions the user in
any given transcript was experiencing. The human experts were chosen based on
their knowledge and experience in the psychology of active listening. The experts
were not restricted to use the same set of emotions as the machine could identify,
instead they were free to mention anything they found appropriate. To compare
with the machine's performance, we mapped similar emotion-describing words
into the same category. For example, "anxious" was mapped to "worried". In
75% of the transcripts, the top emotion chosen by the evaluators matched with
the top experienced emotion as computed by the machine. In the absence of
ground truth (i.e., we did not have information from the user as to what they
were experiencing), this accuracy is reasonable.

It is to be noted that with more information about the user (such as their
conversation history), the machine will be able to uncover more hidden emotions. Also given that human evaluation itself was subjective, machine's result
can serve as an additional source of information. For example, for the user in
Transcript 2, the machine result suggested that sadness was the highest experienced emotion. Interestingly, none of the human experts identified sadness in the
top 3 experienced emotions. However, given the situation of the user, it may not
be unreasonable to say that sadness is likely underneath all her other emotions.

Understanding the User: In this study, one of our goals was to understand the patterns of expressed and experienced emotions in users. Figure 1 is a plot of the highest expressed and experienced emotions at every time interval for the user in transcript 1. Throughout, the expressed emotion seems consistent with the experienced emotions. Also, there isn't any statistically significant difference between the degree of expressed and experienced emotions. Figure 2 is a plot of the lowest expressed and experienced emotions. Except for one time interval (the last time interval wherein the lowest expressed emotion is worried and the lowest experienced emotion is fear), the lowest expressed and experienced emotions are the same, with no statistically significant difference in their intensity.

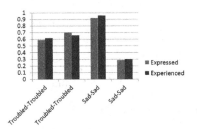
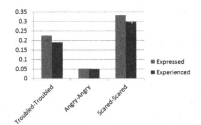

Fig. 1. Highest expressed and experienced emotions for user in Transcript 1.

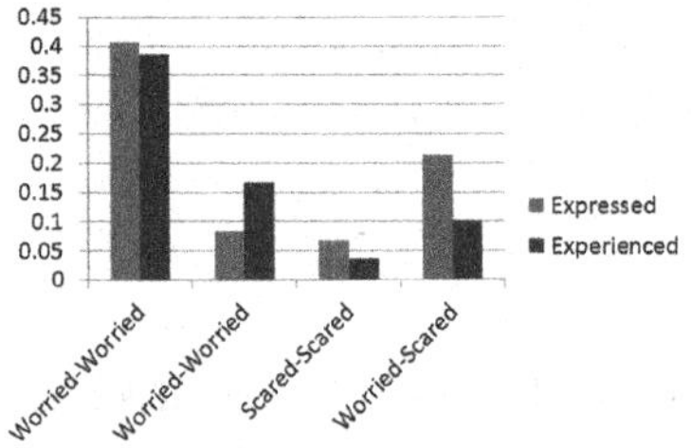

Fig. 2. Lowest expressed and experienced emotions for user in Transcript 1.

Thus, this user is *mostly* expressing what s/he is experiencing. As another case study, consider the user in transcript 2. Figure 3 summarizes the *highest* expressed and experienced emotions for this user. Figure 4 shows the plot for *lowest* expressed and experienced emotions for this user. As can be noticed from Figs. 3 and 4, this user is *always* expressing what she is experiencing.

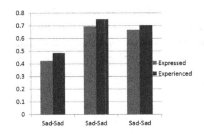

Fig. 3. Highest expressed and experienced emotions for user in Transcript 2.

Fig. 4. Lowest expressed and experienced emotions for user in Transcript 2.

There is generally a gap between what people express and what they experience. The aforementioned case studies were illustrations wherein one user *mostly* expressed what was experienced and the other *always* expressed what was experienced. However, there could be cases where people mostly hide certain emotions or never exhibit them. Thus, such quantitative studies of expressed and experienced emotions, can be useful in constructing "emotion profiles" of users. Emotion profiles can be thought of as some characteristic patterns exhibited by users in expressing and experiencing emotions. Understanding such details can help both the users as well as counselors assisting them. For example, if someone is scared, but only shows anger, it would be helpful to gently show (this user) that his/her underlying emotion is fear so that s/he can address it better. Such insights would also help a counselor in recommending suitable solution strategies.

5   Conclusions

We presented an approach to understand relationship between expressed emotions and experienced emotions during the course of a conversation. Specifically, we evaluated the probability of a user experiencing an emotion based on the knowledge of their expressed emotions. We discussed how the relationship between the expressed and experienced emotions can be leveraged in understanding a user. Such an emotion analytic can be powerfully deployed in conversation platforms, that have machines or humans in the backend. We hope our findings will help in providing personalized solutions to end-users of a CUI by means of augmenting CUIs with an algorithmically guided emotional sense, which would help in having more effective conversations with end-users.

References

1. Perez, D.: Conversational Agents and Natural Language Interaction - Techniques and Practices. IGI Global, Hershey (2011)
2. Ferrara, E., Varol, O., Davis, C., Menczer, F., Flammini, A.: The rise of social bots. arXiv Report, MA (2015)
3. Mackintosh, B., Yiend, J.: Cognition and emotion. In: Braisby, N.R., Gellatly, A.R.H. (eds.) Cognitive Psychology. Oxford University Press, Oxford (2005)
4. Teasdale, J.D., Taylor, R., Fogarty, S.J.: Effects of induced elation-depression on the accessibility of memories of happy and unhappy experiences. Behav. Res. Ther. **18**, 339–346 (1980)
5. Teasdale, J.D., Taylor, R., Fogarty, S.J.: The social context of emotional experience. Behav. Res. Ther. (1980)
6. Hoque, M.E., McDuff, D.J., Picard, R.W.: Exploring temporal patterns in classifying frustrated and delighted smiles. IEEE Trans. Affect. Comput. **3**, 323–334 (2012)
7. Planalp, S.: Communicating Emotion-Social Moral and Cultural Processes. Cambridge University Press, Cambridge (1999)
8. Lee, C., Narayanan, S.: Towards detecting emotions in spoken dialogues. IEEE Trans. Speech Audio Process. **13**, 293–303 (2005)
9. Mikolov, T., Sutsever, I., Chen, K., Corrado, G., Dean, J.: Distributed representations of words and phrases and their compositionality. In: NIPS (2013)
10. Kahneman, D.: Evaluation by moments past and future. In: Kahneman, D., Tversky, A. (eds.) Choices Values and Frames. Cambridge University Press, New York (2000)

11. Darley, M., Gross, H.: Hypothesis Confirming Bias in Labeling Effects. Psychology Press, New York (2000)
12. Lewis, M., Haviland-Jones, M., Barrett, L.: Handbook of Emotions, 3rd edn. Guilford Press, New York (2008)
13. McFarland, M.: What happened when a professor built a chatbot to be his teaching assistant, Washington Post (2016)
14. Isacsson, D.: Author Ray Kurzweil develops a new chatbot with Google based on one of his characters. Digit. Trends (2016)
15. Ba, S.O., Marc, J.-M.: A Probabilistic framework for joint head and pose estimation. In: ICPR (2004)
16. D'Mello, S., Kappas, A., Gratch, J.: The affective computing approach to affect measurement. Emot. Rev. (2017)
17. Zhang, L., Barnden, J.: Context-sensitive affect sensing and metaphor identification in virtual drama. In: D'Mello, S., Graesser, A., Schuller, B., Martin, J.-C. (eds.) ACII 2011. LNCS, vol. 6975, pp. 173–182. Springer, Heidelberg (2011). https://doi.org/10.1007/978-3-642-24571-8_18
18. Bohus, D.: Stochastically-based semantic analysis in human-computer dialogue. Graduate thesis, University of Timisoara (2000)
19. Groen, F., Pavlin, G., Winterboer, A., Evers, V.: A hybrid approach to decision making and information fusion: combining human and artificial agents. Robot. Auton. Syst. **90**, 71–85 (2017)
20. Chowanda, A., Flintham, M., Blanchfield, P., Valstar, M.: Playing with social and emotional game companions. In: IVA (2016)
21. Pan, X., Gillies, M., Slater, M.: Virtual character personality influences participants attitudes and behavior - an interview with a virtual human character about her social anxiety. Front. Robot. AI **2**(1) (2015)
22. Ward, N., DeVault, D.: Challenges in building highly interactive dialog systems. AI Mag. (2016)
23. Ochs, M., Niewiadomski, R., Pelachaud, C., Sadek, D.: Intelligent expressions of emotions. In: Tao, J., Tan, T., Picard, R.W. (eds.) ACII 2005. LNCS, vol. 3784, pp. 707–714. Springer, Heidelberg (2005). https://doi.org/10.1007/11573548_91
24. Walter, S., Scherer, S., Schels, M., Glodek, M., Hrabal, D., Schmidt, M., Böck, R., Limbrecht, K., Traue, H.C., Schwenker, F.: Multimodal emotion classification in naturalistic user behavior. In: Jacko, J.A. (ed.) HCI 2011. LNCS, vol. 6763, pp. 603–611. Springer, Heidelberg (2011). https://doi.org/10.1007/978-3-642-21616-9_68
25. Becker, C., Kopp, S., Wachsmuth, I.: Simulating the emotion dynamics of a multimodal conversational agent. In: André, E., Dybkjær, L., Minker, W., Heisterkamp, P. (eds.) ADS 2004. LNCS (LNAI), vol. 3068, pp. 154–165. Springer, Heidelberg (2004). https://doi.org/10.1007/978-3-540-24842-2_15
26. Likforman, L., Esposito, A., Zanuy, M.F., Cordasco, G.: EMOTHAW: a novel database for emotional state recognition from handwriting and drawing. IEEE Trans. Hum. Mach. Syst. **47**, 273–284 (2016)
27. Mower, E., Mataric, M., Narayanan, S.: A framework for automatic human emotion classification using emotion profiles. IEEE Trans. Audio Speech Lang. Process. **19**, 1057–1070 (2011)
28. Constanin, T.: Machine learning techniques in spam filtering. In: Data Mining Seminar (2004)
29. Guo, S., Sanner, S., Graepel, T., Buntine, W.: Score-based Bayesian skill learning. In: Flach, P.A., De Bie, T., Cristianini, N. (eds.) ECML PKDD 2012. LNCS (LNAI), vol. 7523, pp. 106–121. Springer, Heidelberg (2012). https://doi.org/10.1007/978-3-642-33460-3_12

30. Griffiths, T., Kemo, C., Tenenbaum, J.: Bayesian models of cognition. In: Sun, R. (ed.) Cambridge Handbook of Computational Cognitive Modeling. Cambridge University Press, Cambridge, UK (2008)
31. Lake, B., Salakhutdinov, R., Tenenbaum, J.: Human-level concept learning through probabilistic program induction. Science (2015)
32. Black, M.J., Yacoob, Y.: Recognizing facial expressions in image sequences using local parameterized models of image motion. Int. J. Comput. Vis. **25**(1), 23–48 (1997)

Open Access This chapter is licensed under the terms of the Creative Commons Attribution 4.0 International License (http://creativecommons.org/licenses/by/4.0/), which permits use, sharing, adaptation, distribution and reproduction in any medium or format, as long as you give appropriate credit to the original author(s) and the source, provide a link to the Creative Commons license and indicate if changes were made.

The images or other third party material in this chapter are included in the chapter's Creative Commons license, unless indicated otherwise in a credit line to the material. If material is not included in the chapter's Creative Commons license and your intended use is not permitted by statutory regulation or exceeds the permitted use, you will need to obtain permission directly from the copyright holder.

Standard Co-training in Multiword Expression Detection

Senem Kumova Metin[✉]

Department of Software Engineering, Faculty of Engineering,
Izmir University of Economics, Sakarya Caddesi, No. 156, Izmir, Turkey
senem.kumova@ieu.edu.tr

Abstract. Multiword expressions (MWEs) are units in language where multiple words unite without an obvious/known reason. Since MWEs occupy a prominent amount of space in both written and spoken language materials, identification of MWEs is accepted to be an important task in natural language processing.

In this paper, considering MWE detection as a binary classification task, we propose to use a semi-supervised learning algorithm, standard co-training [1] Co-training is a semi-supervised method that employs two classifiers with two different views to label unlabeled data iteratively in order to enlarge the training sets of limited size. In our experiments, linguistic and statistical features that distinguish MWEs from random word combinations are utilized as two different views. Two different pairs of classifiers are employed with a group of experimental settings. The tests are performed on a Turkish MWE data set of 3946 positive and 4230 negative MWE candidates. The results showed that the classifier where statistical view is considered succeeds in MWE detection when the training set is enlarged by co-training.

Keywords: Multiword expression · Classification · Co-training

1 Introduction

A learning machine and/or the task of learning requires experience in other words a training phase to learn. The method to obtain the experience puts the machine learning methods into 3 main categories: supervised, unsupervised and reinforcement learning algorithms. In supervised learning, a labeled data set is given to the machine during training. Following, the machine that gained the ability to label a given sample, may classify the testing samples. In unsupervised learning, the labels of the samples are not provided to the machine in training phase. The machine is expected to learn the structure of samples and varieties in unlabeled sample set and to extract the clusters it self. In reinforcement learning, the machine interacts with the dynamic environment and aims to reach a predefined goal. The training of the machine is provided by the rewards and penalties.

The supervised methods require a sufficient amount of labeled samples for training to achieve in classification of unlabeled data. However, in many problems it is not possible to provide that sufficient amount of labeled samples or preparation of such a

© The Author(s) 2017
P. Horain et al. (Eds.): IHCI 2017, LNCS 10688, pp. 178–188, 2017.
https://doi.org/10.1007/978-3-319-72038-8_14

sample set is over costing. In such cases, the machine may be forced to learn from unlabeled data. This is why, the notion of semi-supervised learning is defined as a halfway between supervised and unsupervised learning [2].

In semi-supervised learning methods, commonly training is performed iteratively. In first iteration, a limited number of labeled samples are given to the machine to learn. After first iteration, the machine labels the unlabeled samples. The samples that are labeled most reliably are added to the labeled set and the machine is re-trained by this enlarged labeled set in next iteration. After a number of iterations, it is accepted that the learning phase is finished and the machine is ready to label unlabeled data set. In other group of semi-supervised methods, some constraints are defined to supervise the training phase [2].

The earliest implementation of semi-supervised learning approach is probably the self-training [2]. In self-training, a single machine, trained by labeled sample set, enlarges its own labeled set iteratively, by labeling the unlabeled set. An alternative method to self-training, co-training, is proposed by Blum and Mitchell [1]. The co-training aims to increase the classification performance by employing two classifiers that considers different views of the data to label the unlabeled samples during training phase. There exist several implementations of the method that are used to solve different problems such as word sense disambiguation [3], semantic role labeling [4], statistical parsing [5], identification of noun phrases [6], opinion detection [7], e-mail classification [8] and sentiment classification [9].

In this study, we examine the effect of co-training in an important natural processing task: multiword expression detection. The notion of multiword expression may be explained in a variety of different ways. Simply, MWEs are word combinations where words unite to build a new syntactical/linguistic or semantic unit in language. Since the words may change their meaning or roles in text while they form MWE, detection of MWEs has a critical role in language understanding and language generation studies. For example, the expression "lady killer" is a MWE meaning "an attractive man". But if the meanings of the composing words are considered individually, the expression refers to something completely different. In MWE detection, it is believed that the links between the composing words of MWEs are stronger than the links between random combinations of words. The strength of these links is measured commonly by statistical and/or linguistics features that may be extracted from the given text or a text collection (e.g. [10–13]).

In a wide group of studies that aim identification of MWEs, the regarding task is accepted as a classification problem and several machine-learning methods are employed. For example, in [13] statistical features are considered together by supervised methods such as linear logistic regression, linear discriminant analysis and neural networks. In [12], multiple linguistically-motivated features are employed in neural networks to identify MWEs in a set of Hebrew bigrams (uninterrupted two word combinations). Several experiments are performed on Turkish data set with linguistics features by 10 different classifiers (e.g. J48, sequential minimization, k nearest neighbor) in [14].

In this study, we aim to examine the performance change in MWE recognition when co-training is employed. The paper is organized as following. We first present the semi-supervised learning and co-training in Sect. 2. In Sect. 3, experimental setup is given. In Sect. 4 results are presented. And the paper is concluded in Sect. 5.

2   Semi-supervised Learning: Co-training

Semi-supervised methods are proposed in order to overcome the disadvantages of supervised learning when there is a lack of sufficient amount of labeled samples. The methods are reported to succeed in some cases when some assumptions such as smoothness, clustering, manifold and transduction hold.

Semi-supervised methods are mainly categorized in four groups: generative, low-density, graph-based models and change of representation [2]. In generative models, the main aim is modeling the class conditional density. Co-training [1] and expected maximization [15] methods are well-known examples of generative models. On the other hand, low-density separation methods such as transductive support vector machine proposed by [16] try to locate decision boundaries in low density regions and away from the unlabeled samples. The methods presented in [17–19] are the examples of graph based methods where each node represents a sample and classification is performed by measuring the distance between nodes. In change of representation approach, a two-stage training is required. Since labeled samples are considered without their labels in the first stage, it is accepted that the representation of samples are changed by this way. In the second stage of training, unlabeled samples are excluded from the data set and supervised learning is performed with the new measure/kernel.

In this study, the semi-supervised method: co-training is implemented to identify MWEs. The co-training algorithm, given in Fig. 1, that will be named as standard co-training is proposed by [1].

Given
- Labeled data set L
- Unlabeled data set U

Repeat until there is no sample in set U:

Train first classifier, $f^{(1)}$, by labelled data set L, using only $x^{(1)}$ features
Train second classifier, $f^{(2)}$, by labelled data set L, using only $x^{(2)}$ features

Label/classify samples of unlabelled data set U by first classifier, $f^{(1)}$.
Label/classify samples of unlabelled data set U by second classifier, $f^{(2)}$.

Insert n number of negative and p number of positive samples that are most confidently labelled by first classifier to the labelled data set L.

Insert n number of negative and p number of positive samples that are most confidently labelled by second classifier to the labelled data set L.

Remove the samples that are inserted to the labelled set from the unlabelled set U.

Fig. 1. Standard co-training algorithm [1]

In standard co-training, the main aim is building a classifier trained by L number of labeled and U number of unlabeled samples where L is known to be a small number. In order to overcome the disadvantage of having a limited number of labeled samples, L, [1] proposed to split the feature vector in two groups of features where each group of features represents a different view of the regarding data set. Each group of features/split/view is used to train one of the classifiers. The assumptions that guarantee the success of co-training are explained as [1]

- Both groups of features (splits/views) must be available for classification.
- Given the label, the feature groups must be conditionally independent for each sample in the data set.

In several studies such as [6, 20], the researchers investigated to what degree these assumptions and the data set size effect the performance of co-training algorithm. For example, experimenting on the same problem mentioned in [1, 20] reported that even if the independency assumption is not satisfied, still co-training performs better than to alternatively proposed expected maximization algorithm since in each iteration all the samples are compared to others to determine the most confidently labeled ones in co-training.

The standard co-training algorithm is implemented to classify web pages in [1]. The first group of features is built by the words in web pages and the second group includes the words in the web links. In both classifiers, Naive Bayes algorithm is used and the tests are performed with $p = 1$ and $n = 3$. In [1], it is reported that the proposed co-training algorithm reaches to higher classification performance compared to supervised machine learning.

3 Experimental Setup

The experiments to examine performance of co-training in MWE detection require the following four tasks to be performed:

1. Two different views (two groups of features) of data set must be determined
2. The classifier pairs must be chosen
3. MWE data set composed of both positive and negative samples must be prepared/selected.
4. Labeled, unlabeled and testing data set sizes must be set.
5. Evaluation measures must be determined.

We propose to use linguistic and statistical features as two different views on MWE data set. In this study, the linguistic view includes 8 linguistic features listed below:

1. *Partial variety in surface forms (PVSF_m and PVSF_n)*: In MWE detection studies, it is commonly accepted that MWEs are not observed in a variety of different surface forms in language. As a result, the histogram presenting the occurrence frequencies of different surface forms belonging to the same MWE is expected to be non-uniform [12]. We measured variety in surface forms in two different ways that are called as *PVSF_m* and *PVSF_n* features based on the surface form histogram,

similar to [12]. Briefly, the Manhattan distance between the actual surface form histogram of the MWE candidate and the possible/expected uniform histogram is employed as $PVSF_{\_m}$. The ratio of $PVSF_{\_m}$ to total occurrence frequency of the candidate (in any form) is accepted as $PVSF_{\_n}$.

2. *Orthographical variety (OV_h and OV_a):* MWEs may hold orthographical changes due to the use of some punctuation marks such as hyphen. For example, expression "e mail" is commonly written as "e-mail". In this study we considered two punctuation marks and employed a Turkish corpus to obtain the feature values. The first punctuation mark is the hyphen. OV_h value is the proportion of the occurrence frequencies of candidate that is formed with a hyphen and without a hyphen. The second orthographical variety feature is OV_a. In this feature, the occurrences of the candidate with and without apostrophe symbol in the second composing word are counted. The ratio of the occurrences with and without apostrophe is employed as OV_a.

3. *Frozen Form:* It is a binary feature that is one if the MWE candidate has a single surface form in corpus and zero other vice.

4. *The ratio of Uppercase Letters:* The feature is simply the ratio of occurrence frequency of MWE candidate where capital letters are used to the total frequency of the candidate in the corpus.

5. *The suffix sequence (SS):* It is expected that a number of suffixes or suffix sequences are to be used with MWEs more than random word/word combinations. In order to determine such suffixes, a set of Turkish idioms is built. The suffixes of length [3 10] (in characters) that are commonly used with the idioms are determined in a Turkish corpus. And *SS* value of the MWE candidate is obtained by comparing the last n characters of the candidate with these suffix sequences. If there exists a match, the number of characters of regarding suffix is employed as *SS* feature value.

6. *Named Entity Words (NEW):* A list of words (3626 words) that are commonly used in Turkish named entities (e.g. personal names, locations, addresses) is prepared to obtain *NEW* feature values. The list includes 5 different categories of named entities. If a composing word of the given MWE candidate is observed in one of these categories, *NEW* value is increased by one. As a result, for each word in MWE candidate, *NEW* value may be increased to five theoretically.

The statistical view includes 18 features (Table 1). These features are known to be commonly used in many studies (e.g. [10, 13, 21]). In Table 1, w_1 and w_2 represent the first and the second word in given MWE candidate, respectively.

In Table 1, $P(w_1w_2)$ is the probability of co-occurrence of two words w_1 and w_2 sequentially. $P(w_1)$ and $P(w_2)$ are the occurrence probabilities of first and the second words. $P(w_i|w_j)$ gives the conditional occurrence probability of the word w_i given that the word w_j is observed. $f(w_1w_2), f(w_1), f(w_2)$ are occurrence frequency of the bigram w_1w_2, and the words w_1 and w_2 respectively. The different number of words following the bigram is represented by $v_f(w_1w_2)$, different number of words preceding and following the bigram is $v_b(w_1w_2)$ and $v_f(w_1w_2)$, respectively.

In this study, the classifiers *SMO* (Sequential Minimal Optimization) [22, 23], *J48* [24] and logistic regression (*Logistic*) [25] are employed in classifier pairs as presented in Table 2. A Turkish MWE data set that includes 8176 samples of MWE candidates

Table 1. Statistical features

Feature	Formula
Bigram-backward variety	$\frac{v_b(w_1w_2)}{f(w_1w_2)}$
Bigram-forward variety	$\frac{v_f(w_1w_2)}{f(w_1w_2)}$
Bigram–word forward variety	$\frac{v_f(w_1w_2)}{v_f(w_2)}$
Fager	$\frac{f(w_1w_2)}{\sqrt{(f(w_1w_2)+f(w_1\bar{w}_2)).(f(w_1w_2)+f(\bar{w}_1w_2))}} - \frac{1}{2}\max(f(w_1\bar{w}_2)f(\bar{w}_1w_2))$
First Kulcznsky	$\frac{f(w_1w_2)}{f(w_1\bar{w}_2)+f(\bar{w}_1w_2)}$
Jaccard	$\frac{f(w_1w_2)}{f(w_1w_2)+f(w_1\bar{w}_2)+f(\bar{w}_1w_2)}$
Joint probability	$P(w_1w_2)$
Mutual dependency	$\log\frac{P(w_1w_2)^2}{P(w_1)P(w_2)}$
Normalized expectation	$\frac{2f(w_1w_2)}{f(w_1)+f(w_2)}$
Neighborhood unpredictability (*NUP*) [11]	$FNUP(w_1w_2) = 1 - \frac{v_f(w_1w_2)-1}{v_f(w_2)-1}$ $BNUP(w_1w_2) = 1 - \frac{v_b(w_1w_2)-1}{v_b(w_1)-1}$ $NUP(w_1w_2) = \sqrt{FNUP(w_1w_2)^2 + BNUP(w_1w_2)^2}$
Point-wise mutual information	$\log\frac{P(w_1w_2)}{P(w_1)P(w_2)}$
Piatersky-Shapiro	$P(w_1w_2) - P(w_1)P(w_2)$
R cost	$\log\left(1+\frac{f(w_1w_2)}{(f(w_1w_2)+f(w_1\bar{w}_2))}\right) + \log\left(1+\frac{f(w_1w_2)}{(f(w_1w_2)+f(\bar{w}_1w_2))}\right)$
S cost	$\log(1+\frac{\min(f(w_1\bar{w}_2),f(\bar{w}_1w_2))}{f(w_1w_2)+1}$
U cost	$\log(1+\frac{\min(f(w_1\bar{w}_2),f(\bar{w}_1w_2))+f(w_1w_2)}{\max(f(w_1\bar{w}_2),f(\bar{w}_1w_2))+f(w_1w_2)}$
Second Kulcznsky	$\frac{1}{2}\left(\frac{f(w_1w_2)}{(f(w_1w_2)+f(w_1\bar{w}_2))} + \frac{f(w_1w_2)}{(f(w_1w_2)+f(\bar{w}_1w_2))}\right)$
Second Sokal-Sneath	$\frac{f(w_1w_2)}{f(w_1w_2)+2(f(w_1\bar{w}_2)+f(\bar{w}_1w_2))}$
Word forward variety	$\frac{v_f(w_2)}{f(w_2)}$

(3946 positive (MWE labeled) and 4230 negative (non MWE labeled)) is utilized in experiments.

Table 3 presents the sizes of labeled (L), unlabeled (U) and test (T) data sets. For example, in experimental setting no 1, 50 samples are used in labeled set, unlabeled set has 250 samples and test size is set as 100.

The evaluation of the classification is performed by F1 measure. F1 measure is given as

$$F1 = \frac{2TP}{2TP + FN + FP} \tag{1}$$

Table 2. Classifier pair

Classifier pair	Linguistics classifier	Statistical classifier
1	*J48*	*Logistic*
2	*SMO*	*SMO*

Table 3. Data sets

Setting no	L (Labeled set size)	U (Unlabeled set size)	T (Test set size)
1	50	250	100
2	100	200	100
3	200	100	100
4	50	700	250
5	100	650	250
6	200	550	250
7	500	250	250
8	50	950	300
9	100	900	300
10	200	800	300
11	500	500	300
12	750	250	300

where *TP* is the number of true positives (candidates that are both expected and predicted to belong to the same class MWE or non-MWE), *FN* is the number of false negatives, *FP* is the number of false positives.

4   Results

The performance of standard co-training, given in Fig. 1, is examined on test settings by repeating the same experiment 5 times (5 runs) for each setting. The numbers of positive (p) and negative samples (n) that will be inserted to the labeled data set in each iteration are set to one. And in each run of the tests, the data set is shuffled to build the labeled L, unlabeled U and test sets randomly. Table 4 gives the average evaluation results of the regarding tests. In Table 4,

- *Fi*, is the average F1 value that is obtained when classifier is trained by the labeled data set L,
- *Fc*, is the average F1 value that is obtained when classifier is trained with enlarged data set (U + L) (the resulting/final training set after co-training),
- *Fs*, is the average F1 value that is obtained when enlarged data set (U + L) is used in training with the actual (not expected) labels of the samples.
- *CP* column includes classifier pairs employed in the study. The first method in *CP* cells is the statistical classifier and the second method represents the linguistic classifier. For example, J48 is statistical and logistic is linguistic classifier.

Table 4. Testing results of standard co-training.

CP	Test/U+L	L	Statistical Classifier Results			Linguistic Classifier Results		
			F_i	F_c	F_s	F_i	F_c	F_s
J48-LOGISTIC	100/300	50	0,50	0,60	0,68	0,59	0,58	0,63
		100	0,58	0,62	0,68	0,60	0,57	0,63
		200	0,63	0,66	0,68	0,61	**0,63**	0,63
	250/750	50	0,52	0,57	0,65	0,61	0,53	0,62
		100	0,57	0,62	0,65	0,60	0,57	0,62
		200	0,55	0,62	0,65	0,60	0,58	0,62
		500	0,61	**0,67**	0,65	0,61	0,61	0,62
	300/1000	50	0,51	0,57	0,65	0,61	0,55	0,62
		100	0,56	0,61	0,65	0,63	0,56	0,62
		200	0,56	0,63	0,65	0,63	0,60	0,62
		500	0,57	**0,66**	0,65	0,63	**0,62**	0,62
		750	0,60	0,64	0,65	0,63	**0,62**	0,62
SMO-SMO	100/300	50	0,50	0,55	0,71	0,60	0,61	0,66
		100	0,56	0,63	0,71	0,63	0,63	0,66
		200	0,63	0,68	0,71	0,66	**0,66**	0,66
	250/750	50	0,52	0,55	0,68	0,63	0,58	0,66
		100	0,56	0,58	0,68	0,64	0,64	0,66
		200	0,56	0,60	0,68	0,66	0,65	0,66
		500	0,62	**0,68**	0,68	0,66	**0,66**	0,66
	300/1000	50	0,52	0,56	0,68	0,64	0,58	0,67
		100	0,55	0,59	0,68	0,65	0,62	0,67
		200	0,56	0,63	0,68	0,67	0,66	0,67
		500	0,57	**0,68**	0,68	0,67	**0,67**	0,67
		750	0,63	**0,69**	0,68	0,67	**0,67**	0,67

The shaded regions in Table 4 show the settings in which $F_i \geq F_c$, meaning that when training set is enlarged with co-training, F1 value increases. It is observed that standard co-training succeeds for all settings in statistical classifier. The cells that hold bold F1 values represent the settings where $F_c \geq F_s$, meaning that the training set that is enlarged by co-training is more successful in supervising the classifier when compared to the same data set with human annotated labels of samples.

Table 5 gives minimum, average and maximum F1 values of both classifiers for three different cases:

1. *Classification (L):* This is the case where labeled set L is employed in training
2. *Standard co-training:* Standard co-training is employed to enlarge the training set size to U + L.
3. *Classification (U + L):* Classifiers are trained by U + L samples that are labeled by human annotators.

Table 5. F1 results with and without co-training.

		Statistical classifier			Linguistic classifier		
	Classifier pair	*Min*	*Ave*	*Max*	*Min*	*Ave*	*Max*
Classification (L)	*J48-Logistic*	0,50	0,56	0,63	0,59	0,61	0,63
	SMO-SMO	0,50	0,57	0,63	0,60	0,65	0,67
Standard Co-training	*J48-Logistic*	0,57	0,62	0,67	0,53	0,59	0,63
	SMO-SMO	0,55	0,62	0,69	0,58	0,64	0,67
Classification (U + L)	*J48-Logistic*	*0,65*	0,66	0,68	0,62	0,62	0,63
	SMO-SMO	*0,68*	0,69	0,71	0,66	0,67	0,67

From Table 5, three important outputs are observed. These are:

1. Standard co-training succeeds in training for both classifier pairs in statistical classifier. On the other hand, it is observed that for linguistic classifier, co-training generates lower/equal F1 values when compared to training with a limited number of samples (L).
2. Overall, *SMO-SMO* classifier pair outperforms *J48-Logistic* classifier pair in terms of average and maximum F1 values.
3. The highest performance in co-training (0.69) is obtained with *SMO-SMO* pair. It is observed that the increase in F1 value reached to an acceptable level (0.69 − 0.63 = 0.06) for this classifier pair.

5   Conclusion

In this study, we present our efforts to improve the performance of MWE detection by the use of standard co-training algorithm. The results showed that especially for the classifier that employs statistical features in classification, performance is improved by co-training. As a further work, we plan to apply different versions of co-training and run the tests with different types of classifiers.

Acknowledgement. This work is carried under the grant of TÜBİTAK – The Scientific and Technological Research Council of Turkey to Project No: 115E469, Identification of Multi-word Expressions in Turkish Texts.

We thank to Mehmet Taze, Hande Aka Uymaz, Erdem Okur and Levent Tolga Eren for their efforts in labeling MWE data set.

References

1. Blum, A., Mitchell, T.: Combining labeled and unlabeled data with co-training. In: Proceedings of the Eleventh Annual Conference on Computational Learning Theory - COLT 1998, pp. 92–100 (1998)
2. Olivier, C., Schölkopf, B., Zien, A.: Semi-Supervised Learning (2006)

3. Mihalcea, R.: Co-training and self-training for word sense disambiguation. In: Language Learning, pp. 182–183 (2003)

4. He, S., Gildea, D.: Self-training and Co-training for Semantic Role Labeling, New York, Primary Report 891, 13 (2006)

5. Sarkar, A.: Applying Co-Training methods to statistical parsing. In: ACL, pp. 175–182 (2001)

6. Pierce, D., Cardie, C.: Limitations of co-training for natural language learning from large datasets. In: Proceedings of the Conference on Empirical Methods in Natural Language Processing, pp. 1–9 (2001)

7. Yu, N.: Exploring co-training strategies for opinion detection. J. Assoc. Inf. Sci. Technol. **65**, 2098–2110 (2014)

8. Kiritchenko, S., Matwin, S.: Email classification with co-training. In: Proceedings of the 2001 Conference on Centre for Advanced Studies on Collaborative Research, pp. 301–312 (2001)

9. Wan, X.: Co-training for cross-lingual sentiment classification (2009)

10. Metin, S.K., Karaoğlan, B.: Collocation extraction in Turkish texts using statistical methods. In: Loftsson, H., Rögnvaldsson, E., Helgadóttir, S. (eds.) NLP 2010. LNCS, vol. 6233, pp. 238–249. Springer, Heidelberg (2010). https://doi.org/10.1007/978-3-642-14770-8_27

11. Metin, S.K.: Neighbour unpredictability measure in multiword expression extraction. Comput. Syst. Sci. Eng. **31**, 209–221 (2016)

12. Tsvetkov, Y., Wintner, S.: Identification of multiword expressions by combining multiple linguistic information sources. Comput. Linguist. **40**, 449–468 (2014)

13. Pecina, P.: A machine learning approach to multiword expression extraction. In: LREC Workshop Towards a Shared Task for Multiword Expressions, pp. 54–61 (2008)

14. Kumova Metin, S., Taze, M., Aka Uymaz, H., Okur, E.: Multiword expression detection in Turkish using linguistic features. In: 25th Signal Processing and Communications Applications Conference, pp. 1–3 (2017)

15. Nigam, K., McCallum, A.K., Thrun, S., Mitchell, T.: Text classification from labeled and unlabeled documents using EM. Mach. Learn. **39**, 103–134 (2000)

16. Vapnik, V.N.: Statistical Learning Theory. Wiley, New York (1998)

17. Szummer, M., Jaakkola, T.: Information regularization with partially labeled data. Adv. Neural. Inf. Process. Syst. **15**, 1049–1056 (2002)

18. Zhu, X., Ghahramani, Z.: Learning from labeled and unlabeled data with label propagation. Neuroscience (2002)

19. Belkin, M., Niyogi, P.: Using manifold structure for partially labelled classification. In: Nips 2002, pp. 271–277 (2002)

20. Nigam, K., Ghani, R.: Analyzing the effectiveness and applicability of co-training. In: Proceedings of the Ninth International Conference on Information and Knowledge Management - CIKM 2000, pp. 86–93 (2002)

21. Metin, S.K., Karaoğlan, B.: Türkiye Türkçesinde Eşdizimlerin İstatistiksel Yöntemlerle Belirlenmesi. J. Soc. Sci. Turkic World. Summer, 253–286 (2016)

22. Platt, J.C.: Sequential Minimal Optimization: A Fast Algorithm for Training Support Vector Machines (1998)

23. Shevade, S.K., Keerthi, S.S., Bhattacharyya, C., Murthy, K.R.K.: Improvements to the SMO algorithm for SVM regression. IEEE Trans. Neural Netw. **11**, 1188–1193 (2000)

24. Quinlan, J.R.: C4.5: Programs for Machine Learning (1992)

25. Tabachnick, B.G., Fidell, L.S.: Using Multivariate Statistics. Allyn & Bacon, Boston (2007)

Open Access This chapter is licensed under the terms of the Creative Commons Attribution 4.0 International License (http://creativecommons.org/licenses/by/4.0/), which permits use, sharing, adaptation, distribution and reproduction in any medium or format, as long as you give appropriate credit to the original author(s) and the source, provide a link to the Creative Commons license and indicate if changes were made.

The images or other third party material in this chapter are included in the chapter's Creative Commons license, unless indicated otherwise in a credit line to the material. If material is not included in the chapter's Creative Commons license and your intended use is not permitted by statutory regulation or exceeds the permitted use, you will need to obtain permission directly from the copyright holder.

Comparative Study on Normalisation in Emotion Recognition from Speech

Ronald Böck[(✉)], Olga Egorow, Ingo Siegert, and Andreas Wendemuth

Cognitive Systems Group, Otto von Guericke University Magdeburg,
Universitätsplatz 2, 39106 Magdeburg, Germany
ronald.boeck@ovgu.de
http://www.cogsy.de

Abstract. The recognition performance of a classifier is affected by various aspects. A huge influence is given by the input data pre-processing. In the current paper we analysed the relation between different normalisation methods for emotionally coloured speech samples deriving general trends to be considered during data pre-processing. From the best of our knowledge, various normalisation approaches are used in the spoken affect recognition community but so far no multi-corpus comparison was conducted. Therefore, well-known methods from literature were compared in a larger study based on nine benchmark corpora, where within each data set a leave-one-speaker-out validation strategy was applied. As normalisation approaches, we investigated standardisation, range normalisation, and centering. These were tested in two possible options: (1) The normalisation parameters were estimated on the whole data set and (2) we obtained the parameters by using emotionally neutral samples only. For classification Support Vector Machines with linear and polynomial kernels as well as Random Forest were used as representatives of classifiers handling input material in different ways. Besides further recommendations we showed that standardisation leads to a significant improvement of the recognition performance. It is also discussed when and how to apply normalisation methods.

1 Introduction

The detection of affective user states is an emerging topic in the context of human-computer interaction (HCI) (cf. [19,24]), as it is known that besides the pure context additional information on the user's feelings, moods, and intentions is transmitted during communication. For instance [1] discussed that such information should be used in HCI for a more general view on the human interlocutor.

The detection of emotions from speech can be seen as a challenging issue since both, the emotions themselves as well as the way humans utter emotions, introduce variations increasing the difficulty of a distinct assessment (cf. [2,24]). Furthermore, many up-to-date classification methods analyse data based on the distances between the given sample points (cf. [24]). As a consequence of the

© The Author(s) 2017
P. Horain et al. (Eds.): IHCI 2017, LNCS 10688, pp. 189–201, 2017.
https://doi.org/10.1007/978-3-319-72038-8_15

aforementioned aspects, a data handling which scales the given samples in a comparable way has to be considered, leading to the question of data normalisation before classification. Yet, there are many approaches for data normalisation available (cf. e.g. [26] pp. 45–49) which are used in various studies.

The paper's aim is to investigate and to compare the different normalisation methods and to deduce in which situation they perform best. Since we were mainly interested in the *general trend* of the recognition results we did not argue on pure classification results, but *derived more general statements*. We are aware that a highly optimised classifier outperforms the systems presented in this paper. Nevertheless, in such cases, it is hard to identify general statements we are looking for. Therefore, the presented analyses are based on six normalising methods, dominantly used in the literature, applied to nine benchmark corpora well-known in the community of speech based emotion recognition.

The investigation is guided by the following research questions: **Q1:** Which normalising methods are usually applied in the community? **Q2:** Which normalisation approach provides the best recognition results? **Q3:** At which point can and shall normalisation be applied to the data? **Q4:** Can we derive recommendations stating which method(s) shall be used to achieve a reasonable improvement in the emotion recognition from speech?

Related Work. Normalisation is a pre-processing step which is applied to given material to handle differences caused by various circumstances. According to our knowledge, no comparison study on different normalisation methods based on several benchmark corpora was conducted for emotion recognition from speech. Nevertheless, various approaches are used in the community which are the foundations of this paper. Furthermore, we found that in the literature a heterogeneous terminology is used (cf. e.g. [15,31]). Therefore, we will use in the following a unique naming of normalisation methods.

In general, two papers present an overview on normalisation: in [26] normalisation techniques in the context of speaker verification are presented. For emotion recognition from speech, we found a rather brief overview in [31], highlighting that the same names often refer to different normalisation approaches.

Regarding the different normalisation techniques, the most prominent version is the standardisation (cf. [31]), although it is often just called normalisation. In most cases, papers refer to z-normalisation (cf. [7,9,16,21,22,25]) and further, to mean-variance-normalisation (cf. [29]).

Range normalisation and centering are, to the best of our knowledge, just used in the work of [15,31]. In [31], the authors applied these methods only on six data sets (a subset of corpora presented in Table 1) considering only two affective states and further, they do not vary the classifier.

Another approach highlighted in [15] is the normalisation based on neutral data. This idea is invented in [3], and further elaborated in [4]. In [15], the authors apply this approach on all three presented normalisation methods. As this is a promising approach keeping the differences between various affective states (cf. [3]), we included it in our experiments as well.

Several papers like [11, 24, 30] do not use any normalisation at all. This practice is related to the statement that "[f]unctionals provide a sort of normalisation over time" [24], assuming that normalisation is implicitely provided by the selected features mainly based on functionals.

In general, the presented works vary in approaches of normalisation, classification techniques, and utilised corpora. Therefore, a direct comparison of results is quite difficult for readers. The closest related papers for comparison are [21, 31], as they refer to subsets of the benchmark corpora we analysed. Otherwise, as we were interested in the general characteristics of the normalising methods, we thus did not opt on fully optimised recognition results.

2 Data Sets

This study is focussed on the influence of normalisation approaches on the classification performance. Therefore, we decided to apply the various methods described in the literature to data sets widely used in the community. To cover various characteristics in the experiments, the corpora provide material in various languages, speaker ages and sexes as well as different emotional classes. Further, the material is recorded under different conditions reflecting acted and spontaneous (acoustic) expressions. The individual characteristics of each data set are presented in Table 1 and will be briefly introduced[1] in the following.

Table 1. Overview of the selected emotional speech corpora characteristics including information on number of classes (# C.) and if the corpus provides material for neutral speech (Neu.).

Corpus	Content	Samples	Subjects	Emo.	# C.	Neu.	HH:MM
ABC	German fixed	431	8 (4 f)	acted	6	x	01:15
AVIC	English variable	3 002	21 (10 f)	spont.	3	–	01:47
DES	Danish fixed	419	4 (2 f)	acted	5	x	00:28
emoDB	German fixed	492	10 (5 f)	acted	7	x	00:22
eNTERFACE	English fixed	1 277	42 (8 f)	acted	6	–	01:00
SAL	English variable	1 692	4 (2 f)	spont.	4	–	01:41
SmartKom	German variable	3 823	79 (47 f)	spont.	7	x	07:08
SUSAS	English fixed	3 593	7 (3 f)	spont. + act.	4	x	01:01
VAM	German variable	946	47 (32 f)	spont.	4	–	00:47

The *Airplane Behaviour Corpus (ABC)* (cf. [23]) is developed for applications related to public transport surveillance. Certain moods were induced using a predefined script, guiding subjects through a storyline. Eight speakers – balanced in sex – aged from 25–48 years (mean 32 years) took part in the recording. The 431 clips have an average duration of 8.4 s presenting six emotions.

---

[1] The explaining text for each corpus is inspired by [27].

The *Audiovisual Interest Corpus* (AVIC) (cf. [20]) contains samples of interest. The scenario setup is as follows: A product presenter leads each of the 21 subjects (ten female) through an English commercial presentation. The level of interest is annotated for every sub-speaker turn.

The *Danish Emotional Speech (DES)* (cf. [8]) data set contains samples of five acted emotions. The data used in the experiments are Danish sentences, words, and chunks expressed by four professional actors (two females) which were judged according to emotion categories afterwards.

The *Berlin Emotional Speech Database (emoDB)* (cf. [2]) is a studio recorded corpus. Ten (five female) professional actors utter ten German sentences with emotionally neutral content. The resulting 492 phrases were selected using a perception test and contain in seven predefined categories of acted emotional expressions (cf. [2]).

The *eNTERFACE* (cf. [18]) corpus comprises recordings from 42 subjects (eight female) from 14 nations. It consists of office environment recordings of pre-defined spoken content in English. Overall, the data set consists of 1277 emotional instances in six induced emotions. The quality of emotional content spans a much broader variety than in emoDB.

The *Belfast Sensitive Artificial Listener (SAL)* (cf. [6]) corpus contains 25 audio-visual recordings from four speakers (two female). The depicted HCI-system were recorded using an interface designed to let users work through a continuous space of emotional states. In our experiments we used a clustering provided by [21] mapping the original arousal-valence space into 4 quadrants.

The *SmartKom* (cf. [28]) multi-modal corpus provides spontaneous speech including seven natural emotions in German and English given a Wizard-of-Oz setting. For our experiments, we used only the German part.

The *Speech Under Simulated and Actual Stress* (SUSAS) (cf. [14]) dataset contains spontaneous and acted emotional samples, partly masked by field noise. We chose a corpus' subset providing 3593 actual stress speech segments recorded in speaker motion fear and stress tasks. Seven subjects (three female) in roller coaster and free fall stress situations utter emotionally coloured speech in four categories.

The *Vera-Am-Mittag* (VAM) corpus consists of audio-visual recordings taken from a unscripted German TV talk show (cf. [12]). The employed subset includes 946 spontaneous and emotionally utterances from 47 participants. We transformed the continuous emotion labels into four quadrants according to [21].

3   Normalising Methods

We reviewed the literature according to normalisation methods utilised in speech based emotion recognition and found four main approaches, but no direct comparison amongst them. Furthermore, it can be seen that the utilised methods are named differently by various authors although employing the same approaches. Therefore, we structured the methods and harmonised the naming.

Generally, we defined x as the input value representing, for instance, a speech feature, μ as the corresponding mean value, and σ as the corresponding variance.

Standardisation is an approach to transform the input material to obtain standard normally distributed data ($\mu = 0$ and $\sigma = 1$). The method is computed as given in Eq. 1.

$$x_s = \frac{x - \mu}{\sigma} \tag{1}$$

Range Normalisation is also called normalisation and is thus often confused with common standardisation. Therefore, we chose the term *range normalisation* that implies the possibility to vary the transformation interval. In Eq. 2 the interval is specified by $[a, b]$ and further x_{min} and x_{max} are the minimal and maximal values per feature. In contrast to standardisation (cf. Eq. 1) the mean and variance are not used by the approach.

$$x_n = a + \frac{(x - x_{min})(b - a)}{x_{max} - x_{min}} \tag{2}$$

In our experiments we chose the interval $[-1, 1]$ for range normalisation.

The *Centering* approach frees the given input data from the corresponding mean (cf. Eq. 3). Therefore, the transformation results in a shift of input data.

$$x_c = x - \mu \tag{3}$$

Neutral Normalisation is an approach where normalisation parameters are computed based on neutral data, only. It is described in [4], and a logical extension of the idea to use neutral speech models for emotion classification (cf. [3]). Neutral normalisation is used for normalisation purpose in [15]. The methods works as follows: The parameters μ and σ or x_{min} and x_{max}, respectively, for each feature are obtained based on the samples annotated as neutral and are further applied on samples with other emotional impressions. In our experiments this was done separately for each aforementioned normalisation method, namely standardisation, range normalisation, and centering.

Application of normalisation methods is as follows: The described normalising methods were applied to the training material as well as to the testing samples. For the test set two practices are possible and both were examined in our experiments. The first option assumed that both sets are known. Therefore, each set can be normalised separately, where accordingly optimal parameters (i.e. μ and σ, for instance) were used. In the second option, the necessary parameters were extracted only on the training set and applied to the testing set. In this case, it is assumed that the test samples are unknown, and thus no parameter estimation can be previously operated.

4   Experimental Setup

To evaluate the influence of normalisation, we conducted a series of classification experiments. Since one of our objectives was to obtain *reproducible* results comparable to other studies, we decided to employ established feature sets and classifiers.

The *emobase* feature set is well-known in the community of emotion recognition from speech. This set comprises 988 functionals (e.g. mean, minimum, maximum, etc.) based on acoustic low-level descriptors (e.g. pitch, mel-frequency cepstral coefficients, line spectral pairs, fundamental frequency, etc.) [10]. The features are extracted on utterance level, resulting in one vector per utterance.

We decided to employ two different kinds of *classifiers*: the distance-based Support Vector Machine (SVM) and the non-distance-based Random Forest (RF). We expected that normalisation would provide significant improvement if using SVM, and no or only little improvement if using RF. For SVM, we used the LibSVM implementation developed by [5] implemented in WEKA [13]. For RF, we also rely on WEKA.

Since the data sets used in the experiments are very diverse, it would be difficult to impossible to fine-tune the classifiers to fit all the data. Therefore, we decided to use standard parameters for both, SVM and RF, without further fine-tuning. In the case of SVM, we chose a linear kernel (referred to as lin-SVM) and a polynomial kernel with a degree of 3 (referred to as pol-SVM), both with cost parameter $C = 1.0$. In the case of RF, we used 32 features per node, as the square root of the number of input features (in our case 988) is often used as default value in different RF implementations, and 1000 trees.

We evaluated the classifiers in a Leave-One-Speaker-Out (LOSO) manner, using the Unweighted Average Recall (UAR) of all emotions per speaker as evaluation metric.

5   Results

Figure 1 shows the results at a glance for lin-SVM on two of the nine investigated corpora (ABC and eNTERFACE). For the ABC corpus, we could see that some normalising methods such as standardisation performed better than others for nearly all speakers. For the eNTERFACE corpus, we see that the performance of the same normalising method varies remarkably depending on the speaker.

Table 2. Classification results (UAR, averaged over all nine corpora, in %) for all normalising methods (NN - non-normalised, S(-neu) - standardisation (with neutral), RN(-neu) - range normalisation (with neutral), C(-neu) - centering (with neutral)). The best classification result is highlighted for each classifier.

	NN	S	RN	C	S-neu	RN-neu	C-neu	Mean (w/o NN)
UAR for lin-SVM	39.1	49.6	45.9	38.7	47.3	45.1	32.6	43.2 ± 6.4
UAR for pol-SVM	37.4	40.1	22.9	33.5	42.9	27.4	30.3	32.9 ± 7.6
UAR for RF	44.9	47.5	43.2	46.1	45.5	43.2	45.2	45.1 ± 1.7

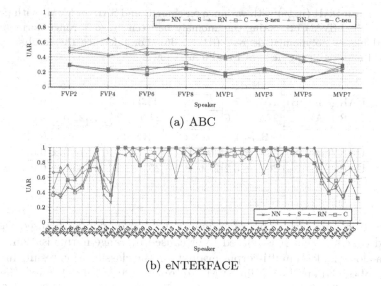

(a) ABC

(b) eNTERFACE

Fig. 1. UAR per speaker in (a) ABC and (b) eNTERFACE for lin-SVM.

In Table 2, the results are shown in a more detailed way, comparing the mean UAR, averaged over all nine corpora for all normalising methods and classifiers. For two of the three classifiers, standardisation outperformed other methods – and in the case of lin-SVM, neutral standardisation worked even better. Also, we see that standardisation and neutral standardisation were the only two normalising methods that always led to an improvement of the classification results.

An interesting point could be found by looking at the mean and standard deviation of all normalising methods presented in Table 2: For both SVM classifiers, normalising data in any kind changed the results (on average, $+4.1\%$ for lin-SVM and -4.5% for pol-SVM, absolute) more than in the case of RF (only 0.2%). There were also noticeable differences between the normalising methods, resulting in a higher standard deviation for both SVM classifiers compared to RF. Both observations support our hypothesis that in the case of SVM, changing the distance between data points by applying any normalising method would influence the classification results, whereas in the case of RF, normalisation would not change the classification results significantly.

There is another interesting point concerning the results using pol-SVM: Applying range normalisation significantly impairs the classification, leading to an UAR drop of 14.5% absolute. Our hypothesis concerning this phenomenon was that there is a non-linear effect induced by the combination of the polynomial kernel and high-dimensional data. To investigate this phenomenon, we conducted a series of additional experiments using polynomial kernels of increasing degrees. The results are shown in Table 3. We could see that the increasing degree of the kernel led to a drop in performance – for higher degrees the performance

Table 3. Mean UAR (in %) with variance on emoDB and SAL for SVMs with polynomial kernel (pol-SVM) presenting the anomaly between usage of range normalisation (RN) and higher polynomial degrees (d1 ... d6). For reference the results on non-normalised material using degrees 1 and 6 are shown.

	NN-d1	...	NN-d3	...	NN-d6
UAR (emoDB)	47.7 ± 7.4	...	45.3 ± 8.3	...	37.5 ± 6.1
UAR (SAL)	27.2 ± 1.6	...	24.9 ± 2.7	...	25.5 ± 2.3

	RN-d1	RN-d2	RN-d3	...	RN-d6
UAR (emoDB)	55.0 ± 7.5	20.0 ± 2.1	14.3 ± 0.0	...	14.3 ± 0.0
UAR (SAL)	30.5 ± 6.2	25.6 ± 0.6	25.0 ± 0.1	...	25.0 ± 0.0

decreases to chance level. This effect does not occur on non-normalised data, so we could conclude that it is related to or caused by range normalisation.

For a closer look on multi-corpus evaluation, the classification results in terms of UAR, obtained employing lin-SVM, are presented in Table 4. Since the data was not normally distributed, we executed the Mann-Whitney-U-Test (cf. [17]) to calculate significance for all classification outcomes. For five of the nine corpora, the improvements of normalised over non-normalised data were statistically significant ($p < 0.1$). But even for the cases where the improvements were not significant, normalising data led to at least some improvements: For all corpora except SAL, standardisation or standardisation on neutral data achieves the best results (cf. Table 4). In the case of SAL, range normalisation achieved the best results – but is only 0.2% better than standardisation. Otherwise, using inappropriate normalising methods could also impair the results. For example, in the case of AVIC, eNTERFACE, and SUSAS, all normalising methods except for standardisation led to minor decreases, although not statistically significant.

Table 4. Results achieved (UAR in %) using lin-SVM on normalised data and non-normalised baseline. Best results are highlighted gray, results below the baseline are given in *italic*. Significance levels: [***]p < 0.01, [**]p < 0.05, [*]p < 0.1

UAR	NN	S	RN	C	S-neu	RN-neu	C-neu
ABC	23.2	44.4***	43.9***	23.6	45.6***	42.1**	*21.8*
AVIC	46.6	47.5	*44.2*	*45.5*			
DES	30.3	50.5*	41.0	30.3	47.5*	44.2*	*27.4*
emoDB	47.4	77.2***	75.6***	51.4	72.4***	70.6***	48.9
eNTERFACE	81.9	89.3	*78.3*	*76.5*			
SAL	23.8	31.2	31.4	25.6			
SmartKom	16.5	19.0*	16.8	16.6	19.1*	17.4	*16.2*
SUSAS	53.4	54.4	52.0	50.4	52.0	*51.3*	*48.7*
VAM	28.6	32.5*	30.4	*28.1*			

Concerning normalising training and test set either using independently calculated parameters or using parameters calculated on both data sets, we could state that there is no significant difference in terms of UAR. There were some fluctuations in the results depending on the considered corpus, but the differences occurred in both directions and did not show a trend towards one option, and they were within the standard deviation. For example, in the case of AVIC, the maximum difference in the UAR achieved using independent versus combined parameters is 1.5% in favour of the former – with a standard deviation of 6.6% and 8.3% for independently and non-independently calculated normalisation parameters, respectively.

6 Discussion

In the current section the experimental results (cf. Sect. 5) are reflected considering the questions Q1 to Q4.

For question Q1, we analyse various works reflecting the state-of-the-art in the community (cf. Sect. 1). From these, we find that mainly two different approaches are used, namely standardisation and (range) normalisation. Less frequently centering is applied to data sets for normalisation purposes. Further, as presented in [3], the normalisation parameters can also be estimated based on emotionally neutral samples. This is tested in our experiments as well. We also find a slight trend towards standardisation in the literature.

Given this overview, we select the three most prominent methods for the experiments, namely standardisation, range normalisation, and centering (cf. Sect. 3). Further, they are also applied in the context of neutral normalisation if possible. Based on our results, the aforementioned trend towards standardisation is valid, since for eight benchmark corpora (cf. Table 1) standardisation produces an improvement in the recognition performance. The same statement holds for neutral normalisation, where standardisation shows the best performance as well (cf. question Q2). In our experiments we apply the LOSO validation strategy. Therefore, we have the opportunity to analyse the recognition performance in a speaker-independent way. As shown in Fig. 1 for ABC and eNTERFACE, the recognition results depend on the speaker to be tested. Of course, this effect is seen on the other corpora as well. Nevertheless, we find a relation between normalisation methods and the performance. For corpora containing mainly acted speech samples, a clustering of particular normalisation methods can be seen (cf. the gap between lines in Fig. 1(a)). In contrast for data sets providing more spontaneous emotions such clustering is not feasible. Further, the different methods are closer to each other in absolute numbers (cf. Fig. 1(b)). From our point of view, this is related to the lower expressivity of emotions uttered in spontaneous conversations, and hence, no particular normalisation approach is able to improve the recognition performance. As presented in Table 4, we can conclude that standardisation provides the best results across the nine benchmark corpora. In the case of SAL, range normalisation outperforms standardisation by 0.2%, absolute, only. Based on the Mann-Whitney-U-Test, we show that the improvement of recognition performance is significant for five corpora (at least $p < 0.1$). For this, we test the significance against the non-normalised classification as well as against the second best results if the difference is low (cf. e.g. SmartKom in Table 4). This statistical significance emphasises the importance of suitable normalisation during the classification process.

Regarding the question how the normalisation shall be applied (cf. Q3), we tested two possible options: For the first one, the test set is normalised independently from the training set, for the second one, we normalise the test set using parameters obtained on the training set. The final results show that the differences in the recognition results are marginal with no statistical significance for either method. Therefore, both options are useful for testing purposes, and thus there is no need to refrain from using separately normalised test samples.

From our experiments, we can derive some recommendations for the application of normalisation approaches (cf. question Q4). First, in a multi-corpus evaluation based on a LOSO strategy standardisation is reasonable since in most cases (six of nine) this leads to a (significant) improvement of classification performances. This is also an indicator that normalisation improves even classification results based on feature sets mainly consisting of functionals (cf. *emobase* in Sect. 4). From our perspective this levels the statement of [24] that functionals already provide a kind of normalisation. Secondly, there is no need to favour either handling approach for test sets as no statistical significance in the differences in performance can be seen. Finally, the classifier influences the effect obtained by normalisation as well. From Tables 2 and 3 we can see that lin-SVM achieved better results than the other two classifiers across corpora. For RF, it was expected that normalisation has almost no influence since the classification is not distance based, resulting in lower standard deviations across corpora (cf. Table 2). In contrast, pol-SVM collapses with higher degrees (cf. Table 3), especially in the case of using range normalisation. We assume that this is related to a non-linear effect between the polynomial degree and the normalisation method. This will be further elaborated in future research.

7   Conclusion

In this paper, we have shown that normalising data in emotion recognition from speech tasks can lead to significant improvements. The extent of these improvements depends on three factors – these are the *general trends* we already discussed in Sect. 1. First of all, we have shown that standardisation works best in almost all cases: Applying it improved the recognition results for all nine corpora, for six corpora it proved to be the best normalising method. Secondly, the results depend on the used classifier: We have shown that, using lin-SVM, significant improvements are possible when applying standardisation as well as range normalisation. But for pol-SVM, range normalisation does not work well. The final factor is the data itself: For some corpora such as emoDB, improvements of up to 30% absolute are possible, for other corpora like SmartKom, only slight improvements of less than 3% absolute are achieved. From these findings we can conclude that standardisation in most cases leads to substantially improved classification results.

Acknowledgments. We acknowledge continued support by the Transregional Collaborative Research Centre SFB/TRR 62 "Companion-Technology for Cognitive Technical Systems" (www.sfb-trr-62.de) funded by the German Research Foundation (DFG). Further, we thank the project "Mod3D" (grant number: 03ZZ0414) funded by 3Dsensation (www.3d-sensation.de) within the Zwanzig20 funding program by the German Federal Ministry of Education and Research (BMBF).

References

1. Biundo, S., Wendemuth, A.: Companion-technology for cognitive technical systems. KI - Künstliche Intelligenz **30**(1), 71–75 (2016)
2. Burkhardt, F., Paeschke, A., Rolfes, M., Sendlmeier, W., Weiss, B.: A database of German emotional speech. In: INTERSPEECH-2005, pp. 1517–1520, Lisbon, Portugal (2005)
3. Busso, C., Lee, S., Narayanan, S.S.: Using neutral speech models for emotional speech analysis. In: INTERSPEECH-2007, pp. 2225–2228. ISCA, Antwerp, Belgium (2007)
4. Busso, C., Metallinou, A., Narayanan, S.S.: Iterative feature normalization for emotional speech detection. In: Proceedings of the ICASSP 2011, pp. 5692–5695. IEEE, Prague, Czech Republic (2011)
5. Chang, C.C., Lin, C.J.: LIBSVM: A library for support vector machines. ACM Trans. Intell. Syst. Technol. (TIST) **2**, 1–27 (2011)
6. Douglas-Cowie, E., Cowie, R., Cox, C., Amier, N., Heylen, D.: The sensitive artificial listner: an induction technique for generating emotionally coloured conversation. In: LREC Workshop on Corpora for Research on Emotion and Affect, pp. 1–4. ELRA, Paris, France (2008)
7. El Ayadi, M., Kamel, M.S., Karray, F.: Survey on speech emotion recognition: Features, classification schemes, and databases. Pattern Recogn. **44**(3), 572–587 (2011)
8. Engbert, I.S., Hansen, A.V.: Documentation of the Danish emotional speech database DES. Technical report Center for PersonKommunikation, Aalborg University, Denmark (2007)
9. Eyben, F., Scherer, K., Schuller, B., Sundberg, J., Andre, E., Busso, C., Devillers, L., Epps, J., Laukka, P., Narayanan, S., Truong, K.: The geneva minimalistic acoustic parameter set (GeMAPS) for voice research and affective computing. IEEE Trans. Affect. Comput. **7**(2), 190–202 (2016)
10. Eyben, F., Wöllmer, M., Schuller, B.: Opensmile - the munich versatile and fast open-source audio feature extractor. In: Proceedings of the MM-2010, pp. 1459–1462. ACM, Firenze, Italy (2010)
11. Eyben, F., Batliner, A., Schuller, B., Seppi, D., Steidl, S.: Cross-corpus classification of realistic emotions - some pilot experiments. In: LREC Workshop on Emotion: Corpora for Research on Emotion and Affect, pp. 77–82. ELRA, Valetta, Malta (2010)
12. Grimm, M., Kroschel, K., Narayanan, S.: The vera am mittag German audiovisual emotional speech database. In: Proceedings of ICME 2008, pp. 865–868. IEEE, Hannover, Germany (2008)

13. Hall, M., Frank, E., Holmes, G., Pfahringer, B., Reutemann, P., Witten, I.H.: The WEKA data mining software: an update. ACM SIGKDD Explor. Newsl. **11**(1), 10–18 (2009)
14. Hansen, J., Bou-Ghazale, S.: Getting started with SUSAS: A speech under simulated and actual stress database. In: Proceedings of EUROSPEECH-1997, vol. 4, pp. 1743–1746. ISCA, Rhodes, Greece (1997)
15. Lefter, I., Nefs, H.T., Jonker, C.M., Rothkrantz, L.J.M.: Cross-corpus analysis for acoustic recognition of negative interactions. In: Proceedings of the ACII 2015, pp. 132–138. IEEE, Xi'an, China (2015)
16. Lefter, I., Rothkrantz, L.J.M., Wiggers, P., van Leeuwen, D.A.: Emotion recognition from speech by combining databases and fusion of classifiers. In: Sojka, P., Horák, A., Kopeček, I., Pala, K. (eds.) TSD 2010. LNCS (LNAI), vol. 6231, pp. 353–360. Springer, Heidelberg (2010). https://doi.org/10.1007/978-3-642-15760-8_45
17. Mann, H.B., Whitney, D.R.: On a test of whether one of two random variables is stochastically larger than the other. Ann. Math. Stat. **18**(1), 50–60 (1947)
18. Martin, O., Kotsia, I., Macq, B., Pitas, I.: The eNTERFACE'05 audio-visual emotion database. In: Proceedings of the Workshop on Multimedia Database Management. IEEE, Atlanta, USA (2006)
19. Picard, R.: Affective Computing. MIT Press, Cambridge (2000)
20. Schuller, B., Müller, R., Hörnler, B., Höthker, A., Konosu, H., Rigoll, G.: Audiovisual recognition of spontaneous interest within conversations. In: Proceedings of the 9th ICMI, pp. 30–37. ACM, Nagoya, Japan (2007)
21. Schuller, B., Vlasenko, B., Eyben, F., Rigoll, G., Wendemuth, A.: Acoustic emotion recognition: A benchmark comparison of performances. In: Proceedings of the ASRU 2009, pp. 552–557. IEEE, Merano, Italy (2009)
22. Schuller, B., Vlasenko, B., Eyben, F., Wöllmer, M., Stuhlsatz, A., Wendemuth, A., Rigoll, G.: Cross-corpus acoustic emotion recognition: Variances and strategies. IEEE Trans. Affect. Comput. **1**(2), 119–131 (2010)
23. Schuller, B., Arsic, D., Rigoll, G., Wimmer, M., Radig, B.: Audiovisual behavior modeling by combined feature spaces. In: Proceedings of the ICASSP-2007, pp. 733–736. IEEE, Honolulu, USA (2007)
24. Schuller, B., Batliner, A., Steidl, S., Seppi, D.: Recognising realistic emotions and affect in speech: State of the art and lessons learnt from the first challenge. Speech Commun. **53**(9–10), 1062–1087 (2011)
25. Schuller, B., Zhang, Z., Weninger, F., Rigoll, G.: Selecting training data for cross-corpus speech emotion recognition: Prototypicality vs. generalization. In: Proceeeings of the Afeka-AVIOS Speech Processing Conference, Tel Aviv, Israel (2011)
26. Schwartz, R., Kubala, F.: Hidden markov models and speaker adaptation. In: Laface, P., De Mori, R. (eds.) Speech Recognition and Understanding: Recent Advances, Trends and Applications, pp. 31–57. Springer, Heidelberg (1992)
27. Siegert, I., Böck, R., Vlasenko, B., Wendemuth, A.: Exploring dataset similarities using PCA-based feature selection. In: Proceedings of the ACII 2015, pp. 387–393. IEEE, Xi'an, China (2015)
28. Steininger, S., Schiel, F., Dioubina, O., Raubold, S.: Development of user-state conventions for the multimodal corpus in smartkom. In: Proceedings of the Workshop on Multimodal Resources and Multimodal Systems Evaluation, pp. 33–37. ELRA, Las Palmas, Spain (2002)
29. Tahon, M., Devillers, L.: Towards a small set of robust acoustic features for emotion recognition: challenges. IEEE/ACM Trans. Audio Speech Lang. Process. **24**(1), 16–28 (2016)

30. Tahon, M., Devillers, L.: Acoustic measures characterizing anger across corpora collected in artificial or natural context. In: Proceedings of the 5th International Conference on Speech Prosody. ISCA, Chicago, USA (2010)
31. Zhang, Z., Weninger, F., Wöllmer, M., Schuller, B.W.: Unsupervised learning in cross-corpus acoustic emotion recognition. In: Nahamoo, D., Picheny, M. (eds.) Proceedings of the ASRU 2011, pp. 523–528. IEEE, Waikoloa, HI, USA (2011)

Open Access This chapter is licensed under the terms of the Creative Commons Attribution 4.0 International License (http://creativecommons.org/licenses/by/4.0/), which permits use, sharing, adaptation, distribution and reproduction in any medium or format, as long as you give appropriate credit to the original author(s) and the source, provide a link to the Creative Commons license and indicate if changes were made.

The images or other third party material in this chapter are included in the chapter's Creative Commons license, unless indicated otherwise in a credit line to the material. If material is not included in the chapter's Creative Commons license and your intended use is not permitted by statutory regulation or exceeds the permitted use, you will need to obtain permission directly from the copyright holder.

Detecting Vigilance in People Performing Continual Monitoring Task

Shabnam Samima[1](✉), Monalisa Sarma[1], and Debasis Samanta[2]

[1] Subir Chowdhury School of Quality and Reliability,
Indian Institute of Technology Kharagpur, Kharagpur, West Bengal, India
{shabnam.samima,monalisa}@iitkgp.ac.in
[2] Department of Computer Science and Engineering,
Indian Institute of Technology Kharagpur, Kharagpur, West Bengal, India
Debasis.samanta.iitkgp@gmail.com

Abstract. Vigilance or sustained attention is an extremely important aspect in monotonous and prolonged attention seeking tasks. Recently, Event Related Potentials (ERPs) of Electroencephalograph (EEG) have garnered great attention from the researchers for their application in the task of vigilance assessment. However, till date the studies related to ERPs and their association with vigilance are in their nascent stage, and requires more rigorous research efforts. In this paper, we use P200 and N200 ERPs of EEG for studying vigilance. For this purpose, we perform Mackworth's clock test experiment with ten volunteers and measure their accuracy. From the measured accuracy and recorded EEG signals, we identify that amplitude of P200 and N200 ERPs is directly correlated with accuracy and thereby to vigilance task. Thus, both P200 and N200 ERPs can be applied to detect vigilance (in real-time) of people involved in continuous monitoring tasks.

Keywords: Vigilance detection · Attention monitoring · Human errors
Brain computing interface · Event related potential · EEG signals

1 Introduction

According to Mackworth, "Vigilance is defined as a state of readiness to detect and respond to small changes occurring at random time intervals in the environment" [1]. In other words, vigilance or sustained attention is an act of careful observation of critical or rare events whose negligence may lead to catastrophe [2]. In today's world, where emphasis is laid on reducing risks and errors, and mitigating the chances of accidents, it seems rational to assess the operator vigilance in real time to avoid human errors. Air traffic control, drowsiness detection in drivers, inspection and quality control, automated navigation, military and border surveillance, life-guarding, cyber operations, space exploration, etc., [3], are some major domains where operators are involved in monotonous tasks for prolonged intervals of time and remaining vigilant is an utmost requirement.

© The Author(s) 2017
P. Horain et al. (Eds.): IHCI 2017, LNCS 10688, pp. 202–214, 2017.
https://doi.org/10.1007/978-3-319-72038-8_16

However, in [4,5], it has been pointed that sleep deprivation, work overload, stress, time pressure, drowsiness and prolonged working hours are the major factors that lead to low vigilance, thereby, human errors.

Till date several concerted efforts have been made in the literature to propose and design new techniques of vigilance detection with the help of features like, heart rate variability [6], galvanic skin response [6], pupil diameter, eye blink frequency [3] and brain activity measurement [7–9] (namely, EEG (Electroencephalogram), MEG (Magnetoencephalogram), fNIRS (functional near infrared spectroscopy), ECoG (electrocorticogram), fMRI (functional magnetic resonance imaging), etc.). Although, the techniques mentioned above are good contender for vigilance detection, yet, they have several serious limitations associated with them. For instance, eye related features show strong inter-personal and intra-personal variability, EEG suffers from poor spatial resolution, MEG requires special operating environment for its functioning, ECoG involves implantation of electrodes in an invasive manner, fMRI is associated with high equipment overhead and fNIRS suffers from low spatial resolution.

Amongst the above-mentioned methods, designed for vigilance detection, EEG is the most commonly studied physiological measure despite of its poor spatial resolution. The prime reasons behind its tremendous popularity amongst researchers are: (1) its high time resolution, (2) its non-invasive nature and simplicity of operation and (3) relatively cheap cost compared to other devices. Furthermore, as vigilance deteriorates with time it seems plausible to study the brain signals in time bound fashion to assess the vigilance status in real-time. In this regard, the Event Related Potentials (ERPs) present in the EEG signals have successfully been utilized to study the changes occurring in the human brain with passing time [10]. For instance, ERP features namely P100-N200 have been utilized for studying emotional information processing in [11]; frontal midline theta and N200 ERP have been shown to reflect complementary information about expectancy and outcome evaluation in [12]; in [13] authors utilized N200 ERP for word recognition; in [14], N100, P200, N200 and P300 ERP components have been used to study the impact of depression on attention. Further, ERPs have also been used for understanding reaction times in response to pictures of people depicting pain [15]; in [16] ERPs have been utilized to understand the state of brain in schizophrenia patients; in [17] authors demonstrated the association of mMMN, P200 and P500 ERP components with artificial grammar learning in the primate brain; in [18], N400 and the P200 components have been utilized in the investigation of semantic and phonological processing in skilled and less-skilled comprehenders; besides, ERPs have also found utility in studying multisensory integration (MSI) ability of the brain in school-aged children [19].

From the above literature, we observe that P200 and N200 ERPs (see Fig. 1) have been instrumental in studying cognitive behaviour of humans and is prospective for real-time assessment of vigilance. Here, concisely P200 ERP refers to a positive spike in EEG signals which is generally observed within 150 to 250 ms after the exhibition of a target stimulus (auditory or visual event) [20], while N200 is a negative potential usually evoked between 180 to 325 ms after the presentation of a specific visual or auditory stimulus following a string of standard (non-target) stimuli [21,22]. In general, P200 latency is a measure of stimulus classification speed and its amplitude represents the amount of attentional resources devoted to the task along with the required degree of information processing, whereas N200 ERP, which is usually evoked only during conscious stimulus attention before the motor response, is helpful in stimulus identification and distinction, thereby suggesting its link to the cognitive processes.

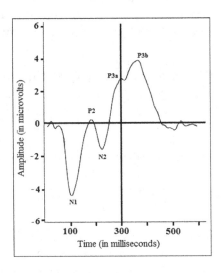

Fig. 1. P200 and N200 components in ERP signal of EEG data

In this work we propose (a) to use N200 and P200 ERPs for studying vigilance, (b) observe the correlation of N200 and P200 ERPs with behavioural accuracy obtained, (c) observe the variation in the amplitude of both N200 and P200 ERPs under the presence of target and non-target stimuli, (d) observe the variation in the active areas of the brain before, during and after the experiment and check whether the hotspots are present in the areas from which P200 and N200 evoke.

2   Proposed Methodology

In the following, we present our proposed research methodology and steps for extracting ERPs (P200 and N200) from the EEG signals.

2.1   Experimental Setup

Subjects: Ten healthy, right handed participants with normal or corrected-to-normal vision, aged between 26 to 33 years volunteered for the experiment (see Table 1). To carefully monitor the vigilance of each volunteer, a proper schedule was maintained. It was ensured that the participants: (a) were not sleep deprived, (b) were under no medication and (c) had no history of mental illness. We also took written consent from each participant, which was approved by the institution's ethical committee, before conducting the experiment. Further, we asked each volunteer to do not consume tea or coffee 3 to 4 h prior to the experiment. Keeping in mind the usual circadian cycle of activeness of each participant, the experiment was conducted in the morning, that is between 7 am and 10 am.

Table 1. Participant details

Participant ID.	P1	P2	P3	P4	P5	P6	P7	P8	P9	P10
Age	31	33	26	29	29	29	28	27	29	28
Gender	M	M	M	M	M	M	M	F	F	M
Sleep duration (in hours)	~8	~8	12	~6	~6	~7	7	6	7	7

Vigilance Task: To study the variation of vigilance over a long period of time, we utilized the computerized version of the *Mackworth Clock Test* as the experimentation tool, wherein the small circular pointer moves in a circle like the seconds' hand of an analog clock. It changes its position approximately after one second. However, at infrequent and irregular intervals, the pointer can make a double jump. Here, the task of each participant is to detect and respond to the double jump of the pointer, indicating the presence of the target event, by pressing the *space bar* key of the keyboard.

2.2 Protocol

The participants were comfortably seated in a quiet and isolated room (devoid of any Wi-Fi connections), wherein a constant room temperature was also maintained. Before conducting the actual experiment, each participant was given proper demonstrations and instructions about the experiment and were asked to relax for ten minutes. Further, a practice session of five minutes was also arranged for each participant to make them accustomed to the task. We utilized a large 20 in. monitor kept at a distance of 65 cm from the user for presenting the visual stimuli to the participant. The beginning of the experiment was marked by an EEG recording of an idle session of five minutes followed by the clock test of 20 min. There were a total of 1200 trials in the experiment. After completion of the clock test, we again recorded the EEG signals for an idle session of five minutes. Besides, to keep track of a participant's responses and to ensure true marking of the target events, we also recorded the hardware interrupt from the keyboard. The entire experimental procedure has been pictorially shown in Fig. 2.

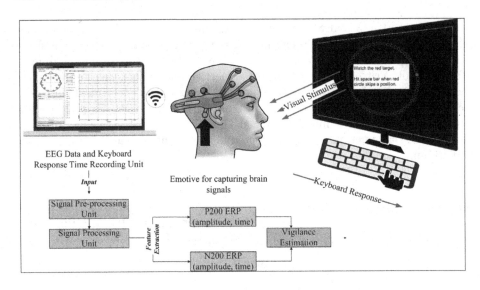

Fig. 2. The overall experimental procedure

2.3 Data Acquisition

The experiment was designed to be completed in 30 min. Further, all EEG data recordings were carried out with the help of portable, user friendly and cost effective Emotiv Epoc+ device which follows the well-known 10–20 international system. This device comprises of 14 electrodes positioned at AF3, F7, F3, FC5, T7, P7, O1, O2, P8, T8, FC6, F4, F8 and AF4 locations and has a sampling rate of 128 Hz. We collected 12000 trials for our experiment with the help of ten voluntary participants.

2.4 Detection of ERPs

1. *Pre-processing*: Usually while recording EEG data, due to various external environmental disturbances, the data gets contaminated with various kinds of artifacts. The extraction of desired/useful features from the EEG signal becomes very difficult under the presence of artifacts. Hence, to minimize the effect of artifacts, it is mandatory to pre-process the recorded raw EEG signals. For this purpose, filters in the standard frequency range of (0.1–30 Hz) are used. Thus, filters help in extracting the desired brain activity by rejecting the other undesired brain signals within a frequency range of (<0.1 Hz and >30 Hz). In the present work, we have used the Chebyshev's high pass filter (having cut off frequency of 0.1 Hz) to remove all disturbing components emerging from breathing and voltage changes in neuronal and non-neuronal artifacts. Besides, we used Chebyshev's low pass filter (having cut off frequency of 30 Hz) to eliminate the noise arising from muscle movements. Further, to ensure perfect rejection of the strong 50 Hz power supply interference, impedance fluctuation, cable defects, electrical noise, and unbalanced

impedances of the electrodes, we utilized (at the recording time) a notch filter with null frequency of 50 Hz.

2. *Feature Extraction*: It is known from the literature that P200 and N200 ERPs are dominant over parietal, occipital and frontal regions, respectively, of the brain. Thus to locate these features, we have used the AF3, AF4, F3, F4, P7, P8, O1 and O2 electrodes. Now, for extracting the features from the EEG signals, first, the pre-processed EEG data is marked to identify the type of event (that is, correctly identified event, falsely identified event and missed event). Next, baseline removal process is carried over this marked data, followed by epoch averaging (500 ms pre-stimulus and 1000 ms post-stimulus) to generate the ERP waveforms. Furthermore, to verify the presence of P200 and N200 ERPs we performed ensemble averaging of the target event epochs and plotted the average waveform.

3   Results and Discussions

The recorded EEG data, of 20 min, has been divided into 10 equal observation periods of two minutes each to carefully observe the pattern of vigilance changes. Next, we observed the amplitude and latency variation of P200 and N200 component of ERPs for those instances where the user responded correctly to an occurrence of the target event. Further, we compared the accuracy attained by each individual, while focusing on the pointer of the clock test and trying to correctly detect the target, with the amplitude of P200 and N200 ERPs to establish a correlation amongst them. The variation of amplitude and latency of P200 and N200 has been reported in Tables 2 and 3, respectively. The amplitude ranges for P200 and N200 ERP are heuristically defined as follows:

$$P200\ (amplitude) = \begin{cases} very\ low, & \text{for } value \geqslant 0.1\ \mu V\ and < 1\ \mu V \\ low, & \text{for } value \geqslant 1\ \mu V\ and < 3\ \mu V \\ moderate, & \text{for } value \geqslant 3\ \mu V\ and < 7\ \mu V \\ high, & \text{for } value \geqslant 7\ \mu V \end{cases} \quad (1)$$

$$N200\ (amplitude) = \begin{cases} very\ low, & \text{for } value \geqslant -0.01\ \mu V\ and < -1\ \mu V \\ low, & \text{for } value \geqslant -1\ \mu V\ and < -3\ \mu V \\ moderate, & \text{for } value \geqslant -3\ \mu V\ and < -6\ \mu V \\ high, & \text{for } value \geqslant -6\ \mu V \end{cases} \quad (2)$$

To evaluate the performance of the participants in terms of accuracy of detection, we sub-divided the recorded EEG data into four categories defined as *true alarm* (TA), *true skip* (TS), *false alarm* (FA) and *false skip* (FS). In terms of Mackworth Clock test experiment, *true alarm* represents correct identification of target stimuli, *true skip* represents correct identification of non-target stimuli,

Table 2. Variation of amplitude and latency of P200 ERP

Observation interval	Parameters	Participant									
		P1	P2	P3	P4	P5	P6	P7	P8	P9	P10
(0–2) min	Amplitude (μV)	10.48	10.75	8.44	7.11	2.11	10.45	0.29	8.25	4.87	5.14
	Latency (ms)	164.1	195.3	218.8	226.6	234.4	203.1	164.1	195.3	187.5	148.4
(2–4) min	Amplitude (μV)	10.91	11.64	11.66	7.09	1.03	12.87	6.75	3.40	10.01	6.31
	Latency (ms)	187.5	187.5	203.1	210.9	179.7	187.5	245.6	171.9	218.8	218.8
(4–6) min	Amplitude (μV)	7.68	12.67	7.16	8.83	9.02	8.95	4.37	3.22	3.42	11.5
	Latency (ms)	203.1	156.3	164.1	242.2	171.9	226.6	164.1	218.8	218.8	164.1
(6–8) min	Amplitude (μV)	1.71	1.47	11.35	8.81	7.26	7.20	5.88	1.46	0.40	7.97
	Latency (ms)	218.8	210.9	156.3	218.8	156.3	171.9	187.5	234.4	187.5	226.6
(8–10) min	Amplitude (μV)	4.63	6.201	4.87	9.94	7.097	6.46	3.52	1.97	5.02	12.78
	Latency (ms)	226.6	218.8	156.3	218.8	164.1	234.4	179.7	164.1	187.5	234.4
(10–12) min	Amplitude (μV)	11.97	10.99	5.44	6.92	5.47	8.94	6.15	1.02	2.92	6.05
	Latency (ms)	226.6	156.6	218.8	171.9	171.9	164.1	195.3	226.6	171.9	187.5
(12–14) min	Amplitude (μV)	11.28	11.02	3.12	4.36	3.64	1.16	6.8	2.19	6.62	9.88
	Latency (ms)	210.9	164.1	210.9	242.2	187.5	195.3	171.9	187.5	171.9	179.7
(14–16) min	Amplitude (μV)	3.22	11.81	2.19	4.86	3.34	3.26	0.99	5.52	6.67	7.61
	Latency (ms)	187.5	148.4	164.1	210.9	156.3	156.3	203.1	234.4	210.9	218.8
(16–18) min	Amplitude (μV)	11.01	9.95	9.62	3.08	7.2	2.31	2.71	7.94	3.61	8.45
	Latency (ms)	179.7	203.1	195.3	242.2	242.2	164.1	187.5	187.5	195.3	203.1
(18–20) min	Amplitude (μV)	8.97	6.16	8.43	3.08	6.81	7.09	2.95	2.55	3.73	4.12
	Latency (ms)	179.7	226.6	218.8	242.2	195.3	156.3	195.3	187.5	156.3	171.9

Table 3. Variation of amplitude and latency of N200 ERP

Observation interval	Parameters	Participant									
		P1	P2	P3	P4	P5	P6	P7	P8	P9	P10
(0–2) min	Amplitude (μV)	−6.11	−3.32	−2.75	−5.22	−4.09	−3.51	−2.58	−1.63	−1.25	−6.44
	Latency (ms)	273.4	289.1	273.4	281.3	281.3	250	203.1	296.9	265.6	203.1
(2–4) min	Amplitude (μV)	−4.08	−1.82	−2.06	−2.05	−1.91	−1.97	−3.53	−4.62	−5.11	−1.06
	Latency (ms)	203.1	210.9	187.5	273.4	195.3	242.2	320.3	218.8	312.5	250
(4–6) min	Amplitude (μV)	−1.77	−3.04	−5.03	−0.34	−0.23	−3.26	−1.75	−1.01	−0.06	−4.78
	Latency (ms)	234.4	289.1	242.2	304.7	210.9	281.3	203.1	289.1	250	250
(6–8) min	Amplitude (μV)	−7.19	−1.42	−1.38	−5.09	−2.54	−0.39	−5.72	−0.89	−4.16	−5.28
	Latency (ms)	281.3	242.2	296.9	273.4	164.1	195.3	265.6	263.1	210.9	257.8
(8–10) min	Amplitude (μV)	−1.8	−1.06	−5.11	−5.32	−0.43	−2.09	−1.59	−5.59	−4.18	−4.02
	Latency (ms)	257.8	328.6	226.6	265.6	265.6	289.1	218.8	273.4	226.6	312.5
(10–12) min	Amplitude (μV)	−2.39	−2.46	−5.82	−5.72	−4.07	−0.95	−0.76	−1.17	−2	−3.88
	Latency (ms)	304.7	234.4	242.2	242.2	195.3	218.8	218.8	257.8	234.4	234.4
(12–14) min	Amplitude (μV)	−3.08	−4.96	−1.71	−1.62	−4.04	−6.08	−3.83	−1.26	−0.64	−5.02
	Latency (ms)	281.3	273.4	312.5	325	210.9	226.6	273.4	210.9	257.8	234.4
(14–16) min	Amplitude (μV)	−1.23	−2.92	−7.71	−3.11	−5.55	−2.45	−2.71	−0.19	−6.97	−3.01
	Latency (ms)	218.8	210.9	289.1	234.4	250	187.5	273.4	312.5	234.4	242.2
(16–18) min	Amplitude (μV)	−6.09	−0.70	−5.42	−1.37	−3.76	−1.25	−3.13	−2.4	−4.13	−2.27
	Latency (ms)	312.5	289.1	234.4	320.3	304.7	210.9	226.6	273.4	265.6	257.8
(18–20) min	Amplitude (μV)	−4.38	−4.44	−2.7542	−1.37	−4.17	−1.99	−1.34	−5.82	−2.97	−3.16
	Latency (ms)	250	304.7	273.4	320.3	257.8	218.8	242.2	281.3	179.7	195.3

false alarm represents incorrect key pressed at non-targets and *false skip* represents non-identification of the target stimuli. Based on these data, the accuracy is calculated by using Eq. 3. The accuracy of detection of each individual who participated in the experiment has been tabulated in Table 4. The latencies of P200 and N200 ERPs were observed to be within the already known ranges; however, no particular trend with respect to amplitude has been observed for the obtained latencies.

$$Accuracy = \frac{TA + TS}{TA + TS + FA + FS} \tag{3}$$

The accuracy (in %) obtained is divided into four classes which is defined as follows:

$$Accuracy\ (\%) = \begin{cases} very\ low, & for\ value \geqslant 0\%\ and < 30\% \\ low, & for\ value \geqslant 30\%\ and < 50\% \\ moderate, & for\ value \geqslant 50\%\ and < 80\% \\ high, & for\ value \geqslant 80\%\ and \leqslant 100\% \end{cases} \tag{4}$$

Table 4. Variation of accuracy (in %) of each participant

Observation interval	Participant									
	P1	P2	P3	P4	P5	P6	P7	P8	P9	P10
(0–2) min	100	94.34	90.78	97.83	84.75	92.75	80.56	91.12	87.83	93.48
(2–4) min	100	95.84	96	92.75	96	90.19	97.29	86.05	98.25	91.94
(4–6) min	86.37	93.48	90.19	94	93.03	93.67	86.96	80.56	86.36	95.56
(6–8) min	81.48	87.83	85.11	100	98.08	87.17	95.75	92	75	100
(8–10) min	90.78	91.67	96.08	100	89.58	88.24	81.48	88.24	97.78	100
(10–12) min	100	98.08	95.92	97.96	90.69	91.43	93.48	75	91.12	97.5
(12–14) min	95.56	97.23	87.24	77.36	89.48	71.43	97.29	74.51	85.72	98.18
(14–16) min	81.48	92	88.24	93.48	91.49	88.64	71.74	91.18	98.08	89.58
(16–18) min	100	77.36	81.52	75.51	86.36	71.41	74.51	93.48	87.83	88.89
(18–20) min	100	98.11	93.48	88.64	91.89	95.56	71.73	76.47	85.71	88.64

From Tables 2, 3 and 4, and using Eqs. 1, 2 and 4, we can see that for participant P2, during an observation interval between (4–6) min the amplitude of P200 is high (12.67 μV) while the amplitude of N200 is low (−3.04 μV), thereby resulting in 93.48% accuracy. In case of participant P6, during an observation interval between (16–18) min the amplitude of both P200 and N200 is low and is 2.31 μV and −1.25 μV, respectively, thereby resulting in 71.41% accuracy. In case of participant P1, during an observation interval between (6–8) min the amplitude of P200 is low (1.71 μV) while the amplitude of N200 is high (−7.19 μV), thereby resulting in 81.48% accuracy. Similarly, in case of participant P1, during observation interval between (0–2) min the amplitude of both P200 and N200 is high and is 10.48 μV and −6.109 μV, respectively, thereby resulting in 100% accuracy. Other values may be verified from the tables in the similar manner to conclude that both accuracy and ERPs (P200 and N200) are correlated to each other, such that, whenever the accuracy of detection is high there is a high amplitude of P200 and N200. In other words, we can say that whenever an individual successfully distinguishes the target stimuli amongst all other presented stimuli, the two ERPs, *viz.*, N200 and P200 are elicited with high amplitude. Besides, we also show the variation of accuracy and amplitude of P200 and N200 with time for participant P1 in Fig. 3. It can be easily observed from Fig. 3 that accuracy of target detection and amplitude of both ERPs are correlated.

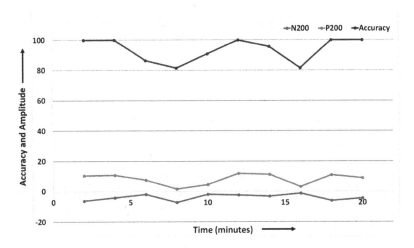

Fig. 3. Plot showing variation of accuracy and amplitude of P200 and N200 with time

To study the variations in the ERPs under the presence of true alarm (when the user correctly identifies the target events) and false alarm (when the user incorrectly identifies the events), we plotted the P200 and N200 ERPs on a single graph with common origin (see Fig. 4). We observed that there is a considerable difference in the amplitude of both ERPs under true and false alarm conditions.

Further, Fig. 5 shows the variation in P200 and N200 ERPs under the presence of target and non-target stimuli.

Figure 6 depicts the variation in the active regions of the brain before, during and after the completion of the experiment. Here, blue spots visible in pre and post experiment scalp images show low brain activity, while the red spots visible during experimentation show an increase in the brain activity of the associated regions. Besides, from instance 1 we observed that during the experiment - parietal, frontal and some parts of occipital region were highly energized and these regions showed the presence of P200 and N200 ERPs. Further, from instance 2

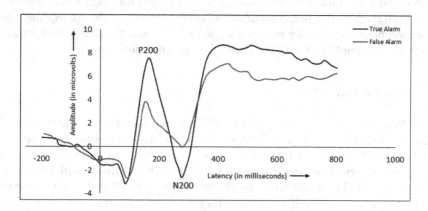

Fig. 4. P200 and N200 peaks during true alarm and false alarm conditions

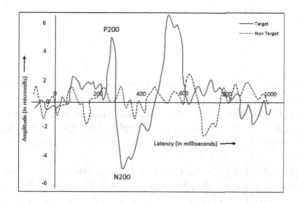

Fig. 5. Variation of ERPs in target and non-target conditions

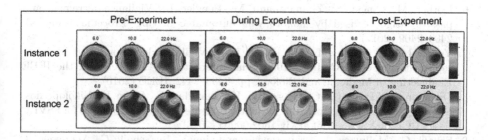

Fig. 6. Variation of scalp plot before, during and after experiment (Color figure online)

we observed that during the experiment frontal region was highly energized and the region showed the presence of N200 ERP. Through this, we verified that our experiment successfully evokes the two ERPs from the designated regions. Hence, we can apply the selected ERPs for vigilance detection.

4   Conclusion

In the literature different features of EEG signals have been utilized to study vigilance level of human beings. In this work, First, we successfully demonstrated that both P200 and N200 ERPs are suitable candidates for studying vigilance. Second, we observed the variation in P200 and N200 amplitude with true alarm and false alarm. Third, we observed the variation in P200 and N200 amplitude under the presence of target and non-target stimuli. Fourth, with the help of scalp plot of Fig. 6 we verified the hot-spots/active regions of the brain from where the studied ERPs originate.

This work may be applied in real-time analysis of vigilance. Besides, in future we plan to extend this work to quantize the level of vigilance instead of indicating its mere presence and absence.

References

1. Mackworth, N.H.: The breakdown of vigilance during prolonged visual search. Q. J. Exp. Psychol. **1**(1), 6–21 (1948)
2. Shingledecker, C., Weldon, D.E., Behymer, K., Simpkins, B., Lerner, E., Warm, J., Matthews, G., Finomore, V., Shaw, T., Murphy, J.S.: Measuring vigilance abilities to enhance combat identification performance. In: Human Factors Issues in Combat Identification, pp. 47–66 (2010)
3. McIntire, L.K., McKinley, R.A., Goodyear, C., McIntire, J.P.: Detection of vigilance performance using eye blinks. Appl. Ergon. **45**(2), 354–362 (2014)
4. Sauvet, F., Bougard, C., Coroenne, M., Lely, L., Van Beers, P., Elbaz, M., Guillard, M., Leger, D., Chennaoui, M.: In-flight automatic detection of vigilance states using a single EEG channel. IEEE Trans. Biomed. Eng. **61**(12), 2840–2847 (2014)
5. Helton, W.S., Russell, P.N.: Rest is best: the role of rest and task interruptions on vigilance. Cognition **134**, 165–173 (2015)
6. Körber, M., Cingel, A., Zimmermann, M., Bengler, K.: Vigilance decrement and passive fatigue caused by monotony in automated driving. Procedia Manuf. **3**, 2403–2409 (2015)
7. Yu, H., Lu, H., Ouyang, T., Liu, H., Lu, B.-L.: Vigilance detection based on sparse representation of EEG. In: 2010 Annual International Conference of the IEEE Engineering in Medicine and Biology, pp. 2439–2442. IEEE (2010)
8. Oikonomou, V.P., Liaros, G., Georgiadis, K., Chatzilari, E., Adam, K., Nikolopoulos, S., Kompatsiaris, I.: Comparative evaluation of state of the art algorithms for SSVEP based BCIs. arXiv preprint arXiv:1602.00904 (2016)
9. Schalk, G., Mellinger, J.: Brain sensors and signals. In: Schalk, G., Mellinger, J. (eds.) A Practical Guide to Brain-Computer Interfacing with BCI2000, pp. 9–35. Springer, London (2010). https://doi.org/10.1007/978-1-84996-092-2_2

10. Samima, S., Sarma, M., Samanta, D.: Correlation of P300 ERPs with visual stimuli and its application to vigilance detection. In: 39th Annual International Conference of the IEEE Engineering in Medicine and Biology Society (EMBC17) (2017, accepted)

11. Dennis, T.A., Chen, C.-C.: Neurophysiological mechanisms in the emotional modulation of attention: the interplay between threat sensitivity and attentional control. Biol. Psychol. **76**(1), 1–10 (2007)

12. Hajihosseini, A., Holroyd, C.B.: Frontal midline theta and N200 amplitude reflect complementary information about expectancy and outcome evaluation. Psychophysiology **50**(6), 550–562 (2013)

13. Zhang, J.X., Fang, Z., Du, Y., Kong, L., Zhang, Q., Xing, Q.: Centro-parietal N200: an event-related potential component specific to Chinese visual word recognition. Chin. Sci. Bull. **57**(13), 1516–1532 (2012)

14. Kemp, A.H., Benito, L.P., Quintana, D.S., Clark, C.R., McFarlane, A., Mayur, P., Harris, A., Boyce, P., Williams, L.M.: Impact of depression heterogeneity on attention: an auditory oddball event related potential study. J. Affect. Disord. **123**(1), 202–207 (2010)

15. Lautenbacher, S., Dittmar, O., Baum, C., Schneider, R., Keogh, E., Kunz, M.: Vigilance for pain-related faces in a primary task paradigm: an ERP study. J. Pain Res. **6**, 437 (2013)

16. Ford, J.M., Roach, B.J., Palzes, V.A., Mathalon, D.H.: Using concurrent EEG and fMRI to probe the state of the brain in schizophrenia. NeuroImage Clin. **12**, 429–441 (2016)

17. Attaheri, A., Kikuchi, Y., Milne, A.E., Wilson, B., Alter, K., Petkov, C.I.: EEG potentials associated with artificial grammar learning in the primate brain. Brain Lang. **148**, 74–80 (2015)

18. Landi, N., Perfetti, C.A.: An electrophysiological investigation of semantic and phonological processing in skilled and less-skilled comprehenders. Brain Lang. **102**(1), 30–45 (2007)

19. Brett-Green, B.A., Miller, L.J., Gavin, W.J., Davies, P.L.: Multisensory integration in children: a preliminary ERP study. Brain Res. **1242**, 283–290 (2008)

20. NeuRA. Factsheet P200 event-related potential (2016). https://library.neura.edu. au/wp-content/uploads/p200/Factsheet_P200.pdf. Accessed 21 June 2017

21. Patel, S.H., Azzam, P.N.: Characterization of N200 and P300: selected studies of the event-related potential. Int. J. Med. Sci. **2**(4), 147–154 (2005)

22. Fonaryova Key, A.P., Dove, G.O., Maguire, M.J.: Linking brainwaves to the brain: an ERP primer. Dev. Neuropsychol. **27**(2), 183–215 (2005)

Open Access This chapter is licensed under the terms of the Creative Commons Attribution 4.0 International License (http://creativecommons.org/licenses/by/4.0/), which permits use, sharing, adaptation, distribution and reproduction in any medium or format, as long as you give appropriate credit to the original author(s) and the source, provide a link to the Creative Commons license and indicate if changes were made.

The images or other third party material in this chapter are included in the chapter's Creative Commons license, unless indicated otherwise in a credit line to the material. If material is not included in the chapter's Creative Commons license and your intended use is not permitted by statutory regulation or exceeds the permitted use, you will need to obtain permission directly from the copyright holder.

Author Index

© The Editor(s) (if applicable) and The Author(s) 2017. This book is an open access publication.
Open Access This book is licensed under the terms of the Creative Commons Attribution 4.0 International License (http://creativecommons.org/licenses/by/4.0/), which permits use, sharing, adaptation, distribution and reproduction in any medium or format, as long as you give appropriate credit to the original author(s) and the source, provide a link to the Creative Commons license and indicate if changes were made.

The images or other third party material in this book are included in the book's Creative Commons license, unless indicated otherwise in a credit line to the material. If material is not included in the book's Creative Commons license and your intended use is not permitted by statutory regulation or exceeds the permitted use, you will need to obtain permission directly from the copyright holder.

Printed in the United States
By Bookmasters

Printed in the United States
By Bookmasters